The Girl's Guide to Homelessness

The Girl's Guide to Homelessness

a memoir

brianna karp

The Girl's Guide to Homelessness

ISBN-13:978-0-373-89235-8

© 2011 by Brianna Karp

The names and identifying details of some characters in this book have been changed.

Library of Congress Cataloging-in-Publication Data

Karp, Brianna, 1985–
The girl's guide to homelessness / Brianna Karp.
p. cm.
ISBN 978-0-373-89235-8 (trade pbk.)
1. Homelessness-United States. 2. Karp, Brianna, 1985-3. Homeless persons-United States-Biography. I. Title.
HV4505.K37 2011
362.5092-dc22
[B]
2010044201

www.harlequin.com

Printed in U.S.A.

To Brandon, Sonia, Vicki and Sage

home·less (hōm'lĭs)
adj. Having no home or haven.
n. (used with a pl. verb) People without homes considered as a group. Often used with *the*.

§11302. General definition of homeless individual:
an individual who lacks a fixed, regular, and adequate nighttime residence; and

an individual who has a primary nighttime residence that is a supervised publicly or privately operated shelter designed to provide temporary living accommodations (including welfare hotels, congregate shelters, and transitional housing for the mentally ill);

an institution that provides a temporary residence for individuals intended to be institutionalized; or a public or private place not designed for, or ordinarily used as, a regular sleeping accommodation for human beings.

—Federal Definition of Homeless, United States Code Title 42, Chapter 119, Subchapter I

The Walmart lot was cold in the night air, even for southern California. I hadn't brought enough blankets and would need to swing by the thrift store and pick up a few more. Everything was well-lit by the streetlamps and eerily quiet. There were maybe a dozen other trailers around when I arrived, but no sign that actual people might live in them at all. I had once visited Calico Ghost Town, an old abandoned mining settlement in the hills outside San Bernardino, and this had that same sense of deathly desertion. I *knew* they were there, perhaps even peeking out their windows at the newcomer, but I couldn't *see* or *hear* any of them.

Were any of the others like me? Were the rest of them just passing through? Was I the only one idiotic enough to think I could pull off a stunt like this?

Irrational fear swept through me. How could I sleep? I was more weary than I'd been in a long time, but I flicked on a solitary flashlight and tried to read a book, although you couldn't exactly call it reading. It was more like staring blankly at the page, eyes racing over the words without comprehension as my mind created scenarios one after the other, each more horrible than the last. What if I awoke to the brisk tapping of police batons on my windows? What if they *knew* I was planning on staying here longer than a night or two? What if they could *sense* it? What if I awoke at a tilt, all my boxes hurtling from one end of the trailer toward my head, as a tow truck dragged me away, screeching for help, muffled and buried under hundreds of books?

I had never much thought about homelessness or homeless people. Sure, there was the occasional "hobo" on the street, perhaps lounging on the sidewalk outside a 7-Eleven, begging for change, ragged, perhaps with a worn ski cap on, maybe missing a few teeth, with scraggly hair and a wizened visage.

"Don't make eye contact with them," my mother would say, jerking me to her side, not even bothering to whisper or even lower her voice. She spoke about them as if they couldn't hear or understand her, or as if they had no feelings to hurt. I never really thought to question that. It was just another stereotype repeated to me, ad nauseam, from infancy.

"They're just lazy bums. Too lazy to get a job. Don't look at them, don't talk to them and don't give them anything. Half of them aren't even really homeless, you know. They're just faking it to make money without actually having to do anything."

I had never thought about how those homeless people ended up there. I had never once thought to ask, "Why would a lazy person choose that life?" It seems like a really hard, scary, uncertain life. It seems like the last kind of life a lazy jackass would choose.

I was ashamed of myself, thinking back on it. In a way, this was my atonement, my penance for being so self-righteous all those years. *Serves me right,* I realized wildly.

It was Thursday, February 26, 2009. I was homeless.

But then, it's not really enough to tell you that I'm homeless, is it? You want to know who the hell I am and how I got here.

Chapter One

I'm trying to decide whether it's fair or not to say that insanity runs in my blood.

Certainly it's a statement with which many of my family members would, shall we say, take umbrage. But I don't know that it's much of a stretch, from an outsider's perspective. I'm not talking about the kooky, madcap, adorably dysfunctional brand of crazy, either. The *Moonstruck*-style family with their over-the-top yelling and gesticulating, followed by reconciliations and hugs and kisses and banquet-reunion meals. The bighearted kind of crazy.

That's not my family. My lineage runs more along the batshit-fucking-nuts crazy train.

As you might imagine, this is enough to give a girl a massive mind trip. There's always that underlying paranoia—wondering whether I have miraculously broken the mold and escaped the curse, or whether the insanity is buried and brewing just below the surface, lying dormant and awaiting the inevitable breakout.

. . .

I was born a fourth-generation Jehovah's Witness. There wasn't much choice in the matter. On my mother's side, the JW heritage goes all the way back to my great-grandparents— Polish immigrants to Canada who met on a bus one day in the early 1900s, discovered they each thought the other looked pretty spicy and married a week later. Mary and TaTa Mazur would later convert to the "Bible Students," renamed "Jehovah's Witnesses" in 1931, and pump out nine devout Jehovah's Witness children up through the Great Depression, one of whom was my grandmother, Iris, the youngest and the black sheep and hell-raiser of the family.

The Mazur clan would later tell stories of their persecution as Jehovah's Witnesses during both world wars, including the ban on the religion in Canada from 1940 to 1943, when members organized an underground resistance. My grandmother would affectionately relate stories of her father's imprisonment when he was caught distributing JW pamphlets, only to find himself the first known believer to be thrown out of jail for singing religious hymns in Polish at the top of his lungs (and horrendously out of tune), distressing prison guards and inmates alike.

I know, I know, it all sounds very charming and "warms-the-cockles-of-your-heart" so far, doesn't it? Believe me, there are plenty more stories where those came from. JWs thrive on the martyr complex, since they believe that the Bible prophesied that members of the One True Religion would be greatly persecuted. Therefore, I've heard every variation of the chuckle-worthy tale in which oppressed Jehovah's Witnesses pull one over on their tormentors.

But.

My great-grandparents also claimed to be "of the anointed." In JW-speak, this means that they believed Jehovah God had spoken to them and revealed that they were among the elite 144,000 chosen ones, selected to go to heaven and reign alongside Him as kings once He brought about a prophesied New Order of Things. This new order, Jehovah's Witnesses believe, involves the brutal destruction of every nonbeliever at a bloody, apocalyptic Armageddon showdown, and the subsequent building of a Paradise Earth populated solely by—you guessed it—the rest of the Jehovah's Witnesses, the ones not chosen to reign as kings in heaven. They don't tell you this stuff on your doorstep, do they?

So. Two ancestors hearing voices and with delusions of kingly grandeur. Check.

My grandmother, Iris, despite a few young years of running wild, raising Cain and living something of a double life few Witnesses would have approved of, remains in the religion to this day. She attends a Kingdom Hall (JWs don't call them churches; they consider churches "pagan" and "of false religion") in California, where she moved and settled down with my grandfather, Jeremiah. They are now divorced, but he is also a Jehovah's Witness and lives a relatively sweet, unassuming life under the radar in Alabama with his second wife.

Iris Wallingford, née Mazur, carried on the precedent of crazy and inflated it to (apologies in advance for the pun) epic biblical proportions. According to family lore, she abused her three daughters physically, mentally and emotionally. Legendary tales of her heaving vacuum cleaners through the air at their heads, dragging them along the hallway by their hair until it came out by the roots in clumps or grinding pencil lead deep into their knees as they squirmed and fidgeted during two-hour Kingdom Hall meeting sessions were a staple of my childhood. This is all, of course, merely what I've gleaned from multiple sources' whispered tales, including those of family members and friends...but do I believe there's at least some truth to it? Yep. All three girls were destined to run away from home at a young age. First Louisa, the eldest, split for Hawaii, followed by my mother, Linda, at age sixteen. Mom dropped out of high school, took her GED exam and lived on Oahu with Louisa (who had spiraled into drug use) for a year or so before returning to California. Charisse, the youngest, possibly had it the worst—she was afflicted with a severe, lifelong form of alopecia, which caused her to lose her hair and endure torment at school as well as at home. Upon leaving home, she searched for solace in the arms of men, hopping from one to another and sinking two marriages with kind, loving (and non-JW) husbands due to compulsive infidelity. As of this writing, she is imprisoned in Illinois for a period of twelve years, convicted of vehicular manslaughter committed while driving under the influence for the third time. I have not seen her in ages, but, according to family members, she has also had problems with illegal drugs for years and has been "disfellowshipped," or excommunicated, from the Jehovah's Witnesses at least twice. Her two young children are cared for by her non-JW ex-husband, so I hold out hope that they may yet have a quasi-normal life, despite everything.

My grandmother, meanwhile, spends most of her time in a rocking chair in front of the TV at home. Once a slim, lovely young woman with mischievous eyes who attracted men like flies to honey, she has ballooned to ghastly proportions and relies on a walker to get from place to place. Her house is in a condemnable, Grey Gardens state—decades of hoarded trash and junk piled from floor to ceiling, with the exception of walking paths hewn out from room to room. I'm pretty sure I've seen McDonald's containers in there dating back to the 1960s. You think I'm kidding? In Iris Wallingford's warped mind, every bit of junk is a treasure or a memory to add to the magpie's nest. In the past, I have attempted to spend time with my grandma, but could only ever handle her in small doses, as her grating chief hobby is living in the past, reliving imaginary grudges and slights dating back some seventy-odd years. Many of these are against her own brothers and sisters, all but one already passed on—respect for the dead means nothing to her. She and my mother hate each other with a passion. Although they attend the same congregation, they don't speak, but always have an arsenal of nasty digs on hand ready to fling at the other. Despite Iris's extraordinary disregard for her own health, which would seem to invite the most massive heart attack in the history of heart attacks, my mother jokes grimly that Iris will outlive us all out of spite.

I tell these stories because I think it's important for me to establish up front, before I go into my own saga, that I believe I understand, or at least try to understand, why my mother is the way she is. For much of her life, she was indeed victimized—pair cult indoctrination from birth with unabated abuse by a bitter, raving 350-pound maniac, and you've got a recipe for disaster. To this day, I don't know exactly how much of my mother's own particular instability is a product of nature or nurture, but I've got my suspicions that one didn't exactly help the other.

Having returned from her less-than-successful jaunt to Hawaii, which left her broke and disillusioned for such a young kid, my mother endured a brief period of abuse again at home with Iris. At eighteen, by Jehovah's Witness standards she was actually an old maid, though she was young, lovely and vivacious—popular at school, something of a class clown in compensation for the dark home life of which she was so ashamed. She finally escaped (or so she thought) by marrying the first man she could at nineteen, and getting pregnant with me right away.

Bob Neville. Bob was not short for Robert. Just plain Bob. He was a gawky, scarecrow-esque kid a year older than my mother, most often said to resemble Peter Pan. He definitely didn't *look* like a monster.

Mom met him at the moped repair shop after an unfortunate accident in which a neighbor backing out of his driveway neglected to notice her coming up the street and ran over her scooter. She would later point out to me the hedge that had obscured the driver's vision: "If it weren't for that hedge, you would never have been born!" She would come to regret that damn hedge.

Jehovah's Witnesses don't date non–Jehovah's Witnesses, and they definitely aren't supposed to marry them. They view it as marrying a walking corpse—what's the point of falling in love with someone the great and powerful Jehovah is just going to roast with a flaming meteorite at Armageddon, anyway? Members can be privately counseled, publicly reproved, disciplined or even disfellowshipped and shunned for pursuing a relationship with a nonbeliever. Ergo, Bob accepted a "Bible study" with my mother, toward the goal of conversion, and they married quickly and furtively. I was born March 6, 1985.

Bob turned out to be the classic wife beater, belying his sweetly youthful appearance. My mother claims that a week after their wedding, he woke her up in the middle of the night, accused her of cheating on him, bundled her into the car and drove her out to the desert in silence, pausing to open the door and shove her out into the sand, dumping her in only a T-shirt and no underwear. Then he drove home and went back to sleep while she walked until her feet were bloody, finally hitching a ride home from a concerned passing motorist and his wife around dawn. Other stories centered around the time Bob put my mother through a wall in their house, leaving a perfect Linda-shaped indent, and when he picked up a set of heavy stone coasters from the coffee table and started bashing his own forehead in during an argument until blood spurted and coated the furniture, all the while screaming at her as though bestowing an unavoidable curse.

"Look how much I love you! I'll even hurt myself for you! Look what you're making me do to myself! Look what you're making me do to you!"

I hurt you because I love you. Of course. It was a constant refrain of his, definitely not the most original line ever thought up by an abusive husband. Interestingly, it would turn out to be a recurring theme in my own life as well, that persistent, lingering stench you just can't get rid of no matter how hard you scrub.

My mother became pregnant again with my little sister, Molly, mere months after my birth. My sister was born on May 7, 1986 with a congenital defect requiring open-heart surgery, which set the local congregation elders in a tizzy. At that time, only a handful of infants had ever received bloodless heart surgery, and Jehovah's Witnesses apply the archaic biblical command to "abstain from blood" (Acts 15:29) to the ultimate possible literal interpretation— blood pudding isn't the only no-no! The command was previously misapplied to organ transplants, considered cannibalism, for many years. However, "new light" from Jehovah eventually revealed to the old men in the head honcho seat in Brooklyn, the Governing Body of Jehovah's Witnesses, that—oops!—organ transplants (and later blood fractions, though not whole blood itself) were OK after all. Sorry about all those faithful Witnesses who died (or allowed their children to die) under the "old light," folks. Move along, nothing to see here.

At the time of my sister's birth, however, even the use of medical treatments utilizing blood fractions, such as plasma, albumin, immunoglobulins and the like, were not an option for members (they didn't become a "conscience matter" for Jehovah's Witnesses until 1989, when Molly was three years old), and my mom, barely more than a kid herself, was beset upon by elders waving power of attorney forms in her face. Molly's primary hospital insisted that she required a blood transfusion, and that they were prepared to go to court to seek and enforce an injunction making sure she received it. The circus reached its peak when my mother snatched my little sister from the local hospital and took her to Texas, where Dr. Denton Cooley, the world's foremost "blood-free surgeon" (and at the time, one of only two in the United States who performed such procedures on children), completed the two operations that would save Molly's life and leave her with her two scars: a thick, ropey one all the way down from sternum to belly button, and a thin crescent-shaped one under her left breast, toward her armpit. Though only a year old at the time, I distinctly recall the sight of my frail, emaciated sister in a hospital crib, wailing, covered in tubes and surrounded by stuffed animals my mother purchased for her. Her crib and hospital apparatus were all covered in large stickers bearing the words "Jehovah's Witness—No Blood!" Moll's recovery and success story were heralded by Jehovah's Witnesses everywhere as a triumph of Jehovah over Satan, and proof that their religion's ways were the best after all.

Though Mom attempted to escape her abusive marriage, however, the congregation elders were having none of it. Despite the angry bruises and welts covering her from head to toe, and an "unpleasant incident" in which Bob leaped up on the hood of our van in the parking lot of the Kingdom Hall (in front of dozens of witnesses) as my mother attempted to flee and I screamed in confused terror in the backseat, they advised her to "wait on Jehovah, be a better wife and perhaps things would get better." Divorce is scripturally prohibited for Jehovah's Witnesses, except in the case of adultery. Even abused spouses are advised to remain in their dead-end marriages and "set a good example" for their abuser, "that he might be won over without a word." (*Read:* Maybe if you're really, really nice to him, he'll realize what a jackass he's been, feel sorry and repent. Even if it takes a decade or three.)

And, they said, if he did kill her, as he threatened and she feared, she would be resurrected to Paradise. God would fix everything eventually. Just not right now.

Despite the ire of the elders, my mother finally filed for divorce when I was two years old, amid the debacle of Molly's operations. The congregation warned her that, though she might be legally free, scripturally Jehovah still considered her married. She was not allowed to date or remarry until Bob shacked up with another woman and admitted infidelity. Still obsessed with her, and as a particularly sadistic form of torment, he stubbornly refused for the longest time to give her grounds for a scriptural divorce in the eyes of the Witnesses.

In the meantime, the courts ruled for weekend visitation with Bob, who had moved into his mother's garage. I, and sometimes Molly—when she wasn't in the hospital— would visit him on and off for another year or so (when he would actually show up for pickup). During much of this period, I suppose you could say I found myself the object of my father's affection, the apple of his eye. Without preamble, he apparently developed a taste for some of the more repugnant, deviant acts known to man, and foisted upon me the sort of fondlings and sexual acts that are normally reserved for awkward, fumbling sixteen-year-olds in the back of cars, except that I was two and very much confused by the entire thing. I knew one thing, though. If I wanted my Happy Meal toy, I would be a good girl and kiss Daddy's cock and let him put his fingers (and on one memorable occasion, a striped yellow-and-red McDonald's soda straw) inside me without crying while he showed me how he could make it do special tricks, like peeing thick white globby stuff instead of regular yellow pee. Then I would fall asleep feeling oddly wrong, wondering whether that blue plastic toy camel with wrinkled knees at the bottom of the bag was worth it all. This was our special secret, though, and I couldn't tell Mommy or very bad things would happen to Daddy. I didn't want that, did I? Of course not. Besides, with all the attention swirling around Molly and her health since her birth, I often felt lonely, with nobody to play with. At least somebody was spending time with me again. I took it as proof that Daddy really did love me, even though he made lots of mistakes with Mommy when they were married.

. . .

I vividly remember pointing to my mother on our front lawn one day as she watered the plants with a long, curved garden hose, and giggling at the stream of water.

"It looks like you're holding Daddy's penis in your hand!" Her face clouded over, and she shook her finger at me.

"That is *not* a nice thing to say! That's not funny, we don't use words like that in public."

Oops. I knew immediately that I had made a mistake. I had almost ruined Daddy's and my special secret. I had almost precipitated *very bad things*. I resolved to keep my mouth shut and not let it happen again. A few days later, when my mother sat me down and explained to me about private parts and the proper words for them, and how I was never ever to let anybody touch me down there, and tell her immediately if they did, I nodded my head serenely and gave her my chubby-cheeked cherub smile. Nobody was going to trick me into giving up our special secret ever again.

In any event, Bob soon found himself a girlfriend, Charlie, about my mom's age and type: brunette, innocent, wide-eyed and naïve. My mom was overjoyed—she was scripturally free, and she correctly surmised that Charlie would take her place as the object of his obsession, slowly removing him from our lives. Charlie was a kind, warm-hearted person and she seemed to adore Molly and me. I liked her so much I didn't even mind when they got an apartment together and she took my place in Daddy's bed at night, and the attention from him quickly waned. She did sweet things like read us stories and make us sandwiches when we visited: Bob was now too busy to play with us. The visits grew further and further apart, until finally he just didn't show up at all, ever again, without my ever fully noticing or comprehending.

. . .

My mom went on to marry Joseph Karp, from a neigh-
boring congregation, when I was six. Joe was the exact
opposite of Bob, to a fault. He was the human equivalent of Kermit the Frog—harmlessly pleasant, somewhat
oblivious, mild-tempered, sweetly goofy and a redheaded
twenty-seven-year-old virgin. His day had finally come.
Even as a single mom with a heretofore rough past and two
young children, Linda Simpson was still gorgeous.

After a careful year of courtship, quite prolonged according to JW standards, my mother bucked the tradition
of marrying humbly and quietly in the local Kingdom Hall
and instead chose to hold the ceremony at a rose garden
in Anaheim, spawning a rash of clucking henlike gossip
from all the high-and-mighty elders' wives. The wedding
was the event of the decade in JW-land; three hundred at-
tendees strong. Molly and I were the flower girls, in peach
velvet-and-tulle dresses and baby's breath hair wreaths,
drawing coos and "awwwwws" as we held hands and
wicker baskets of peach roses, carefully preceding my mom
down the aisle in her sequin-appliquéd white, mermaid-
style dress and poufy curled pompadour. I was excited to
have a new daddy. I had been nervous at first, hoping that
this daddy wouldn't require any embarrassing and painful
special nighttime activities, but Joe did only nice things,
like give me wild, bucking horsey-back rides on the fluo-
rescent-orange carpet at home; tickle me until I screamed
with laughter; and teach me how to play chess. He would
make a good daddy, I thought.

I guess it was inevitable, though sad, that their marriage would be a star-crossed affair, though not apparently
doomed from the start.

For one thing, Joe was considered pretty wishy-washy as

far as the Jehovah's Witnesses' interpretation of the biblical arrangement of *headship* went. In other words, he was just too damn nice to keep his hotheaded hussy of a wife in line, as God required of him. My mother, on the other hand, didn't seem to know what to do with herself in a relationship with such a passive man—she had gone from one marital extreme to another. Formerly, she had been fighting to protect her daughters and herself from a psychotic monster. Now she felt she had to continue fighting, even though there was little to fight over, other than Joe being something of a weak-willed, meek wuss. She believed what she had been taught all her life, that she should be "in subjection to her husband," but she also had not a single submissive bone in her body. So slowly that we barely noticed it happening, until it seemed like one day it burst out into the open and tore our life asunder, my mother began to take on the persona of a nagging, abusive harpy.

There were three good years of marriage between them, up until I turned nine. Prior to then, I remember my mother the way many others still do—the youngest, prettiest mommy of all the mommies in the world. A woman who loved and fiercely protected Moll and me. Even when life was rough, before meeting Joe, and she had to bundle us sleepily into our old Plymouth Voyager at 4:00 a.m. and go polish FedEx drop boxes to earn money to feed us, she found ways to make it fun, not allowing her desperation and misery to seep through the cracks and poison her daughters. Though she took discipline seriously, when we were little it was never harsh or unwarranted. We always felt loved and adored by our mommy.

That would change.

Chapter Two

It was mid-January 2009, in Brea Jamba Juice, while begging my cheating ex-boyfriend not to leave me for his costar in a chintzy murder mystery dinner theater, that I learned that my biological father had offed himself with a Remington12 gauge. I was twenty-three years old.

One moment I was self-medicating, drinking in, like a carefully rationed narcotic, Dennis's placid voice asking me how I was, what was new, placating me with the tired words I had come to dread: "I just need more time to make up my mind" (ask me now why I never threw a pomegranate smoothie over the asshole's head and walked out for good—I have no answer for you). The next, my BlackBerry rang, a Los Angeles number, and I picked it up, assuming that it was a call for an interview from one of several LA jobs I had applied for.

"Ms. Karp? My name is Joyce Cato. I'm calling you regarding a Bob Jason Neville," the woman on the end of the line began. She had a kind voice, but I was immediately on the defensive. *Oh, my god, he's tracked me down.*

I couldn't understand why or how, but he had done it. I knew it.

My mind was a maelstrom of panic. I didn't want to allow any of this back into my life. I had spent the previous week telling my therapist the little that I remembered about this man, about the things that he used to do to me, to my mother, and the nightmares that had burst into my head six months earlier—some long-delayed trauma reaction that forced me awake, sobbing several times a week, terrifying me so much that I couldn't go back to sleep, setting me on edge and completely annihilating my once-comfortable relationship with Dennis, who couldn't handle disturbances of this kind. He promptly decided that starting a relationship with some common actress (without the convenience of actually breaking up with me first) was somehow the most sensible plan of action. Mysti, I believe was her name. *What the hell kind of a name is* Mysti, *anyway?* I wondered, bitterly. I had no idea what she looked like, but in my wishful thinking she was a trampy bimbo with blonde extensions, a horsey face, fake boobs and a SoCal tan, spouting the platitudes that so many actors keep handily tucked under one arm to prove their depth to the skeptical world.

I found out about Mysti two days before Christmas. In some subconscious layer of being, I knew, and when I asked, "Who is she?" I prayed that Dennis would respond that he hadn't the foggiest idea what I was talking about. Instead, he looked stricken, but didn't deny it; he later told me that, having paused for far too long before responding, he realized that he could no longer make up a convincing enough lie. I threw his Christmas present at his head. Unfortunately, it was an envelope containing two skydiving tickets (he desperately wanted to leap from a plane and I, picturing myself plummeting like a screaming grapefruit, only to splat open on the Lake Elsinore hills, had psyched myself up to do it with him). The envelope had fluttered harmlessly to the ground at his feet, and my life had officially fallen apart.

Joyce Cato's voice had trailed off expectantly, bringing my scrabbling thoughts back to the situation at hand, but I wasn't biting. I remained noncommittal.

"...Yes?"

"Are you the daughter of Bob Jason Neville?" Well, fuck. No skirting that one.

"I, um, sort of. I haven't seen him for years. About twenty-two years. I don't—I mean—my mother remarried. I don't have anything to do with him. That's why my last name is Karp now, instead of Neville."

If she was a private detective, hired to track me down so this man could reenter my life, I wanted to head her off at the pass. Perhaps she would hang up the phone and leave me alone now. That's when she informed me that she was with the Los Angeles County Coroner's Office, that Bob had passed away and that she was so sorry.

Sorry? I wasn't sure what I felt. I was seated with my ex at a Jamba Juice patio, there was a man smoking to our right, the fumes were bugging me a bit and, by the way, one half of my DNA was dead. Forever. Never to return. Certain questions could never be asked, certain mysteries never solved, doors closed forever. Did I care? Did I feel sorry? I didn't know. Detachedly, I wondered if I sounded callous to Joyce Cato as I asked, "Was it an overdose?"

Across from me, Dennis looked up suddenly, his dark eyes pooling with concern. The consummate actor. I paused, absorbing the tinny voice emanating from the phone, then confirmed, "Suicide. Shotgun. Mmm-hmm. Well, right. I guess I can definitely see that. I mean, that makes perfect sense. From what I know of him, that's exactly the sort of thing he'd do." My voice was flat, matter-of-fact, even a little chipper. I was cucumber-cool, could have been conducting a job interview. If anything, I imagine I would have appeared a mite too still to the casual observer. Too collected and serene, with a cruel edge, even.

"You're the next of kin," Joyce Cato informed me. "His mother, Jesse, and his sister, Carol, were notified two weeks ago, when he was found. Jesse told us that there were four children and two ex-wives. We tracked down the other wife and two children fairly easily, since they shared his last name, but you and your sister were harder to find. You're the oldest, and the next of kin. There was no will or suicide note found, so we need you to come down to the coroner's office to take care of some things, tell us what kind of arrangements you'd like to make for the body. Unless you were ever legally adopted by your mother's husband, in which case you would no longer legally be the next of kin. Were you adopted?"

"No," I whispered. "Never formally."

"Again, I'm so sorry for your loss, Ms. Karp."

"I…you know, I didn't know him. We were never in contact. Not for two decades. Thank you for calling, but this is all very surreal. If you'll excuse me, I think that I need to call my mother and let her know. I'll give you a call back about coming down and seeing what needs to be taken care of." As an afterthought, I asked when he had killed himself. She hesitated, and then said that they had found him a few days later, but New Year's Eve was the assumed date, based on the evidence at hand.

In this way, I learned that I had two younger half sisters, both under eighteen, and that I was to be responsible for the details of my estranged drug-addict father's property distribution and cremation. I thanked Joyce Cato for her time and hung up. Inappropriately and without warning, I began laughing hysterically. Dennis's eyebrows shot up in actorly alarm.

I don't think that death is funny, obviously. In fact, death pretty much sucks. But laughing at my worst experiences has long been a favorite coping mechanism of mine. It's one of the myriad ways (too many, in my opinion) that I am like my mother, although it is definitely among the more useful traits I've picked up from her.

I cried often as a kid, when life turned dark at nine years old and any shred of childhood that I had left abruptly vanished in search of sweeter pastures. In time, hearing *Shut up and quit crying you sniveling little bitch you make me sick,* as I was soundly beaten around the head with an umbrella, spatula or the occasional cutting board, rubbed off and I grew a thicker skin. Tears morphed into scathing, sarcastic wit. I wouldn't give her the *satisfaction* of crying, dammit. *Ha. How do you like me now?* were the words I would spat out in my mind. I didn't say it aloud—didn't have to. My venomous, defiant attitude was evident in the lack of the very waterworks that my mother railed against, and the beatings grew steadily more brutal. Long gone were the days of the simple spanking with the paddle that was adorned with a picture of a fawn followed by a shambling bear cub on it. "For the little dear with the bare behind." I hated that paddle but I would eventually come to regard it with a certain nostalgia. The good old times of a smack or two on the bum were over. *Floggings will continue until morale improves,* I thought bitterly. It was only after fleeing the scene and locking myself in my room that

I would allow myself to disintegrate into red-faced, snot-running misery.

My mother was silent at first when I dialed her number to tell her about the hasty shuffling off of Bob's mortal coil. Then she asked me to come home.

"I'm with Dennis at the moment. We've got some things to talk about briefly, and then I'll come back and we can call the coroner together." Brattily, I relished the dig a tiny bit. She disapproved of Dennis, and long before he'd started boinking another chick, too. As a matter of fact, she disapproved of any man I dated, simply because none of them were Jehovah's Witnesses, although I have often wondered if she would even have given her blessing had I taken up with a JW boy. To some degree, I have always had the nagging feeling that seeing me happy with any man bothered Linda Karp to the extreme. For another human being to have loved me unconditionally would have meant that her own marital discord, the blame for which had often been placed squarely on my tiny preteen shoulders, was her own fault after all. She was content to predict doom and gloom for any and all future relationships—her regular proclamation that nobody would ever love me left the deepest and most lasting welts on my psyche that I am ever likely to sustain. I continue to be haunted by that prediction: Those just aren't the sort of words a person forgets.

As for the Witness boys, you couldn't have tempted me to go there if you'd paid me. They were generally self-righteous, quietly arrogant milquetoasts. Jehovah's Witnesses advocate inequality of the sexes—the complete subjugation of women to their husbands' every decision, even if blatantly unjust or flat-out wrong. Countless Jehovah's Witness women have thus quietly endured every form of abuse at the hands of their husbands for years, being told by congregation elders to "wait on Jehovah" in the hopes that someday the injustice would be addressed—by God, of course. Not by, say, police or social workers. Trained and certified domestic violence authorities had nothing on a group of old men in a windowless room and the all-knowing Big J upstairs. Thinking about submitting to some soppy fundamentalist boy playing head of the house made me want to pluck out my own eyeballs like grapes off a vine and stomp on them. Luckily for me, I suppose, the fundamentalist boys in question sensed my obstinacy, because they gave me a wide berth and pursued less opinionated girls in the congregation, which was fine by me. When you're a Jehovah's Witness kid, and sex is verboten before marriage (and not in the usual religious "Gee, we'll be really, really upset and/or disappointed if you have sex, but if you must, use a condom" way, but rather in the manner of "You will be excommunicated and shunned by family and friends if you have sex"), pickings are slim and marriages happen quickly. Very quickly. Courtships are rushed, flushed with the normal raging hormones, and you'd think that the other girls in the congregation would have appreciated my utter lack of interest in competing with them for a "suitable marriage mate," but they were as disconcerted by me as anyone else. I had not had a close friend in the congregation since childhood. I was a lonely, frustrated island at each of our several weekly meetings at the local Kingdom Hall. The very words *marriage mate* made me shudder. It was all too clinical, too passionless for me. I wanted love. And passion. And sex. Especially sex. As an early bloomer, I engaged in frequent and urgent masturbation, which eased me through a sexless, guilt-tinged decade before I would finally throw my arms up in defeat (or triumph, depending on how you look at it) and toss my beribboned virginity at age eighteen to a pushy twenty-four-year-old, non-JW boyfriend. Coincidentally, he was also an arrogantly religious milquetoast. I guess programming dies hard.

Dennis and I sat on a grassy patch near the Jamba Juice parking lot. Suddenly, he was inquisitive. He wanted to know what was going through my head, how I was feeling, and this time he meant it. I assume it was an odd thing to be present and watch such an intimate moment in anybody's life, much less his ex-girlfriend's. Now, of course, I look back and wonder if he was mining this scene for future monologue fodder, but at the time I was grateful for the conversation. Pathetic wimp that I was, I desired nothing more than to keep him by my side, regardless of his value as a person or a companion. I didn't want to be alone, needed to be loved in the most heinously desperate way, and indiscriminately. I couldn't stand to lose anything else, even if it was dead weight that clearly should have been jettisoned.

So I talked. I rambled and spilled out everything I was feeling or, rather, not feeling, about Bob's death. I talked about some of the crazy things Bob had done while hopped up on drugs. I reminisced about the pet hamster I named Benjamin that Bob had bought for me, that I merrily would drop off my top bunk bed onto the floor, watching it bounce and then scurry away, terrified, while I giggled as only a two-year-old can, unaware of my own cruelty. Then, emboldened by my own stream of verbal diarrhea, I spoke about Dennis and how he had hurt me. I spoke of the pain I experienced every day knowing that a man who was, by all accounts, honorable and sensitive would cuckold me. His own father had left his mother and run off to Italy with another woman. Dennis abhorred infidelity, swore time and again that he could never cheat—it was against his very nature. I finished off by telling him that he wasn't the man I thought he was, and that I missed that man. To my surprise, he agreed.

"I'm not the man that I thought I was, either." He said regretfully, tinged with a hint of melancholy and self-loathing, perhaps. "Please believe that I've stayed up late nights wrestling with this, with everything that you've said here today, and I don't like myself any better for it. We both may need to accept that I'm not necessarily a good man anymore; that I'm an asshole and that's just how things are."

"But why would you want to be an asshole? Why would you want to accept being anything less than the best version of yourself? I don't understand. There's plenty I don't like about myself—it's an uphill battle against my worst urges every day. I fight them constantly, though, because settling for less, becoming the very person I hate, would sicken me to my core. So why?"

He had no answer.

My mother greeted me at the door upon my arrival home. "I called Joe about Bob. He let Moll know. She burst into tears when she found out."

Molly. Molly, Molly, Molly. Blonde, tiny, beautiful, zealously preachy Molly. My little sister, off in Arizona knocking on doors, trying her darndest to convert as many unsuspecting saps to Jehovah as she could (before Armageddon came and burning meteors whipped from the heavens to destroy the other 99 percent of the human race), and stalking some poor nineteen-year-old kid in her congregation she had decided was her future husband nearly the second she had laid eyes on him. Even for a fundamentalist cult member, she can be a little nutty. I had a hard time reconciling how one person could be simultaneously so highly intelligent, as I know her to be, and yet exhibit all the awareness of a sack of rocks—nearly every sentence she utters a parroting of one or several Jehovah's Witness buzzwords and catchphrases, in place of her own independent thoughts and ideas, her creativity and potential quashed in the face of intense pressure to conform.

I also had difficulty reconciling our two wildly different reactions to the same news. Molly would only have been a year and a half, maybe two years old, the last time she saw Bob. Although I harbored some very vivid images of him, I wasn't sure how much she could possibly have retained. On the other hand, perhaps that was why she cried.

My mother acted relatively blasé about the news, but there was a trembling undercurrent to her voice that belied her words. I knew that she had lived in constant fear of him showing up again one day, the man who had driven her out to the desert in the dead of night, and left her in only a T-shirt to grope her way back home. The man who had taken Molly and me as covers on trips to Mexico, stuffing large quantities of hard drugs into our car seats on the way back, to resell them in California. The man who had suggested that my mother let Molly die when she was born with a life-threatening condition requiring open-heart surgery, because they just couldn't afford the medical bills. The man who had taken me and Mom out to the garage, held a gun to our heads and threatened to blow our brains out all over the Plymouth Voyager, before killing himself, too.

Now, he really had killed himself, and I could see that Mom didn't quite know what to do with the two decades of fear she had nursed to the point of paranoia.

"I'm just so glad he didn't take anyone else with him. You know he so easily could have," she kept repeating, over and over. Yes, I knew.

The following morning, I received a frantic voice-mail message from a young girl. While I still couldn't feel anything for Bob, it broke my heart.

"Um, hi, this is Patricia Neville—Patty—and I live in Texas and I think you knew my dad, Bob Neville, that is, I think that you're maybe my older sister, and I've actually been looking for you for a few years, and my mom was helping me, but we didn't know your last name so we couldn't find you but now the coroner found you. My mom is Charlie, I think you used to know her when you were little. She married my dad, our dad, and basically I'm trying to find out anything that I can. The coroner said that you're kind of in charge of things from here, and if you can tell me anything about my dad, please, please, please give me a call back."

She rattled off her cell phone number.

Her voice had cracked at a few points and I agonized for her. There was very little I could tell her about Bob since the time I'd known him, and certainly nothing of great comfort from what I did remember. I didn't feel like a sister to this stranger, not yet, but I did feel considerable pain on her behalf, and that was something.

Over lunch at Marie Callendar's that afternoon with my parents, I broke the news of the call. My mother immediately launched into a diatribe.

"I don't think that you should contact her! There's no reason that you should contact her! You have nothing to tell her. Let her mother tell her whatever she wants to know about Bob—that's *her* responsibility! Did you ever think of that?! It's not your place to tell her all the negative crap about Bob! You don't even know what kind of people these *are!*"

Quietly, I pushed some peas around with my fork. "I wasn't planning on going into gritty details with her, Mom. I just thought, you know, she reached out. Perhaps I can drop a kind word or two, and if they want some input as to arrangements for the body, let them give it. Besides, I might eventually have to speak with them anyway, if I have to divvy up any property. You didn't hear the message. She was *pleading* with me. She's a kid, Mom. She just lost her father. It would be rude just to ignore her call."

"No, I don't think it would be rude at all. There's nothing rude about it. You're under no obligation to her, and I'm sure she'll understand that." I stared at her. Her face was impassive, but danger was lurking there. The anger I knew all too well bubbled just below her skin. Her eyes had gone empty and cold as they did whenever she wanted to slug me. I decided it was best not to push her in this mood, and shrugged lightly, choosing instead to snorkel through my minestrone soup. Abruptly, she stood and left the table for the restroom.

I looked at my mother's husband, Joe. *Poor, poor Joe*, the Jehovah's Witnesses all murmured in the congregation, and at times I was inclined to agree. Rarely did anybody ask Joe what he thought. Meek and pale, with fading reddish hair and a sunburned balding spot on top of his head, Joe was generally considered to be quiet, humble and unassuming. Or, more often, a wuss who couldn't keep his damn wife in line as the Bible commanded. I felt for Joe, as I often felt for my mother. The ill-suited match had taken its toll on both of them.

"Dad. What do *you* think? She's already made it clear what she thinks, but you haven't said anything since this whole thing began. What's your take?"

He was surprised that I asked him. I caught just the briefest glimpse of a double take, but he gazed back at me calmly and scrunched up his forehead, rolling his eyes heavenward and quirking his mouth as though the answer were obvious.

"I think you should call her back. I think it would be rude not to. You need to understand, your mom has lived in fear for a long time. Now he's dead, but the fear is still there, and these two girls are a link to that fear—evidence of it. Perhaps if they had contacted you while he was still alive, my answer might be different. But he's dead now and I don't see how just a phone call to see where things lie can hurt."

"That's what I was thinking, too. Thank you, Dad. I'll call her back. I don't think Mom needs to know just yet." We locked eyes. We had an unspoken agreement.

Patty Neville was seventeen and her sister, Penny, was fourteen. Bob had dropped out of their lives when Patty was eight and Penny was five. Their mother, Charlie, had remarried after divorcing Bob and moved the family to Texas. Bob ignored all phone calls from the devastated girls. He reappeared four years later, urged on by a new girlfriend's prompting. Since then, he had been part of Patty and Penny's lives—to a degree. They would visit him in California for holidays and school vacations, sleeping in his mother's garage as Molly and I had as toddlers (although she was a kind and hardworking woman, Jesse had OCD, which did not permit potentially messy children to enter her house; she kept a rake by the door, should somebody step on the carpet and reverse the direction of the piling). A year before his death, Bob would put Jesse into a nursing home and, as trustee of her financial affairs, refinance her paid-off house. He took the $200,000 the bank gave him and blew it all on drugs and toys before the year was out.

My half sisters last visited their father just before Christmas, mere weeks prior to his death. At the airport for their return flight, Patty claimed Bob had stooped to her and his voice had halted with emotion as he admonished, "Don't be an idiot and do drugs like me, Patty." I tried to picture this scene in my mind, but had a hard time doing so. All I knew about Bob was an amalgam of pain, molestation and neglect. It's fair to say that I never much fantasized about any possible human side that he might have.

The girls became concerned when they called Bob to wish him a Happy New Year, and received no response. Even more troubling, he failed to call and acknowledge Patty's birthday a few days later. Right around the same time they were repeatedly dialing his cell phone, Bob's tenant, an old man renting his mother's garage, called 911 and insisted that something was wrong. He had not seen Bob for days, and that was unusual. Knocks at the front door went unanswered. Hearing Bob's cell phone ringing nonstop inside the house, the man begged the police to come. They arrived, entered the house through the bathroom window and found his body.

"A lot of people had problems with my dad," Patty said when I called. "I know that not a lot of people liked him. But…do you think he was a good man? Carol called us a couple of nights ago and started right in, nagging on about how horrible he was. I know that he did some very bad things…but do you think there was good in him?"

Er…he kinda sorta molested me for several months. And was on drugs. And beat my mother to a bloody pulp. But besides that, oh, yeah, he was a great guy. A real stand-up character.

Patty had thrown me for a loop. She was clearly desperate for consolation, and grasping for straws. I considered lying my head off. At any rate, I couldn't relate my version of Bob to her. She was a grieving kid who had just lost her father. Finally, I gave her the best answer I knew how.

"I didn't know him all that well, Patty. I hadn't seen him since I was little. I do know that he clearly had some demons of his own to battle, as we all do. But forget what I think about him. What's more important is how *you* want to remember him. It sounds to me like you think he did his best to be a good dad to you toward the end. It sounds like you loved him very much, and you feel that he loved you back. And it's not my place, or Carol's place, or *anybody's* place, to try to take that away from you. If you have good memories of your dad, hold onto them. Remember him as you knew and loved him."

I waited, suddenly feeling dumb and sentimental—*My god, that answer was cheesy beyond belief, even for me.* But it was the best I could come up with. A long, long pause.

"Thank you, Bri. That was perfect. That was exactly what I needed to hear."

Charlie, Bob's second wife, was delighted to speak to me. I still remembered vague bits about her—her name, her living in an apartment with Bob at some point while he still had visitation rights, how kindly she had treated me and Molly—but that was about it. It turned out that she had told Patty and Penny about Moll and me several years earlier. Patty, in particular, was intrigued and wanted to track us down. Charlie and Patty tried for about three years, but couldn't find anything on us—they didn't know my mother's new married name. Now Charlie was gushing over the phone, sweet as ever, and planning a visit out to California with the girls.

"I didn't communicate much with Bob," she confessed, "other than making arrangements for the girls to visit. Things were strained there. But the girls are taking it very hard, so I was thinking of bringing them out there for a sort of mock funeral."

"That reminds me," I interjected. "I wanted to talk to you guys and find out if you had any specific wishes for his body. I can't afford a burial, but perhaps you or Jesse might want that. If not, we can look into cremation."

"We've already spoken to Jesse. None of us can afford a burial, so she said to go ahead with cremation. The coroner told us over the phone that you have the sole right to release the ashes to us. Would you be willing to do that?"

"Oh, gosh, yes, of course. Absolutely. I don't want them."

"Great. We'd love to come out there and let them go over the sea. He had a little boat, you know. He loved sailing and fishing, so I think it would go a long way toward helping the girls heal."

"About the boat. I'm also going to be stopping by the coroner's and the public administrator's offices. I'll find out what we're looking at as far as property. I don't imagine he left a lot, but of course I would want you and your girls to get your fair share. I don't…I didn't expect any of this. I'm not out to get anything. Clearly, you guys would be far more entitled to anything he left than I would. To them, he was actually a father. I'll keep you posted on what I find out from the coroner and the public administrator."

Charlie hesitated, as if she wanted to bring something up but didn't quite know how. "We aren't too interested in property; if anything, the most important thing to the girls is that they get some photos that he took on their last trip out. He took them to the lake and he rode his old Jet Skis. If you go by the house, could you look for the photos?"

The house. That was a little unnerving to me—the guy had killed himself there. Still, I assumed I'd have to go by at some point if there was any property to be dealt with.

"Sure, I'll do it. Where would the photos be?" I hoped against hope that she would say the garage or the living room or...

"They'd most likely be in his bedroom."

His bedroom. Where he blew his brains out. Oh, *thanks*.

I met with the coroner on a gray, rainy Saturday. I wasn't sure what to expect. It turned out to be a large, courthouse-style building in Los Angeles with very cool turn-of-the-century architecture. Not particularly scary to me—more awe-inspiring than anything, fascinated with old buildings as I am. My parents accompanied me, and I nervously cracked death jokes the entire way there, lightening the mood. We all laughed, the reality of the whole thing not having quite set in.

My mother had been furious when I revealed that I had contacted my half sisters. I tried to assure her that they were very nice and just your average grieving family, but she had locked herself inside her room and refused to speak to me for several hours, which was actually quite minimal for her—she was famous for going weeks or even months on end doling out the silent treatment, positive that the deprivation of her presence was killing all of us. This started when I was nine and my sister eight. It always made Molly sob. She would camp outside my mother's door and pound on it with her tiny fists, begging her mommy to love her again. Molly did not get beaten as I did, so the worst punishment that she could ever fathom was the complete withholding of our mother's sparse affection.

As for me, these times were the calmest in my existence. There was nothing quite as relaxing as a minivacation from Mom. The horror would only begin again when the sticky double doors to the master bedroom would open and she would reemerge, calmly speaking to us again as though nothing had happened. I never understood how Molly and even Joe regarded her siestas as a negative habit. Sure, it couldn't be healthy for my mom to hole herself up in bed, her hatred toward all of us emanating through the cracks of the locked doors like oozing pus. But surely, it was better for *our* mental health to be free of her for a bit, right? So what exactly was the problem?

In any event, my mother's sojourn was abruptly curtailed by her curiosity. She couldn't keep herself mad enough at me to miss out on the excitement of the Saturday matinee production of *Brianna's Fun with the Coroner,* so off we went, as a family.

Joyce Cato was a tiny and calm woman with a soothing voice. I assumed that the soothing voice was a necessity if you were going to work in the Decedent Notification Department. She provided us with a copy of the coroner's report and kindly explained our options as far as funeral arrangements and cremation. She gave me the public administrator's contact information, and an envelope containing the only item that had been on the body at the time of death—his cell phone.

"His keys were in his pocket, but they have to be sent over to the PA first; they need to decide if probate is necessary. I don't know if you want…the gun, but it's legally yours if you do. You have to pick that up separately—we don't give firearms to family members here."

Horrified, I hastily assured her that I had no interest in the shotgun.

"No, I didn't think you would, but we have to ask," she explained.

I winced. I knew how my final request would sound. "I know this is going to seem weird, or gross, but—I'd like to see the mortuary photo, please. If you don't think he's too...mangled...or anything. If it's something I could probably handle, I'd like to see it."

"It's not weird or gross—believe me. Many relatives ask to see the death photo. We get all kinds of requests in here—I've heard it all." She pulled out a piece of paper. "I don't know what you can or can't handle, of course. Every person's threshold is different." She studied the photo. "I can tell you that it's not as bad as many that I've seen. His face is all still there, there's no jaw missing or anything."

Kindly, Joe reached out and took the photo from her. "I'll look first," he said. My mother looked away. She didn't want to see it.

Joe looked for about thirty seconds, then handed the sheet to me. "It's OK. I think you can handle it."

I looked.

The man on the slab looked like nobody I had ever known. I couldn't find the slightest hint of similarity between him and the scarecrow-gaunt young man with the mop of blond hair and the glittering, often fanatical eyes who had once been my father. This man was obese, well on his way to three hundred pounds, and mostly bald. One eye was closed, the other partially open and rolled up into his head. His mouth hung open, teeth crowded and fleeing in all different directions, like scared goldfish; black blood spatters swallowed most of his face. Offhandedly, I wondered why they didn't wipe down his face or something before taking the picture. The room suddenly smelled like death, whereas moments before, it had simply been a regular office with a conference table.

"Thank you," I whispered, handing back the photo and feeling queasier than I expected.

For several nights, unable to sleep, my thoughts would revert back to that face on the mortuary drawer, and I would try to imagine what was going through his mind when he pulled the trigger. Was it planned? Spur of the moment? Was he drunk? High? Did he, at any point, feel the cold gun barrel against the inside of his mouth, and think, "I can still back out of this, I don't have to do it..." before deciding "...yes, yes I do," and pulling the trigger?

Once, at fourteen years old, I was left behind at the house while my mother took Molly on a trip to Palm Springs. She had instructed me not to read any books— books were my lifeline to sanity, my passion and my escape, so as punishment, she liked to deprive me of them as often as possible. She drove the hour back from Palm Springs that night and peeked through my bedroom window, to make sure that I hadn't disobeyed her edict. She discovered me deep in study, preparing for my NMSQT, an optional scholarship test being administered at Troy High School the following week. Jehovah's Witnesses do not approve of pursuing higher education, the reasoning being that college is a waste of time—after all, the apocalypse is coming any day now. It's not as if God will understand that you were just too busy getting a degree to convert the poor sinners before it's too late. Besides, the Governing Body of the Watchtower, Bible and Tract Society likes to point out, going to college turns people into atheists. Mind control of this sort, keeping members in darkness and ignorance, never sat very well with me. I did well in school and part of me wanted to go on to college, even though I knew it was a very heathenish, pagan desire, this frivolously airy-fairy "pursuit of knowledge" that the Witnesses scoffed at.

I was jolted from my studies by my mother screaming through the window. I was in for it now.

Fifteen minutes of beating later, she spat on me and stalked out of my room, with the parting shot, "And just think, I was coming back to pick you up and bring you with us to Palm Springs. You don't deserve it, you little whore." I lay on the floor in fetal position, keening, the pain and outrage too much to tamp down. I could not be callous and detached that night. I waited for her headlights to dim as she sped off, and I bolted to the downstairs bathroom. I couldn't explain what came over me. I was just *done*. I was a fourteen-year-old kid who had been writing bad, angst-ridden poetry for five years just to cope and something had finally snapped. My mother's medicines were all locked up in her room—otherwise, I would have had my pick of Vicodin, Valium and any number of other prescription sleep aids, which she often unwisely mixed with her cheap boxed wine from Long's Drugstore. I flung open the medicine cabinet and rummaged. A jumbo bottle of Tylenol. That was it. Bawling like a wounded hippo, I poured out handful after handful, cramming them into my mouth, holding my face under the sink faucet, water splashing everywhere, and swallowing, swallowing, swallowing. Large doses of Tylenol would cause liver failure, right? It couldn't be all that bad. Maybe it would be easy. Like drifting to sleep.

Fifty or sixty pills later, I had finished off the bottle, and for the first time qualms set in. Then the first waves of agony hit my abdomen and I cried out, bringing my mother's tenant, Alfie, running from the guestroom, where he found me sprawled on the bathroom floor, legs akimbo, waiting to die.

"What did you do?" he asked.

I motioned toward the empty Tylenol bottle. "I...took some Tylenol. All of them." I clutched my stomach. "It hurts."

Alfie dialed my mother's cell phone and explained the situation. I heard the pause on the other end of the line, the interminable chasm of dead air as she thought. The warped cell phone voice finally replied.

"Tell her to stick her finger down her throat and throw them up. I don't have time for this." Click.

Alfie propped me up against the toilet and encouraged me to throw up the pills. I dry-heaved for several minutes, but couldn't seem to make anything come up. Finally, he shook his head sadly and left me there. I laid down on the cool tile and passed out.

I awoke the next morning, cheek pressed and stuck to the floor, drooling a little, exhausted and aching from head to toe, and from the inside out. Trembling, I climbed on my bike and rode to school. Suicide, I decided, hurt. *A lot.* Clearly, this had been a bad idea. I wouldn't be trying *that* again.

My mother returned from her trip to Palm Springs a few days later and neither of us ever mentioned the fact that—oh, by the way—I had tried to kill myself. Overdramatic histrionics were to be saved for serious offenses like forgetting to put the lids on the garbage cans or spilling a glass of water. We danced around all those pesky, silly little issues like suicide.

Perhaps by scrutinizing the mortuary photo of My Father Who Was Not My Father, I was searching for some kind of connection with this man, attempting to establish even the slightest understanding of his anguish, how he must have felt when he irrevocably, irreversibly, exploded his life out from the back of his skull. But, try as I might, I couldn't comprehend it. I could only feel ill, as though I had once again overloaded my liver with Tylenol.

Bob's death was no longer a game to me, a mystery to be pieced together, an opportunity to experience different facets of the law and the death process from the most fundamental level. It had begun that way, my curious detachment insulating me from any gut-wrenching emotional reactions, but quite suddenly, it all pivoted and began to seem more distasteful than I ever could have imagined. I didn't want to play anymore.

The public administrator's office informed me that, as the house did not belong to Bob, but to his mother, his assets totaled less than $100,000. As such, the estate would not pass into probate and whatever belonged to Bob legally passed on to me, as his next of kin.

"Do you have any idea what he left behind?" I queried.

"We haven't been to the house, but I do think somebody mentioned that there are a few recreational vehicles. You have full permission to go through the house and take anything there that you have reason to believe is his. Perhaps he will have left titles lying around, and any other useful information."

Ugh, the house again. My stomach turned a slow flip as I asked when I could pick up the keys that were on Bob's body.

That was when I learned that the keys had been lost somewhere between the coroner's office and the PA's office. Both offices swore that they didn't have them. Presumably, they're still floating in the back corner of somebody's desk drawer, lonely for their former owner from whom they were so drastically and violently parted.

"Um, how exactly am I supposed to enter the house or drive any of the vehicles?"

"We can authorize you to enter the house by any means necessary. That means that you can go in through a window or break the lock, if you like. As far as the vehicles, you'll need to pay a locksmith. That's just not our responsibility."

Two days later, I found myself hanging half-in, half-out of the window of a tiny house, one of dozens of identical, Crackerjack-box style houses on an idyllic *Edward Scissorhands*-esque block in Lakewood. It was the same window that the police had entered through. The window screen and the screwdriver that had been used to pry it from its frame had been carelessly tossed to one side on the backyard grass below. The house was on a raised foundation, and the window was quite high and narrow. Joe looked up at me, having boosted me up. This was most uncomfortable. My mother leaned casually against the back gate, chatting with the locksmith we had called to create a key for the Dodge Ram parked on the curb, collecting parking tickets on the windshield issued by a month's worth of annoyed street sweepers.

I rolled into the window, landing with an "oof!" onto the vinyl flooring. The bathroom was Pepto-Bismol pink.

I remembered how much Jesse loved pink. It was her favorite color.

The house smelled like rotten meat and decay. I wondered how much of it was my mind playing tricks on me. Opening the bathroom door, I realized something disconcerting. The house was bare. There was no furniture, or anything at all. I assumed that perhaps Carol had gotten there first, or maybe Jesse's sisters, but I never found out for sure. It was just one of those things that I ended up writing off as too petty and unimportant to create a stink about. Walking into the living room, I saw no sign of the big-screen TV that Patty had told me would be there, no couches or tables. Only an old record player against one wall and a woman's purse (one of Jesse's, I assumed). Also…what was that on the floor, near the doorway leading to the hall? I was sickened as I read the word Remington in red lettering across the long, skinny, empty box. It lay where he had left it.

A shudder ran through me, unbidden, and I hastily scurried to the back door, unlocking it and letting Joe in. My mother did not want to enter the house. I wondered what kind of nightmares, if any, this would all bring back for her, and felt a few pangs of solidarity on her behalf.

Joe and I examined the house. It was tiny, and it was easy to see at a glance that it had been completely cleaned out. Drawers were half-open in the kitchen, the occasional trinket left behind on the floor, but nothing of value. I poked my head into Jesse's room, her pride and joy. Only a 1950s crystal prism chandelier remained, kitschy perhaps, but I knew that as a child I would have loved it, a frosted cake sparkling against the pink icing walls, and it must have been lovely to Jesse as well. She had worked at the Vons down the street for over fifty years, scraped together everything she had to painstakingly pay off her tiny house. She had understood her only son's imperfections too well, but she had overlooked them as only a mother can. She had dearly loved the boy who never strayed far from home, always returning after another ruined relationship, after throwing another wife through a wall. Inexplicably, her chandelier made me sad. Such a simple joy clearly meant nothing to whoever had razed the home—perhaps Carol, or another family member. I would later learn, from Jesse herself and her caretakers, that Carol had not even visited Jesse in the nursing home when she learned of Bob's death.

We paused at the closed door to Bob's room. We had to look for Patty and Penny's pictures, although I wondered if there would be anything left. Joe pushed the door open, and promptly turned green. Peering past him, I understood why. I also knew why the house was still clogged with the stench of death and rot—it had not been my imagination, after all.

It was a HAZMAT scene. A month past Bob's death, and the room had not been cleaned. In my conversation with the coroner, I was given to understand that the responsibility of cleaning the house was the owner's, which meant that Jesse, or whomever was handling her affairs, would need to hire a crime scene cleanup crew. From some covert calls to the nursing home in Downey, I learned that Jesse's two sisters had obtained power of attorney, and were in the process of selling the house. I had therefore assumed that they would take care of that very important detail.

I was wrong.

The room was cramped, perhaps ten feet by eight feet. A queen-sized bed took up the vast majority of it and an armoire stood just to the left of the doorway. Rivulets of dried blood, like tiny fingers, dribbled down the entire front of the armoire. A long, thick maroon stain, twice as thick as my arm, snaked across the carpet, trailing off as it went. Clearly, this was where Bob's head had dragged along the floor as the officers who found him had attempted to hoist his considerable mass onto a stretcher. I had read in the coroner's report that a female officer had been the one to enter through the little window and find him. Was she horrified or was it just another day at work for her?

The closet was cleared out, racks of hangers still bearing shirts tossed on the bed. The drawers of a dresser next to the closet had clearly been ransacked, clothing still hanging out of it. The mattress had been stripped of its sheets and comforter—they were wadded in a heap by the far wall. Had the police turned it all upside down in search of a suicide note? Or had it been Carol, leeching anything of value, scouring even under the mattress and in the corner of the closet? Could she really have stood it, tramping through the blood-soaked suicide scene of her own brother? She had known him far more deeply than I had. She must have loved him once, mustn't she?

At the base of the armoire, I saw scattered, crumbly, gray bits. Pieces of skull? Of congealed brain matter? Joe tried to hold steady, but I could tell he was losing it. I told him I would be OK—I thought I could handle it from here. Blankly, he nodded his head and turned around. Joe had a strong constitution, but I thought I heard him gag a little as he escaped.

God, the smell. It was putrid. I went into automatic mode. *Don't think about it don't think about it don't think about it just do it don't think about it.* In the kitchen I found two limp washcloths, left behind in the chaos. I held them in my palms like pot holders and returned to Bob's room. *Not thinking about it not thinking about it not thinking about it.* I had lost all hope of finding anything of use in here, as someone had clearly already scoured the area, but I still needed the photos that I had promised to locate for my two new half sisters.

I palmed the knobs of the armoire, carefully searching every drawer, feeling the bloodstains burning through the washcloth to my skin below. *Not thinking about it not thinking about it not thinking good fucking god don't let there be blood-borne pathogens not thinking about it.* Nothing in the drawers. I checked Bob's laundry hamper, the dresser, nothing. I walked over to the corner, avoiding stepping in the pool of blood on the carpet, and lifted the wadded bed linens. Startled, I saw what they had been covering. I inhaled sharply and immediately wished that I hadn't; tasting decomposed air. The white wall was sprayed with blood. Someone spilled maple syrup. It's just maple syrup. Look at that, that's not blood. That looks nothing like blood. That's maple syrup, even if it smells like death and disease and blood-borne pathogens and my dead sperm donor's brain fluids.

Nothing. My search had yielded no photos. I felt angry on behalf of Patty and Penny, and a little bit angry for myself, too. I had gone through all this for nothing. I had failed them. Poking my head out the front door, I called to my mom that there were no photos, and nothing of value left in the room, except for a tiny TV set on top of the armoire.

"You should take the TV," she responded. "They might want it." I doubted it, but wasn't much in the mood for argument. Feeling like a vulture, I held my breath and darted back, reaching behind the splattered armoire and unplugging the television. I reached up to pull it down, and it caught on the corner, which to my surprise jiggled open. It was then that I realized: The top bar of the armoire was a shallow, secret pull-out drawer. It wasn't immediately obvious; Carol would have missed it. My washcloth hands probed inside, and came up with sheaves of papers— vehicle registration titles, insurance cards, bank statements, checkbooks, receipts, mail…a wealth of information. My eyes bugged into Ping-Pong balls, Muppet-style.

The titles were for two old Wave Runner Jet Skis, a beat-up dirt bike we found in an outside shed, a large GE delivery/moving truck with an electronic lift, a fourteen-foot Bayliner boat and the Dodge Ram. All these vehicles were on the premises. There was also a title for a thirty-foot Fan Coach trailer, which was not. All the items were older, mid-'80s to early '90s, except for the 1999 Dodge Ram. The locksmith we had hired cut new keys, and I clambered into Bob's former Dodge as my parents hooked up the boat and Jet Skis for towing. It felt strange to be sitting there, in a dead man's truck. It was filthy; buried in dust, paperwork and random odds and ends. I began sorting, throwing out the trash and keeping little items I thought might prove sentimental or meaningful to Patty and Penny: a pair of sunglasses, a wristwatch, a baseball. I also analyzed the bank statements and checkbooks. From what I could tell, there was no money left in any of his accounts, including the joint ones he shared with his mother. He had not only blown every last dollar of his own, but her entire hard-earned life savings.

Disturbed, I continued my methodical digging through the truck. In the center compartment between the seats, my hand brushed against a Walmart photo pack. My heart skipped a beat. I pulled out the photos. Bob with hunting buddies. The bed of the truck down, tiny decapitated doves lined up as trophies. A deer carcass. I flipped past these impatiently, squinching my eyes shut, perceiving tinges of cruelty from him even now. Photos of the inside of a trailer, which I guessed was the Fan Coach, possibly for insurance purposes. And then...I had them. Images of Patty and Penny, wearing orange life jackets, astride the two Wave Runners on the lake. All toothy smiles and gangly limbs. He had loved them. Again, I thought back to Molly, bursting into tears on the phone. I had told her about Patty and Penny and she wanted to speak with them. Perhaps she wondered why he could love them and not her, dying in a hospital crib, a "Jehovah's Witness— No Blood!" sticker humorously stuck to her soft infant forehead. I hoped against hope that such a thought would never occur to her, although I feared it already had.

Patty and Penny decided that they would like to have the Jet Skis. They would be towed out to Texas, a tangible reminder of their father. The dirt bike and boat would be sold and they would also receive the money from the sale. My mother and sister would take the delivery truck and sell it, keeping the proceeds from that sale. Molly also expressed an interest in the Fan Coach camping trailer, but couldn't come up with the time or funds to have it towed to her in Arizona, so she gave up on getting that. The entire division of property was settled quickly, in a completely amicable way and devoid of resentment or greed, for which I was thankful. That left me with the Dodge Ram and the trailer, if we could ever figure out where the trailer was stored.

The truck could definitely come in handy, I knew. *But what the hell will I do with a damn trailer?!* It was the proverbial big white elephant of Bob's property. *Meh. Probably sell it, when I get a chance.*

Dennis called me a couple of nights later, the evening before he was to fly up to San Francisco to audition for admission to the Juilliard School of the Performing Arts.

"Wish me luck, babe."

I did so, quietly. We began a long talk in which I regaled him with my adventures swanning through a suicide scene, laughing bleakly at the absurdity of the whole thing.

And then he told me that he wanted to move on with Mysti.

Tears. Anger. Accusations.

And finally, "Look, Bri, I want you in my life. I'm not opposed to us trying again at a later date, if this doesn't work out. But this is what my heart wants. I know it's wrong and I know it makes me a bad person, and I might despise myself for it. But my heart *wants* it, don't you understand?"

Fuck you. Fuck you to hell, I cried out bitterly, deep in my splitting rib cage.

"Yes. I understand, Dennis."

"You're my best friend, Bri. You know more about me in so many ways than anybody else. I don't want to lose this closeness, this amazing friendship we have. I want you in my life. Please stay in my life."

Fuck you, you goddamn son of a bitch.

"Yes. I'll stay. I love you and I'll wait." I hated myself for my weakness, my pathos. I should have been stronger than this and I knew it. Looking back, I probably didn't even really love him—I was just a sap who couldn't lose my final tenuous grip on the possibility of happiness and love.

Pause.

"OK, then. I'll call you when I get back from San Francisco. I promise."

I believed him.

He didn't call.

I never heard from Dennis again.

Chapter Three

I had chosen to leave home as soon as I was legally able to at eighteen, but was once again grudgingly living with my parents. The only reason I had returned was that suddenly, and unexpectedly, I was unable to continue making rent payments following the loss of my job, despite my struggle to do so using my unemployment checks. If I had felt I had any choice in the matter, I would never—*never*—have returned to that house, the site of so many deeply rooted, discomfiting memories.

It was an incongruously gorgeous day, the afternoon I was laid off. I had been the executive assistant to the VP of Human Resources and admin to the entire HR department at Kelley Blue Book for just under a year. And I loved—*loved*—my job.

I had held many positions before this one. At the age of ten, I was sent by my mother to work at a tanning salon she frequented. They were looking for a front-desk girl. At first glance, it was easy for me to pass as a little older than I was—maybe fourteen. I carried myself well and was a quiet, solemn kid with a formidable vocabulary for my age. Nobody ever questioned it. I was paid under the table for eleven months and proved myself capable of taking on ever-increasing responsibility, even being left alone in charge of the salon. One day, I wheeled my bike into the building, direct from my routine sixth-grade schoolday, to find movers shuffling out hairdressing stations and tanning beds like blubbery white whales. Lily and Tina, the two stylists who had become my closest friends and confidants, hovered helplessly, fuming and confused. Rachael, the salon owner, had decided to return to her home country of Israel. Without notice, the three of us were out of work.

I went on to work for my mother's husband's company, Hill & Canyon Aquatics Services—a pool/pond/waterfall maintenance service, which also operated a store called the Koi Pond Shoppe, dealing in various brands of koi fish. All unpaid, natch. I learned administrative and accounting principles from the ground up by trying to balance the books of my dad's chaotic office, buried under invoices and files dating back to the late 1980s. I even learned how to give medical injections to new shipments of fish added to our inventory, without feeling squeamish at gripping their glistening, flapping wet bodies in one hand and plunging a needle in with the other, before flipping them into their new tanks.

The Koi Pond Shoppe eventually closed down due to lack of business, but I continued working with koi. Hill & Canyon had performed the maintenance on Disneyland Hotel's ponds and waterfalls for several years, and I took over the Disney account at age twelve. My mother obtained a work permit for me and persuaded Disney security to provide me with an employee badge. Disney would not hire employees under sixteen, but the technicality was that I worked for a subcontractor, so the Happiest Place on Earth did not bother to check my age. I ended up with a photo ID of myself, heavily made-up with dark lipstick and mascara to make me look older, and free access to Disneyland at any time.

I also found myself performing a koi fish feeding show at the hotel pond one to two times a day, depending on the season. This involved answering (or at least, making up plausible-sounding answers to) the most common questions that guests asked about the fish, and trying to keep people from flooding the feeding platform. "One person at a time, please!" "I need you to stay behind that line until it's your turn, please, ma'am!" I became used to shouting above the din of tourists bedecked in white jean shorts, purple fanny packs and Mickey Mouse ears. One by one, guests would step onto the feeding platform, take a fistful of food and lean out above the pond. Three hundred koi, ranging from a few inches long to a few feet (my favorite, fondly dubbed "André the Giant," was the largest at nearly four feet long with a smooth, abnormally bulging yellow forehead—a freak like me, I thought), popped their mouths open and closed expectantly. It was at this point that many would lose their nerve and simply toss the food in. The bravest, who chose to believe my assurance that the fish would not, *could* not hurt them, would thrust their hands into the sea of sucking fish and generally let out a squeal of delight and/or surprise at the sensation of the Hoover-esque mouths drawing the food from between their clenched fingers, accompanied by a very satisfied smacking noise that made the crowd laugh. Flashbulbs went off, capturing laughing relatives and, more than once, screaming children insisting that the fish did have teeth and were biting their fingers off (yet, they always stood in line for a second turn).

One might rightfully wonder just how I made my way to work every day. My hometown of Fullerton bordered Anaheim, but it was still a good ten-mile drive to the Disneyland Hotel. The truth is, I started driving at twelve. My mother, sick of driving me to work and losing valuable sleep time, taught me to drive an automatic transmission. This was not as easy as I initially supposed. The mechanics of operating the car were easy enough—I was a tall kid and could reach the pedals—and I quickly grasped the rules of the road. My mom's teaching skills, however, left much to be desired. I vividly remember an incident on the freeway where I, not seeing another car in my blind spot, signaled a lane change and found my mother's hand snarled in my hair, my face smashed over and over into the steering column as I screamed in pain, desperately grasping the wheel and holding it as straight as I could to keep from swerving all over the road. Eventually, I managed to pull off to the freeway shoulder and weep hysterically, shaking, as my mother continued crushing my head against the wheel and window, blood flowing from my nose and smearing my bruised face. Finally, she stopped, instructed me to start up the car and continue driving to our destination. She would only snap shortly, "Don't ever do that again. Watch where the fuck you're going."

Once I was thoroughly trained and trusted with the car, however, I was sent out daily to work, or to drop off and pick up my sister at school, or just to run the odd errand for my mother. I was only told, "Don't get pulled over." And I never did. In the beginning I was terrified that a cop would catch me and that I would be in huge trouble for operating a freaking piece of heavy transportation machinery a full four years before I was authorized to get my license. It never really occurred to me that my mother could get in trouble for this. My mother might as well have been God, for all I knew. If anything, I assumed that if I were found out, she would tell police that I had stolen her car. Eventually, though, I got more comfortable with the whole arrangement, even cocky. I became an incredibly safe driver and stopped worrying about being caught. I wasn't allowed to take the car out on my own wherever I liked, but I would often stay for hours at the Disneyland Hotel, far longer than it took me to complete the koi feeding show, leaning on the locked gate and staring down at my fish. They knew me, I liked to think. They would conglomerate into a great mass and stare up at me with buggy eyes, wrestling and bumping each other to get closer to me. Probably hoping for more food, I knew, but in my fantasies they had built-in, individual personalities in each of their fishy little brains. They were happy to see me when nobody else was. They were my friends. They were calm amid the hurricane.

Throughout my teens, I continued to work several evening and weekend part-time jobs. I was a restaurant hostess at Bobby McGee's, parading through the foyer, soft curling ostrich feathers flopping in sausage-curled hair, grandly waving a fake wooden shotgun as "Sinful Sal," the resident saloon girl. A customer later complained about the implications of an innocent, blue-eyed, fifteen-year-old proclaiming herself "sinful," and I was renamed "Shotgun Sal," which was somehow apparently much better and more tyke-appropriate. I proudly kept two more cap pistols in satin garters next to my fishnet stockings, which I would pull out at inappropriate moments to fire at other servers or at small children. I went on to host at Orange Hill Restaurant, a four-star affair perched atop a winding hill with a breathtaking view of Orange County. I worked as a receptionist for a veterinarian, for Blockbuster Video as a manager, for an insurance company, for a law office and for another salon as a shampoo girl. My tenures averaged one to two years; I simply worked two or even three jobs at a time in addition to attending school full time. The more I could work, the less I would have to be at home. I didn't get to keep much of my earnings—every pay period I would sadly watch my paycheck swallowed up into my mom's hand. "You know we need this, Brianna," she would say, catching my eye once or twice as I gazed sadly at the $15 or $20 she would hand me back as spending money with which to buy myself clothes or school supplies. *Why won't you work, too?!* I always wanted to ask. *Why do I have to support all of you? Why do I have to be so tired, work so hard and watch it all disappear—all for nothing?* I tried to console myself with the thought that the money was buying food for Molly and me. But oftentimes Mom would simply go on a manic spending spree and bring home something beautiful but completely impractical and unnecessary. *My money bought that,* I would realize, too exhausted even to be indignant.

I was twenty-two when I hopped onboard at Kelley Blue Book in 2007. My boss was Liz Haut, VP of Human Resources and all-around Mama Bear of KBB. Liz was easily the most beloved person at the company. The year I was hired, she celebrated her fortieth year of employment with KBB. Liz knew the name of everyone at an expanding company of over five hundred people, and they could enter her office at any time with problems or in search of a shoulder to cry on, and they would find it. Human Resources tends to get a bad rap. They're viewed as the superficial, uncaring, empty-headed bimbos of the corporate world. HR, I have come to find out, is often all about how to screw over an employee with a smile plastered on your face, in favor of the company itself. It was not so with Kelley Blue Book. Despite its sheer size, there was a family feel to the place. Coworkers liked and respected one another; in the time I was there, it was very rare to see personality conflicts or egoist pissing matches. Perhaps best of all, the Human Resources department *cared* about seeing everybody happy. It was new for me to work for a company that I believed in. I had never done that before. While there have been both positive and negative aspects to every job I had ever held, it was all just filler until I could find my permanent position. I knew full well that I wasn't going to be a shampoo girl or a receptionist forever. When restaurant managers would encourage me to work my way up from hostess to server, I would recoil in horror. There was nothing wrong with serving—it's a good, honorable profession—but I didn't love working in a restaurant or in retail. It didn't thrill me to my core and make me think *This is it. This is where I'm going to work my way as high as I can go and then retire.*

At KBB, for the first time I *did* think that I could see myself working here until I was old and gray. I could still enjoy coming into this company, to these people, ten or twenty years down the road. I didn't want to leave. Running committee meetings, planning company Halloween and Christmas bashes, the thought recurred to me: *I. Fucking. Love. My. Job.* I had made it. I had arrived. I was twenty-two, pulling in $50K a year, for the first time working only one full-time job instead of three part-time ones, and it could only go up from here. I had the entire package: boyfriend, home and a killer job. I plastered my cubicle with a collage of artwork—funny photos that spoke to me, stills from old black-and-white films, animals, acquaintances, me and Dennis at county fairs. I established my mark, my permanence. This cubicle would always be my area, my sanctuary—I wouldn't allow myself to lose it.

I rented myself a tiny six-hundred-square-foot craftsman cottage in Costa Mesa, California, boxed in by tall, carved Indonesian gates. I also adopted a giant, slobbery, jowly Neapolitan Mastiff puppy as my companion and guardian.

The dog was listed on Petfinder.com by Karma Rescue of Los Angeles under the name of Dre. He had been turned into an LA shelter by a furtive couple who swore, with averted eyes, that he was not theirs—they had just found him running loose. Honest. Dre was about a year old, wore a rather expensive black leather collar studded with silver spikes and was still in possession of an impressive pair of swinging balls. The shelter was hours from putting him down when Karma Rescue pulled him out, swiftly neutering the goofy lug and placing him in a foster home with Barbara DeSantis, wife of director and TV writer Larry Charles.

A large-breed dog lover, I was passively searching for a Great Dane or Newfoundland when I came across Dre's photo. It was love at first sight, and my passive interest immediately became an active one. I fired off an email inquiring as to his availability and waited tensely. I was lucky. Karma had posted Dre's photo online mere minutes before I stumbled across it. Mine was the first inquiry, and following a meet-and-greet and a home inspection, I was approved to adopt him.

Dennis and I navigated the posh, exclusive neighborhoods of Los Angeles before pulling up in front of the mansion containing my new best friend. I had already decided to rename Dre—he would be called Fezzik, after the gentle giant character in *The Princess Bride*. Fezzik seemed to approve. Barbara welcomed us into her home, and the dog bounded into the room as though he were on a trampoline, nearly knocking us over in his exuberance.

"He...needs a little work, obviously," Barbara said, shoving him off her. "We've been working with him on training. But he's still a puppy and has a ways to go."

I didn't care. I adored my new 104-pound puppy.

Fezzik would reach 160 pounds or more at maturity. Yet, as he grew, and as I worked with him on training, he mellowed. He would jump up less and less, although he remained as excited as ever to see me return home from work. Settled into my cottage, he would nestle at my feet on the hardwood floors nightly, despite the fluffy bed I had set up for him on the other side of the room, drool pooling around his monstrous, bubbling dewflaps as he snored loud enough to wake the dead. Fezzik wanted to be where I was, and that was fine with me. I took him to the Costa Mesa dog park often, where he cultivated a fan club. Initially slightly emaciated at adoption, he filled out quickly and became a stunning, glossy, blue-gray beast. Men on the street admired him, but from a distance, giving him a wide berth. Fezzik rarely growled, but he was alert around strange men. His tail would slowly stop wagging and he would fixate on them with his beady yellow eyes before letting out a deep and menacing-sounding bark that reverberated throughout your very bones. Eventually, he would overcome his fear of strange men (I assumed it was rooted in some unknown past experience), but in the beginning, he was very protective of me, which comforted me in an odd way. I was a woman living alone. But nobody would fuck with me as long as Fezzik was around. He sensed my shy awkwardness at navigating the outside world and he was more than pleased to guide me through it.

So wrapped up was I in my new life that I failed to take particularly seriously the rumors of trouble for the auto industry in early 2008. This was Kelley Blue Book's bread and butter, but I wasn't worried. The company had been stable for over eighty years and had just begun a major collaboration with Carfinder.com. Surely things were peachy keen. While sorting through confidential documents in employee files, I stumbled across three or four layoff notices in May, but shrugged them off as isolated cases. At company meetings, the president and CFO shared revenue stats and assured us that KBB was doing just fine, hale and healthy as ever.

Which is why it came as a shock when Liz called me into her office in early July 2008 to lay me off. It was a gorgeous, sunny day. The night before, I had attended my first Angels game with Dennis. I had just bought a BlackBerry Curve and marveled at this tiny palm-sized gadget that could do practically anything, short of cooking breakfast. I used the $300 phone to snap photos of the two of us—grinning happily at the baseball game, me in a red-and-white baseball cap with a rally monkey hanging around my neck—now ensconced in my cubicle. Life was beautiful, fantastic.

"Bri...," Liz began, and I knew by her face that something was very, very wrong. "The company...has not been doing so well lately. And that means that we have to make some changes around here. We've looked at the structure of the company in depth, and we're being forced to eliminate 260 out of the current 500 positions."

Two hundred sixty? That's more than half! I thought in shock. I still didn't quite get it, though. *How horrible for all those people! What will they do? Where will they go?* Liz looked uncomfortable and then continued. "I've already spoken to Kailea and Sandhya in the HR department, and now you…" My face crumpled like paper as the impact of what she meant hit me. I sobbed as if my best friend were dying. Liz reached out and grasped my hand, tears filling her eyes.

"I am so, so sorry, Bri. Truly. And I want you to know that this is not because you were a bad worker. You have the ability and the willingness to constantly try anything and everything to succeed. And I have the feeling that perhaps in the future our paths may cross again."

I nodded, vainly attempting to get a grip and suppress my spastic snuffles. I was ashamed that I couldn't handle this in a more adult manner. I hadn't heard a peep from Kailea or Sandhya. Then I realized, *Oh my god, Sandhya just had another baby.*

Liz went on to explain the layoff process. I would receive a generous severance bonus of six weeks' pay. My last day would be in two weeks, but they were willing to allow me to take those two weeks off with pay in addition to my severance. The other employees had opted to accept this offer. I felt awkward about the arrangement, though. Who would do my work? I wanted to know. Who would finish the projects in my inbox? I took pride in my work. I didn't want to leave a mess for somebody else to fix. It was the most bewildering thing—my main fear was who would get stuck cleaning up after me. I left work and drove to Dennis's house, bawling, in need of consolation.

I came into work the next two days. I ground my fingers to nubs, boxing up my beloved collage, returning my cubicle to its bland, standard grayness and methodically completing the tasks in my inbox. I would learn that I was the only employee who had offered to stay the remaining two weeks. On the second day, one of the HR managers called me into her office.

"You don't have to stay the two weeks."

"I know. But I need to finish my stuff."

She chewed on the inside of her cheek for a moment. "You need to start worrying about yourself, Bri. You've always worried about everybody else around here. Now you need to think about *you*. It's hard out there right now, and it may get much worse very soon. Use those two free weeks to look for another job. Nobody here will think any less of you if you leave your tasks unfinished and take the time off."

She was right. I knew she was right. But dammit, couldn't she understand the hurt, the shame of having failed? I may have lost my job, but I couldn't fail. I had to prove my work ethic to myself as well as to the company that had laid me off. I had to prove that I didn't *deserve* to be laid off. So I did the only thing that I could do. I agreed to leave at the end of the day and accepted the severance check that she cut for me. Then I stayed hours past five o'clock, finishing the final scraps of work on my plate, bolting out the back door through the lunchroom, one last look back at my beloved desk, an empty slate.

Chapter Four

Having lost my job, my thoughts shifted, focused on continuing to make the $1,500 rent payments on my cottage. This is Orange County, after all; $1,500 is quite decent, even for an apartment, much less a little house.

I filed for unemployment benefits and was approved for the maximum—$450 a week. I suppose there should have been some consolation in knowing that I was receiving the same amount in unemployment benefits as, say, a laid-off CEO. But there wasn't. The total monthly amount was barely enough to cover my rent, let alone utilities, a hungry dog and a horse.

Yes, a horse.

Growing up, I had been fascinated with horses. I wanted one more than anything, or at least to take riding lessons. My mother refused. Horses were dangerous and expensive, she told me. I was allowed to ride a bombproof old trail horse once, on a family vacation to the rural mountain town of Ramona. I would not sit atop a horse for many more years after that, until one day in my early twenties, when I impulsively picked up the phone and called Kelly, a horse trainer in Santiago Canyon.

Kelly was a tiny, short-haired, spunky ball of pure energy and devout Christian platitudes. She was also a damn good rider and understood horses innately. She worked tirelessly with me on my riding skills. Her horse, Mystery, was a pleasant little Paint, still green but placid and eager to please. I reveled in my newfound hobby, reclaiming for myself some fanciful, impractical childhood wish.

One day, I showed up at the riding ring to be greeted not by chocolate-brown Mystery, but by a galloping, stocky, muscled mare, Lucy, named for Lucille Ball. Lucy was a flaming red dun American Quarter Horse. Solid and compact, she was clearly a highly intelligent and responsive horse, well-trained, but I would come to learn that she had a stubborn streak a mile wide. She was Kelly's other horse, had been boarded at a separate ranch and was being reboarded with Mystery.

"I thought you were ready to start on Lucy," Kelly greeted me. "She's a little more advanced than Mystery and, who knows, I may even sell her to you some day."

I watched Lucy canter around the ring. She kept one ear swiveled in my direction, watching me out of the corner of her eye. She looked suspicious.

"Um, you know, she's cute and all, but I'm kind of set on a draft. Some big-butted Shire or Percheron with a back like a cushy couch. Slow and docile," I qualified.

"Well, those drafts, they sure do eat a lot." I knew this, but damn if I cared. I had a decent salary; I could afford a little bit of extra feed, when I was finally ready to buy a horse.

"Climb on into the ring. I'm going to go grab the saddle," she called as she clambered up a dirt dune toward the tack shed.

I stooped and crawled between the horizontal railings, leaning against the bars and watching Lucy galloping. She didn't slow down for nuzzling and scratches, as Mystery would have. She sped up, passing me four times on her mad sprint around the pen. She passed as close as she could each time, seemingly testing how near she could get before I freaked out and bailed from the ring. I held my ground. Kelly wouldn't have sent me into the ring with a dangerous horse, right?

That was when Lucy passed by me for a fifth time and, without slowing a whit, took methodical aim and *kicked me.*

It was so fast and unexpected that I wasn't quite sure it had happened. The kick was light, aimed to warn and not to hurt, and landed on my hip like the lazy swatting of a fly. I was flabbergasted.

The little bitch.

From then on, it was personal. Goddammit, I was going to show this horse she couldn't just go around *kicking* me.

All in all, Lucy was an obedient horse. She knew her commands, knew what every slight pressure on the reins and stirrups meant. Occasionally, though, she would get a bug up her butt. Kelly assured me that this was typical mare behavior. On one occasion, Kelly sent me on a gallop up the trails near the stable. Having galloped to the tree she wanted, I turned around and assumed that I was to head back. All hell broke loose, however, when Lucy's return gallop broke into a full-on, all-out bolt, as if she were trying to take us both to hell. Screaming, I yanked on the reins harder and harder, begging, "Whoa! Whoa! *Fucking WHOA!*" At the last moment, Kelly turned her own horse into Lucy's path, blocking her, and Lucy pulled back. I, however, kept going, soaring magnificently heels-over-helmeted-head through the air and landing with a blunt thump on my side in the dirt below, where Lucy, still in the process of stopping, trampled on my leg and then backed up, realizing her error.

The wind knocked out of me, I moaned on the ground, clutching myself and feeling for broken bones. Kelly looked down at me, serene, from atop Mystery's back.

"Yeah, sorry, I probably should have told you—you never gallop a horse homeward. They get all excited, thinking, 'Woohoo, I'm about to get fed!' and then they bolt for home and you can't control them. Always walk a horse home." She dismounted.

"Get up."

"Just a second...I can't...it hurts. Just give me a second." I tried to force air into my lungs. Everything was excruciating.

"No, Bri. Get. Up."

I rolled over and staggered to my feet. My right leg protested in pain. I rolled up my pants leg. I was bruised from hip to ankle, with a couple of lovely hoofprints as a bonus.

"Get back on her."

Clearly, she was insane. "Yeah, about that...think I'll just walk back beside you guys." I made as if to grab Lucy's reins.

"Nope. Get back in the saddle. You know what they say: When you fall off a horse..."

So I put my leg in the stirrup and almost cried at the pain in my hip socket as I pulled myself up onto Lucy's back again. She stood stock-still. We walked back to the stable.

I don't know whether it was coincidence or what, but I never had a problem with Lucy again. After that, she began to warm to me considerably, and in perhaps the strangest twist of fate of all, I found myself her owner soon after, when Kelly gave her to me as a gift.

• • •

I'm sorry, Lucy. I stroked her red nose, textured and soft as crushed velvet, and stared into her brown eyes, whimpering out my goodbye. I simply couldn't afford to keep her. I didn't know if or when I'd have another job that could help pay for her board, food, tack—any of it. I didn't know how I'd ended up loving her so much, but I knew that she deserved someone who could take care of her.

I thought back on the many days I had spent exercising her in the turnout pen, riding her up the street to O'Neill National Park, watching her toss her head and strut, showing off to the other horses that would show up at the public ring. All fiery impudence and heart. I remembered her meekly padding along under Dennis on his first and only attempt at riding her around the pen, seemingly sensing his complete and utter terror, taking tiny, mincing steps as if to assure him that she wouldn't hurt him for anything. I had wrapped my arms around Lucy's sinewy neck and cried over more than one disappointment or broken heart, as she stoically munched on her alfalfa hay. She understood then. I convinced myself that she did.

I didn't know whether she understood now. I hoped so.

Selling my beloved horse lightened my financial load a little, but it did not prove enough to save my cottage. For a couple of months, I struggled to keep afloat. I was drowning, but I kept assuring myself, unconvincingly, that something would come along. I occasionally picked up temporary work through an agency, but never anything that lasted for very long. Nobody was hiring; even the companies that I would take temp assignments at were laying off masses of workers and simply calling in temps to clean up unfinished remnants of projects before cutting the temps loose as well.

As if in a foggy nightmare, I tried tallying up my finances about twelve different ways. Surely I could make this all work. Except that I couldn't. I quickly spent my meager savings on rent payments as I frantically searched for more work. And then there was no more money. Only the meager unemployment check, vanishing as quickly as it came, invested in car payments, insurance, gasoline, utilities and Fezzik.

My mother badgered me to move back in with her and Joe.

"Oh, god…no. You know we get on so much better when we don't live together, Mom."

It was true. I was able to maintain a casual, even fun friendship with my mother as an independent adult. I was free of her "my house, my rules" mentality when I lived on my own, and she knew it. Although she didn't necessarily approve of my lifestyle, she was wont to rant about it less, and the opportunity for physical abuse had been stripped from her when I moved out. The occasional mom-daughter thrift store shopping trip or lunch at BJ's Pizza could even be plenty of fun. At these times, we could laugh with each other, truly enjoy the dry sense of humor that we shared and leave the past, not forgotten, but lying undisturbed, as if shallowly buried underneath a pile of brittle, brown leaves.

These were the times I saw clearly just how lovely my mom must have been as a young, vivacious kid, beloved by all her friends and classmates, if not by her own mother. It was so easy to say "water under the bridge" when I didn't have to cohabit in close proximity with my mother's demons as well as my own.

Yet, she persisted. Where else would I go? I couldn't make my rent payments. I would just ruin my already dipping credit if I added an eviction to my record.

After two months of demurring, I finally called my retired, gray landlord, Dave, and informed him that I had to end my month-to-month tenancy. He was saddened, as he had grown fond of me and even of mistrustful Fezzik, whom he inexplicably adored and had gradually befriended with hot dogs and biscuit treats. Dave had hoped that I would eventually sign a one- or even two-year lease, as he was rarely gifted with single, quiet tenants, but alas, it was not to be.

"You know, I've been doing this a long time, and you're by far the best tenant I've ever had," he told me, over and over again. "I'll rent to you again in a heartbeat, if you're ever able to come back. And if you need a letter of reference, don't hesitate to call me."

I spent a week cleaning out my beautiful little vintage cottage. My parents came over and helped. I shuddered, seeing my baby grand piano, Ingrid (a once-in-a-lifetime FreeCycle gift from a woman who could no longer keep the 1934 relic and thought it was wrong to sell something that had been in her family for generations and brought her so much pleasure), dismantled and packed into a storage van.

I had taken a few months of piano lessons as a child, but mom cut them short because Molly lost interest, and there was no room for extracurricular activities unless both of us were willing to participate—or, at least, that was the case for me. I suspected that my mom insisted on Moll accompanying me to keep an eye on me, to make sure that I didn't get too close and friendly with "worldly people." It was definitely a double standard because she trusted Moll to pursue solo activities. Perhaps she felt that my sister was too goody-goody to dare make friends outside the Organization. My teachers told me that I showed a fair amount of promise and encouraged me to go further. I picked up music and dance very quickly and evidenced a strong, innate love of art and culture—qualities frowned on as frivolous and ungodly by Jehovah's Witnesses, highly suspect even as mere recreation, much less potential career choices. My artistic aspirations were further hampered because Molly got bored quickly and never stuck with anything very long. I had been pulled out of ballet, jazz and piano in quick succession when Moll quit and, after that, I realized the hopelessness of the situation and gave up on even trying anymore. She went on to attempt guitar, flute, horseback riding, drama and ice skating, dropping out of each one and rapidly hopping onto the next.

Ingrid was a major unexpected windfall for me. I named her for Ingrid Bergman because *Casablanca* was one of my favorite classics. Immediately upon bringing her home, I had her tuned and painstakingly set about trying to reteach myself piano. My brain was no longer quite so much of a sponge as it had been when I was little, and I struggled to make my fingers obey my mind, even having trouble with simpler pieces that I could play easily as a child. To this day, I play very, very badly and rudimentarily. It sounds like I'm playing by numbers—extremely plonky and deliberate. I'll never be a good pianist or even a decent one; that chance has passed me by. But I still take a great deal of pleasure in playing privately, as long as nobody is listening. It has a calming effect on me and gives me something to aspire to, something to improve.

And now Ingrid was being shuttled off to storage. No playing at my mom's house.

I lovingly swept the hardwood floors free of any lingering dog hair and mopped them until they glistened. I scraped the ashes from the fireplace and scrubbed the counters and kitchen tiles until they were snowy-white.

I made sure to be the last to leave my cottage, spending an hour inside sitting on the floors and working up the will to leave and turn in the keys. Having said goodbye to so many things that I loved in such a short span of time, it was all beginning to feel like just more of the same. I was nearly numb; only the faintest drooping inside my chest betrayed the ache of giving up my home and my privacy.

I was resigned. I was moving back in with my parents.

Chapter Five

I probably shouldn't have been shocked to learn that Mom had been stealing money from me. Her sense of self-entitlement occasionally reared itself when she coveted something I owned. For instance, an eBay package mistakenly delivered to her house after I had moved out was opened without regard to pesky little details such as federal postal laws or statutes dealing with mail fraud. When she discovered the soft vintage Italian scarf inside, she confiscated it, refusing to return it even when confronted.

"I spent twelve agonizing hours forcing your fat head out of my vagina. I fed you for years, cared for you, loved you, and now you won't even give *me* something! Selfish, selfish girl. I deserve this."

Or she would wheedle.

"I remember you liking that brooch/skirt/necklace/barrette of mine. If you let me keep this scarf, I'll give you that instead."

Most of the time, it wasn't worth the inevitable argument, fallout, screaming and crocodile tears, so I would just give up, throw my hands in the air and concede the desired item. History may not have proven appeasement to be a particularly effective strategy in the long run, but, so help me, I just didn't want to deal with it. I chose my battles, for all the good that did.

My parents had also been having money problems for, well, ever. Mom often threw hapless Joe out of the house, thus shooting herself in the foot as far as financial support went for the weeks, months or years he was gone. Even when Joe was there, however, money from Hill & Canyon Aquatics was scarce. His head swam with visions of his own successful empire, but Joe lost many of his clients in the recession of 2008–2009, and had never been particularly good at managing his money anyway. The little that he made he was forever investing and losing in some far-fetched proposal or another—stocks, commodities, pyramid schemes, you name it. I had moved back in with my parents only to be conscripted into driving my dad around from midnight to 5:00 a.m., so that he could nail signs to telephone poles, signs promising a Tidal Wave of Wealth. He tried to explain how the business model was *not* a pyramid scheme, but it sounded exactly like one to me.

"Dad, how long have you been putting up these signs?"

"About a year."

"Mmm. And have you received any results in that year?"

Almost indignant, he retorted, "I've gotten ten phone calls inquiring about it."

"I see. Did any of these ten phone calls come to fruition? Did they lead to you making any money whatsoever?"

He looked at me blankly. "Well, no, not yet. But they will. These things take some time to yield results."

"Come on, Dad. How much money did you spend having these signs made?"

"Dunno. A few hundred, maybe."

He didn't get it. He just couldn't seem to make the connection that he had spent hundreds of dollars and spent countless hours lugging his butt all over town for an entire year, with nothing to show for it. Zero. Zilch. A goose egg. Not even a goose egg. A negative amount of capital.

"Your mom won't work, either," he went on accusingly. "She keeps saying that Jehovah won't help her get a job because she hasn't been a very good Witness lately; she hasn't spent much time in service or going to the Kingdom Hall meetings the way she should."

I dryly pointed out that billions of people the world over managed to obtain and hold down jobs without being Jehovah's Witnesses, so surely there was hope. He sighed.

"Yes, I tried to tell her that, too. It was no use. It's *so freaking frustrating.*" You knew the situation was dire when Joe used an expletive substitute as strong as "freaking." "We're going to lose the house within sixty days if she doesn't get a job. I've tried telling her, but it's no use. She won't listen to me."

"Maybe this is a silly question, Dad, but why don't *you* go out and look for a job? I'm looking too right now. I'll check out some good stuff for you, too, and mail out some résumés if you need me to. It can't hurt. Clearly, you guys are struggling. And you haven't had any Hill & Canyon jobs in ages."

I wasn't used to seeing anger in my dad's eyes, but there was a hint of it now, although he remained nearly as mellow as ever, raising his voice only slightly.

"You don't understand what I've always known, Brianna. Once you take a job working for someone else, for a boss, you're screwed. You no longer belong to yourself. You work for the man, and you'll never do as well or make as much money as you will being your own boss."

It made me sad to think that Joe might, in his quest not to lose himself, lose everything else instead. For himself *and* for my mom. It also made me frustrated. It was, as with many conversations I've had with Jehovah's Witnesses, like clobbering my brains out against the Great Wall of China.

And then the roof caved in. The morning after a tempestuous (for southern California, anyway) rainstorm, I arrived home to a shaft of light beaming down on the living room couch. I looked up and saw clear blue sky through the hole. My mother was in hysterics, arms full of lumpy, spackled cottage-cheese ceiling. The ceilings in other rooms were soaking through, turning a mildew yellow and threatening to collapse as well. I spent hours helping my parents shovel sand into sandbags and hoist them up a ladder to the roof to hold down great black tarps. My mother cried and insisted that a new roof would cost at least $25,000, and where would they get it?! Joe said nothing.

My mother had allowed me two rent-free months staying with her, but March and onward were to cost me $500 a month in rent, which motivated me to find work and an apartment ASAP. Things were already tense in the house. I found myself relapsing into the pretransformative Cinderella role that I had become so accustomed to in childhood, and I didn't like it. I had already broken up with Dennis and was in therapy dealing with my grief and anxiety, as well as the trauma of sexual abuse, rape, dealing with Bob's suicide, various childhood scars and feelings of deep self-loathing and inadequacy. My mother begrudged me my weekly therapy session, harping to Joe incessantly, "I don't understand why she needs therapy. What the hell does she have to complain about? You'd think that she's had a crappy life, the way she's always in therapy. She probably goes to whine and lie about what a terrible mother I was. You know that's what she thinks. She's always had such a twisted, warped view of me. She doesn't know what real pain is."

My mother didn't like therapists. Joe had coaxed her to take me to one when I was nine, the first year their marriage was on the rocks, and I, in fourth grade at the time, had watched the young, beautiful mommy that all my classmates envied slip away. My grades had plummeted from straight As to Cs and Ds, and I withdrew into myself and into books. My teachers were concerned, to say the least.

I wasn't quite sure why I was sitting in the nice psychologist lady's office. She gave me some toys to play with, and then started asking me questions. I can't remember what they were or what the answers were; I only remember that it all seemed like pretty innocuous stuff.

Then the lady spoke to my parents. Most of it seemed to be along the lines of how I was a relatively normal kid, how they might have possibly had a hand in my rapid decline and how, perchance, to improve things. My mother listened quietly, a look of pseudo-concern frozen onto her face. She nodded and smiled, *Yes, of course,* and promised that they would work with me some more and be proactive in their relationship with their child, yada yada yada.

Then she took me home and whaled the ever-loving shit out of me. I, being nine, blamed the mean old psychologist lady. *She* had clearly told my parents that I was bad or something. I hated her. Luckily, we never went back. It was very hard for me to admit that I needed therapy, and voluntarily reenter it at the ripe old age of twenty-three.

While I felt sympathy for my parents' financial woes, and pangs of guilt that I couldn't help out more, I also knew that I couldn't stay and drown with them. If I did, I would never escape. I needed to put every bit of money I accrued toward moving out on my own again, and once I started paying my mother rent, I knew that would be far more difficult, if not impossible—the vast majority of my money was slated to go to her anyway.

My mother, I should probably explain, also had an annoying habit of buying me "presents" on her manic spending sprees and then insisting that she be paid back for them. "You'll be needing this," she would say, tossing a blender or a comforter or a set of dish towels or a crystal decanter into a shopping cart. If I was present, I would often try to refuse, knowing full well what would be coming next.

"No, this is too adorable. Don't worry, you can just pay me back later."

Half the time, though, I wouldn't be out shopping with her in the first place. Then, she would show up at home with anywhere from one to a dozen items for me, singsonging, "I'll just put it on your tab!"

My "tab" was a sheet of paper, a legally binding contract on which each item was faithfully noted in order and signed by me. My mother, no dummy when it came to legal matters, was scrupulously neat and organized about noting each item down, complete with date of purchase. Frustrated, I watched my "tab" grow as I paid off meager amounts from my unemployment checks.

On February 21, 2009, I cashed my latest unemployment check of $900 and used part of it to pay bills before returning home. My mother was in a foul mood, and had been for some days. I don't remember exactly why or whether it was directly related to me, per se. Joe had pulled Molly and me aside nearly a year earlier and told us that medical doctors, therapists, friends, family—all had pointed him to the unmistakable symptoms of bipolar disorder. I can't accurately speculate on just how correct his purely armchair diagnosis was, but it *was* obvious that my mother's behavior was increasingly abnormal and unhealthy. She refused to admit that she had a problem, however, and nobody ever intervened to get her the help she clearly and desperately required. In these moods, she was indiscriminate in her loathing and contempt.

I had barely walked into the house when my mother accosted me. "I want you to pay your tab. *All* of it. Today!"

"Sure." I pulled out my wallet, counted out just over $600 and placed it in her hand.

She started shrieking, demanding "the rest." I gaped at her in shock. "What are you talking about, Mom? That's *it*. That's everything."

She darted up the stairs, screaming for Joe, who eventually came downstairs. Clearly, she had told him another story.

Here's what happened next. My mother insisted that I owed her more than the actual contract stated. I showed Joe the amount I had given her. When she insisted that it wasn't the full amount, I printed out bank statements proving the direct deposits I had previously made into her own bank account as payments on my "tab."

Caught in a lie, she paused for about half a second before insisting that those payments were on a *second* contract, *not* the one she was now holding. Shaking and trying to remain collected over cake layers of tears, I asked her to produce the contract, knowing full well that there was no such contract. She left the room for about two minutes and then returned. There was no change to the twisted, snarling look on her face.

"I can't find it. But it exists. And she will pay for it *now*." She implored Joe to make me give her my remaining money, a little over $100, and come up with another few hundred, which she claimed that I also owed.

I then found out that Alfie, our family friend and mechanic, who had been kind enough to replace the brake pads on my car and do some other tune-up work, had approached Joe and claimed that he had never been paid.

I flashed back to two weeks prior, when I had received another unemployment check, cashed it, arrived home and asked my mom for Alfie's address so that I could swing by his house and pay him the $250 for the work.

"Oh, I already paid him by credit card," she declared (too hastily, upon reflection). "So now you just owe me the cash."

It didn't occur to me that it might have been a lie. Clearly, that would be too brazen, even for my mother. She would have known that she was certain to get caught out on it, when Alfie showed up looking for his money, so why bother lying? I gave her the money.

Now Joe looked uncertain as to whom to believe. I related the date I gave my mother the money, the time, the amount, the clothes I was wearing at the time, the specific conversation verbatim. My mother looked me straight in the eye and denied it all.

She was screaming louder and louder, bursting into ugly crying hollers, her face purple-red and pinched, distorted, perverse. There was not a hint of anybody I had ever loved in the monster before me. Overcome, I finally let loose, rupturing into great jagged, hard-breathing sobs.

"You see that, Joe? Look at her—stupid, sniveling little liar that she is!" She rounded on me. "You're not fooling anybody! You're not crying because you're sorry. You've always been the same revolting, selfish little brat and you always will be! Get out of this house!"

This was not new. It was not the first time I had been thrown out of the house—once at fifteen, once at seventeen—but it was the first time I had no idea where to go. My friends were no longer as capable of taking me in as they had been in our teens. Most now lived with roommates or significant others, and had no room for me. Or for Fezzik.

I sucked in my breath and tried to speak calmly.

"That's fine, I'll leave. However, you should be aware that, by law, you need to give me thirty days' notice."

"I don't have to give you anything, you *fucking cunt!* Get out of my house!"

"If I've resided here for over a month, I am legally a tenant, whether I pay rent or not. You have to give me thirty days."

Working for a lawyer had served me well.

"You can call the police and check it yourself, Mom." She pulled out her cell phone and stormed out of the room, talking too loud as she did so.

"Hello? Fullerton Police Department?"

I politely requested that she make the call in the same room, but she refused. She slammed her bedroom door shut. Joe and I waited, not speaking. I was sickened that he wouldn't stand up for me. She returned to the room, insisting that she had spoken with the police.

"Nope, they said it's my house, you're not a tenant and

I can put you on the fucking sidewalk if I like. You'll take that damn dog with you, too! If Fezzik isn't gone with you tonight, I'll have him in the pound tomorrow! I'll make sure they put him to sleep myself. I'll watch them do it and I'll laugh!"

Quaking inwardly and outraged on behalf of my beloved dog, I reached for my purse, pulling out my cell phone. "OK, I'll call the police to verify that myself."

My mother's frivolous police calls were infamous in the precinct. A few years earlier, she had beaten me around the face in a fit of sadism. I held my arms up to shield my head and stepped out of the doorway I had been standing in. Her momentum carried her through and she landed on the floor. She pulled her cell phone from her pocket and called 911, telling them that her violent daughter was standing above her, threatening her, about to bash her brains in. My sister huddled in a corner, howling in terror like a frightened puppy and begging my mother to stop. The police arrived to find me sobbing on the curb. After entering the house and trying to get an answer out of my sister (who wouldn't say a word, torn between the truth and self-preservation), they came out, patted me on the shoulder and told me not to worry. They knew I had never touched her. I grasped the hand of one of the officers and covered the poor man in snot and tears, insisting that I wouldn't, *didn't* hit her, that she had attacked me and I only wanted to get away.

"We know," they said.

At my suggestion that I call the police myself, Mom lunged at me, knocking the phone from my hand.

"You sick little bitch! You sick, sorry, dis*gu*sting little *fucker!* You know how it will all end, don't you? You're truly your father's daughter! You're exactly like Bob, and you'll end up the same way! It's inevitable. Exact same

DNA. One of these days you'll stick a shotgun down your throat, too. You should just do it and get it over with. You're beyond help and beyond love!"

I was used to being slapped in the face, but this was the final straw. I bolted from the house in a frenzy, drove to a local park and curled up under a tree on the grass by the lake, rocking back and forth and whimpering with pain and fear until it grew dark.

I returned to my mother's house hours later. She was locked in her room, but Joe had taken some of the money from her and handed it to me. It was about $300. "You'll need this. I was able to get you an extension. Five days. That's how long you can stay here. After that, you need to make other arrangements."

His jaw solidified in anger or anguish, I'm not sure which.

"Why, Bri? *Why* couldn't you just agree to pay her the extra money?"

I was bowled over.

"But…I don't owe her that money. I *proved* it. If she had needed money, she could have asked. You know I would have lent or even given it to her anyway. I always do. It was *wrong* of her to steal it, and to make up lies about the amount owed. And I'm not going to admit to lying or stealing just to placate her. You seriously want me to sell out and say in front of her, in front of you, 'Yes, I'm a liar, and a thief, and I'm bailing on my debt to you,' when that's completely false? It's *wrong,* Dad! Don't you *get* that?!"

"Fine. I hope you're happy. Sometimes you have to capitulate in order to keep the peace. You know what she's like, and if you were smart you would have just forked over the money and kept your mouth shut."

"Did you even *hear* the part where she said that I should shoot myself? She's lucky I walked out. I don't even know what I could have done to her right then, if I hadn't walked out."

"Well, now, that was uncalled for. She shouldn't have said that. But still, you've brought this on yourself."

I had never felt so alone or so aggravated. The veins in my head throbbed. I was so tired of crying and thinking and trying to wrap my head around the insane world of lies and power plays that my mother lived in, and the wimpy pacifier—even to the point of being stepped on and stolen from—that was Joe.

I snapped. "You know, Dad, you helped create this. *You* knew she was a monster, a sick person, and yet over and over *you left us with her!* You couldn't stand to be with her yourself, you were so full of relief and calm and peace every time she threw you out, because you couldn't stand to be with her, so *why did you leave us with her?* We were *kids!* And she abused me, abused *us*—Moll got to watch it all for years and deal with the guilt of letting her big sister fry, so *why did you do it?*"

He was caught. His jaw dropped open.

"I…I didn't know. I wasn't around when a lot of that stuff was happening. I only learned about it later." He sounded subdued, tired, humbled. Guilty.

"You were around when *plenty* of it was happening. The school sent a goddamn social worker to the house because I had a lump on my head and left a pool of blood on my chair, bled straight through my pants, where she had lacerated my ass to fucking mincemeat! How could you leave us with that *thing* and still sleep at night?"

It was true. The overweight bottle-blonde had visited our home twice before, declaring my mother's actions (the result of my lack of comprehension as she tried to explain my long division homework to me) a one-time slip and closing our case. Though a teacher had reported my state to the authorities, my parents blamed me and told me that now it was my fault they could never take in any foster children from the state, as they had hoped. Though I would twice be kicked out of my house at ages fifteen and seventeen—both times scooped up by Josh Bogy, a friend from high school, and put up for extended periods of time at the home of his best friend David Roth, another high school pal who is now a brilliant up-and-coming law student—and Troy High School would become aware of my abuse, no teacher or other authority figure would ever again rise to my defense by reporting this state of affairs to the police or Social Services. My mother's reputation for wrath and threats preceded her and had become well-established with the school's administrative staff, who were quite frankly exasperated by the entire situation and desperately wanted nothing more than to be kept out of the drama.

Like so many people in my life up until this point, Joe had no answer to my questions. I was no stranger to frustration with him, but now I wanted, for the first time ever, to hit him.

Chapter Six

I had only a small handful of close friends. Trusting people has been difficult for me for a very long time, so I tend to value quality over quantity. There wasn't anybody who could take me in, and I knew it. The few people I knew either lived at home with their parents or with roommates, and had no spare space to take in an extra person, much less the inclination to harbor Fezzik as well.

Burdening others with my problems was one of the fears foremost in my mind. The 2008–2009 recession was in full force, and everyone's world seemed to be crumbling around their ears. Many of my friends had lost their jobs as it was, or were struggling to hold onto their positions as their companies hinted at layoffs. None of us seemed to have the time, money or energy to spend with one another anymore; most of us kept in touch via Facebook status updates and semiannual emails. Relationships had been downsized, too, it seemed. All of us were simplifying our lives, stripping down to the barest necessities and going into survival mode, and I couldn't blame anyone. I didn't feel hurt that nobody was there to come through for me. I was in no position to expect something of that magnitude from them. They were wrapped up in their own problems and I knew that forcing one of them into a situation where they felt like a long-suffering schmuck and I felt like a selfish mooch wouldn't help either one of us.

So I didn't tell them what was about to happen. Some of my friends had known for years how things were with my mom; some had even witnessed her bad behavior, so they vaguely assumed that the situation of my living at my parents' home was somewhat shaky, but when they heard I was leaving, most of them didn't ask where I was going next, and I didn't volunteer the information, except to my two closest friends. They assumed I'd be fine, and I felt I didn't have the right to tell them otherwise, to put that kind of onus on them when they had so much on their plates already.

In those few days of panic, though, I realized what I *did* have. And I knew, almost as if by instinct, exactly what I needed to do.

Three days later, I made the 2½-hour drive to Blythe, California. There, stored at a national park by the Colorado River, sat Bob's 1984 thirty-foot Fan Coach travel trailer. I'd tracked down the storage location via the insurance policy, which had been among the vast amount of jumbled papers stuffed in Bob's armoire drawer.

The park rangers were distressed to hear the news about Bob, as I produced the title transferred into my name. "Oh yeah, Bob. That's such a shock. He used to come up here all the time," said the mustachioed warden, shaking his head sadly. The bizarre thought occurred to me that somewhere, Bob had been *liked*. Even had *friends*.

The rangers gave me a set of spare keys and I entered the

trailer. I was hit by the stench of rot and disease. It seemed to follow Bob wherever he went. I assumed that he must have done a lot of fishing and hunting up here at the park. Probably gutted and skinned the animals himself in the trailer. My kingdom for a can of Pine-Sol.

Junk piled high, filling the cabin. There was barely any walking room; tubs full of trash, coolers, spare accessories—an awning, a rusty old satellite dish—littered the floor. I was going to be carting all this out tonight, so that I could load up my own boxes.

The trailer, I had realized in a blinding epiphany, was probably my most likely asset as a source of shelter. I knew that I would have nowhere to go. There was no getting around it. Still, perhaps I didn't have to sleep in my car.

"Can you please hitch it up to the truck for me, please? I don't know how," I implored, instantly switching into golly-gee-helpless-li'l-old-me mode. That occasionally came in handy, especially when I had no idea what the fuck I was doing.

"Aw, sure, little lady. Where you gonna put this thing?"

"Um…I'm going to take it to a trailer park near home," I lied.

When you first find out that you're going to be homeless, there's a lot of initial prep work to be done—figuring out how to meet your barest, most essential needs, and then going from there. Sleep is a pretty darn essential need—and perversely, sleeping in public is illegal just about everywhere. I mean, go figure, right? But there you go. There will always be NIMBYs calling cops, and there will always be cops telling homeless people, "It doesn't matter where you go, but you can't stay here." Oh, they might sympathize, sure, but their need to follow the rules will generally win out over common sense, which dictates that a human being cannot control the need to sleep simply because she has no access to a place worth sleeping in.

It's just as illegal to sleep in a car in public as it is to sleep on a park bench in public, but one is far less conspicuous than the other, doubles as shelter and transportation, and can be more easily hidden. Obviously, the best plan of attack, if I could manage it, was to stay under the radar in stealth mode, out of homeless shelters and off curbsides/freeway underpasses and the like. I couldn't believe it, but Bob's death provided me with the Holy Grail of homelessness.

Yet where does a person *put* a thirty-foot travel trailer? It's illegal to just park them on most public streets, especially overnight. I had considered a trailer park. Electricity and plumbing hookups? Yes, please. Except, I had only a few hundred dollars, and over $100 of it would go into the truck's gas tank to get me to Blythe and back. Possibly more. The gas mileage would decrease dramatically with the heavy-ass trailer strapped onto the back, I knew. After that, I simply couldn't afford the monthly expense of staying at a trailer park or campground. My unemployment benefits were running low and the possibility of an extension had not yet been mentioned. The price of a valid RV park—at $40 and up per day—would accumulate to nearly as much as steady rent in a cheap apartment. Which put me right back at square one. The chances that I could pull it off were slim, even without considering food and auto fuel.

I had spent two days browsing the internet frantically, googling "cheap RV campgrounds," and then, "free RV campgrounds." Sitting in a Starbucks with my laptop and my best friend Brandon Quan, frantically poring over alternatives, we stumbled across the Walmart policy.

For many years, Walmart has allowed traveling trailers and RVs to park in the stores' private parking lots overnight. The practice was put into effect by Sam Walton, the founder of Walmart and an avid RVer himself. Policies varied a bit according to the individual store and local city ordinances, and store managers were allowed to interpret the rule loosely and set time limits and regulations if they wished. Still, it was a start.

I had phoned the closest Walmart store to my home, the Anaheim store. "No, sorry, we don't allow that here. Anaheim city ordinance."

Blegh.

I moved on to Brea Walmart. The girl who answered the phone wasn't sure of the answers to my questions. I asked for the store manager. She transferred me to another woman. "This is Elizabeth. How may I help you?"

"Hi, Elizabeth. I was wondering if you allow trailers to park overnight in your lot. I read that a lot of Walmarts do it."

"Yes, that's right. You can park over in the corner, on the east side of the parking lot, at the intersection of Kramer and Imperial Highway. You'll see the other trailers there."

"Thank you, ma'am. I also need to know...is there a limit on the amount of time that I can stay? You see, I don't really have anywhere to go at the moment and I may possibly be around for a while. I'm more than happy to buy my food and supplies at Walmart, of course, and give you my business. I'm just afraid of being towed or outstaying my welcome."

She assured me that there was no reason to worry; store officials did not keep track of which RVs came and went, and as long as I stayed in the corner of the parking lot and didn't bother customers or draw attention to myself, I could practically stay forever, if I wished.

I thanked her profusely, and hung up. I had my parking lot.

"You know," Brandon mused thoughtfully, "you should totally start a blog or something about this."

I scoffed. "Yeah, right. I haven't written since my angst-filled, bad high school poetry days."

It was true. Throughout junior high and high school I always kept a notebook with me, and would write constantly, stream-of-consciousness style. Sometimes it was completely nonsensical (but dark—ooh yes; dark, angry, Tim Burton-esque) poetry. Other times it was just rants on how much I hated my life, how alien and alone I felt at school, how much of a crush I had on that hot senior, Jason Mejia, how intense I imagined sex might actually be if only I weren't a Jehovah's Witness freak prohibited from having it...and so on and so on. By the time I was eighteen, I had amassed a tower of notebooks and bound journals that I hoped to look back on in a decade or so and laugh about, marvel at how far I'd hopefully come from that point. After leaving home, however, the products of my short life's work were nowhere to be found when I unpacked. A year later, Molly would admit what I already suspected—that she and my mother had secretly gone through my moving boxes, removing items that Mom had wanted or felt entitled to. They had taken and read every one of my notebooks, then thrown them away. I was gutted. Everything I had ever thought and felt and pains-takingly recorded—for a decade—was lost forever. Nothing was my own any longer, even my most private thoughts and moments. The betrayal and loss was overwhelming. I would not write again for the next six years.

"I'm not kidding," Brandon went on. "You never know—people read this stuff."

Laughter burst from me. One thing about Brandon, he's always there for me, and he always knows just how to cheer me up with ridiculous ideas like that. We'd gone on a few dates back when we first met two years earlier, but I just wasn't feeling it. I felt bad about it occasionally—if anybody would make the perfect boyfriend, it would be Brandon—but you just can't force chemistry for whatever reason, and we ended up as best buddies instead. Oddly, it works out perfectly for us. He's absolutely the greatest guy out there: quiet, sarcastic, highly intelligent and a film buff. We've watched *Forgetting Sarah Marshall* together more times than I can count. Plus, he holds the distinction of being the only 6-foot-6-inch Asian man I've ever met. If life were a movie, we'd be the two platonic confidantes who suddenly realize at the eleventh hour, after being screwed over by countless prospective jackass significant others, that we were meant to be together. But life isn't a movie, and what we've got going now is just right.

Humorously going along with the joke, I opened my laptop right then and there, setting up a blogger account. "How about 'The Girl's Guide to Homelessness?' Kind of like 'The Girl's Guide to Hunting and Fishing,' but for women about to embark on life in a Walmart parking lot?" I stared at the screen, and then tapped out:

In three days, I will be homeless.

"Well, I'll leave you to it," Brandon said, hugging me and rising from the Starbucks couch. "I gotta get home—work in the morning."

"Yeah, see you tomorrow when I'm the world's most famous homeless chick, all thanks to your brilliant blog idea," I teased.

He left. I screwed my mouth sideways pensively, and then words began to pour out onto the screen, care of the anonymous pseudonym, ~B~. I liked the flourish of the framing tilde marks. In my mind, they gave me a dainty quirkiness I certainly was not feeling at the moment. Nobody would ever read this stuff anyway, and I had lost faith that I was ever any good at it in the first place. But I had forgotten how cathartic it felt to write.

In three days, I will be homeless.

This is not by choice (although many individuals before me have chosen this lifestyle and enjoyed the freedoms that it can offer, and if that's what works for them, kudos!). Personally, I enjoy having a permanent residence and the sense of stability and security that it gives me. I look forward to living in an actual house again. However, it is what it is—in three days, I will be homeless. There are no caveats here, no 'maybe' or 'unless' or 'possibly I can come up with something before then.' Come Thursday, February 26, 2009, I will be making my way on the streets of Orange County as best I can, and I will be considered that most stigmatized of people—a homeless woman.

Initially, this idea terrified me. Here is a summary of the commentary that first ran through my head: This would never happen to me. I am not the kind of person who lives on the street. I have a life, I have friends, I have a dog, I have stable employment and a residential history, references, education, skills, talents—I have worked hard all my life to ensure stability for myself. How did this happen? HOW CAN I DO THIS?!?

So, I cried for a few hours. I cried and I let the panic run its course. Then, I started planning.

I wonder how many other people like me are out there. People who had the stereotypical idea of a homeless man or woman, who believed that it would not, could not, happen to them. The truth is, we never know the whole story. We don't know other people's circumstances. You can speculate that the wino sitting outside the 7-Eleven begging for change is there because he's too lazy or stupid or uneducated or selfish or mentally ill. But will we ever truly know? Look at me. I've worked hard all my adult life (and throughout my adolescence), sought out a college education, worked for corporations and executives, built a life and a 'secure' foundation to fall back on. Yet, here I am. So, now what?

If you're an individual in a similar situation (especially a single, vulnerable woman), I hope that by detailing my experiences in this blog, I may help you come up with tips and ideas for survival and safety for however long your present circumstances may last. Perhaps you didn't choose for this to happen, but it is what it is. It is happening and you must stay strong and levelheaded, so that you can make opportunities happen for yourself and dig yourself out of this hole.

Perhaps you're not homeless, have never been homeless and are currently not faced with the threat of becoming homeless. Maybe you are reading this because homelessness is a topic close to your heart or maybe you just feel that you should cultivate some knowledge on survival skills because, with the economy the way it is right now, who knows what will happen in the future? In any event, I hope that my postings will give you something to think about and/or something to laugh about, for humor can be mined from even the most dire of circumstances.

I have just over $300 cash to my name, in addition to various personal belongings. I have three days to take my plans for the coming weeks/months and put them into motion. I have never been homeless before and I will not deny that I am afraid, but I plan to face this with humor and dignity. I can do this. I can do this without becoming a casualty or a stereotype. I can be homeless and still be clean, nourished, confident, well-dressed, dry in the rain and warm at night. I can make wise and preventive decisions that will help protect me and keep me safe in tenuous circumstances. I can and will continue to bring in revenue, interview and locate permanent employment. I can be a tall woman with flaming red hair, with a jowly and imposing Neapolitan Mastiff and a thirty-foot RV in tow, and still manage to remain inconspicuous and under the radar (...right?). I think that if a wussy chick like me can do all this, then anybody can.

I scrambled into my truck with trepidation. I had thirty feet of train hitched to my bumper and I could feel it, even before turning on the engine. It was a massive presence that blocked out my rearview mirror and made me feel very tiny, insignificant and prone to accidental vehicular manslaughter.

"Now then, yer all good to go, ma'am. Just take the corners wide and slow, and when you want to back up, just remember to turn the wheel the *opposite* direction of the way you normally would to back up."

Terror thrummed through my every nerve. Tentatively, I revved the truck to life, and inched forward. OK. This wasn't too bad, right? The kind rangers cheered me on and waved goodbye. OK. This was good. All good. Yup, yup. *Holy mother of god, what have I gotten myself into?!*

The 2½-hour drive to Blythe became a 5-hour drive back. The truck, bogged down by the trailer, could only go a maximum of 50 mph on the freeway. Downhill. The rest of the time, it chugged along at about 40 mph, or even 25–30 on a hill. Although I stayed in the far right lane, road-raging motorists sped around me, occasionally yelling or flipping me the finger. At a couple of very scary points, the transmission began to overheat and I had to pull off to the shoulder of the road and allow it to cool down. Even scarier, I had to reenter the freeway from the shoulder, without the luxury of being able to build up speed, weighted as I was.

I had left Blythe around 11:00 a.m. I arrived at my mother's house at 4:00 in the afternoon, achy in every single muscle from the sheer tense terror of constantly bracing, trying not to wipe out entire lanes of people on the freeway. Mom wasn't home, and had locked me out, so I began the sweaty, thankless job of yanking all Bob's crap out of the trailer. Trash pickup was scheduled for the following morning, and there were several empty garbage cans by the side of the house, so I pulled them out to the curb and began loading them up with the junk. It took over an hour.

Drained, and knowing that I had several hours' more work to do loading up my own boxes, I lay on the grass in the front yard, trying to relax enough for my muscles to unlock. I didn't have long to wait. My mother pulled her van into the driveway and stepped out coolly. Gone was the screaming rage, replaced by still, inhuman coldness. She must have been surprised at the enormous trailer pulled up by the curb, but to her credit, she didn't show it.

"Get all this *shit* out of my garbage cans and back into your truck. Take it and dump it somewhere else."

"Trash pickup is tomorrow. It doesn't matter."

"The hell it doesn't. You'll pull every last item out of the trash and load it right back up, or you won't enter this house, and you won't carry out a single box of your things."

"You aren't allowed to keep my things from me. I'm here to pick them up, well within my rights, and the law prohibits you from withholding them."

She smirked.

"Watch me."

She stalked in and locked the door.

My back breaking in half, I dragged all the trash out of the cans and threw it into the truck bed. I knocked. Nothing. I rang the doorbell. She wouldn't let me in. After several rings, she shouted through the door, "You're not coming in here until Joe comes home. I'm afraid for my safety."

You've got to fucking be kidding me.

Another hour passed before Joe's silver Tacoma pulled up and he let me inside. I was too dead to care.

Joe cornered me upstairs in my former room, where I shoveled anvil-esque boxes of books, which constituted the vast majority of my belongings, through the window. It was a shorter path through the window and across the lawn than carrying boxes down the hall, down stairs (my parents' home is trilevel), through the foyer, out the front door and across the driveway to the trailer. It also minimized the number of trips I'd have to make past Mom.

"I just want to let you know that I'm proud of how you behaved today. You didn't engage her. You just sat back, remained calm and did what she demanded, instead of fighting. I think she's proud of you, too, even if she doesn't say so."

Tears dropped silently down my cheeks, partially because he'd never before told me he was proud of me and I
had assumed for years that he didn't really care, and partly
out of disappointment that the only way I could ever gain
his approval was by acting like a doormat, allowing myself
to be degraded, humiliated and crushed when I was already so exhausted and felt I had nothing left to give.

I thanked him, though.

He began to help me load books, but my mother flung
open the door and ordered him to drop the box he was
carrying.

"Don't you dare help her. She thinks she's better than
everyone else. Let her do it all alone."

Too stubborn and proud to argue, I wrenched my back
over and over again, lifting box after box and staggering
to the car, entreating any non-specific higher power out
there, if it existed, to keep me from passing out from fa-
tigue, just until I was done and could pull the trailer out
of their sight. Anger spurred me on; it was now dark—
the light hours had been wasted by my mom's little mind
games—and I could barely see the inside of the trailer, or
where I was putting things.

Last of all was Fezzik.

I had set up his crate in the trailer with a fluffy bed and
an area for his food and water. I would worry about what
to do with him later, if and when I found a job. For now,
though, he could stay with me in the trailer. I would exercise him every day. I couldn't give him up—not now. Not
only would he keep me safe and give me companionship
(I was sure the experience to come would get very lonely),
but I could never forgive myself if I gave him away to a
new home and days or weeks later managed to restabilize
my life, having to start over again without my best friend.

I ambled into the kitchen and out onto the patio with Fezzik's leather lead. I clicked it on to his collar ring and led him back through the house. Almost free.

My mother stepped into my path.

I was half-dead. I was emotionally fried. I didn't want to deal with any of her shit. I never wanted to see her again. I just wanted to be free.

"I just want you to know that I love you. I don't approve of your life, or your choices, or the person you are, or anything about you…but I do love you, and I'll always love you." Her eyes grew moist. I felt a very faint stirring in my chest. This should mean something to me. This should make me cry, too, bawl and throw my arms around her and beg for her forgiveness, confess that I loved her back. Shouldn't it?

It was too little, too late.

"When I swallow a shotgun, I'll dedicate my suicide note to you."

Her eyes widened.

I felt evil.

I left.

It was Thursday, February 26, 2009. I was parked in a Walmart lot in a trailer with my dog. I was scared and alone. I was homeless.

Chapter Seven

Despite the restlessness and the cold, I eventually conked out and passed the night relatively peacefully and uneventfully. Fezzik settled into his crate and didn't make a peep all night, and when I awoke, the sun was shining and there were no parking tickets or tow notices on my windshield. Perhaps irrationally, I had half expected that there would be. It was becoming natural to expect the absolute worst possible scenario. But so far, so good. I seemed to be blending.

If you are homeless and living out of a vehicle, you may think that it's a good idea to find some isolated spot to park, since it is illegal to sleep in your own personal vehicle. This is an insane rule. You can eat in your car, listen to music in your car, just sit there for hours and read in your car, but sleep in it? You'll get branded as a "transient" by the police pretty darn quickly, and then you'll be asked to move on. So I can understand the logic involved in trying to find somewhere obscure and isolated—you just want to sleep without the police bugging you.

However, parking somewhere isolated is also incredibly dangerous, and a good way to put yourself in harm's way. Especially as a woman, my main fears included being mugged, raped or killed. Crazy and bad people seek out isolated victims. Police are also likely to be checking isolated spots—a single vehicle illegally parked on a quiet dirt road stands out. Sometimes the best place to "hide" is right in plain sight. Think about it—how often while walking through a busy grocery store parking lot do you look around and take stock of other vehicles or people? You're in a rush, there are cars looking for spaces, you don't have time to notice if there's someone sleeping in his car. You're wrapped up in your own little world, your needs and wants, whatever errand brought you there. Before learning about this Walmart rule, I had never even realized that there were RVs and trailers parked in their lot. I had been to this Walmart countless times, and I'm a pretty observant person, but I had never actually *noticed* the giant campers just sitting there. How can you miss something that huge? But I did.

Apparently, so did everyone else. It would be months before I was disturbed on the lot.

Over time, there were several unwritten rules I learned about camping at Walmart.

The first rule was to keep clean. No littering. No pulling out a barbecue or awning, playing Frisbee in the lot or similarly tacky behavior. This wasn't a regular campground—it was a place of business. Occasionally, in some communities, residents complain about Walmart's policy, and attempt to pass city ordinances forbidding RV parking. The most commonly cited complaints that they back this up with are: homeless people camping for a long time and litter/trash. One rude camper (long term or not) can ruin it for everyone else.

The second rule: Keep quiet and remain faceless. To me, it was important for people to be able to walk past my trailer and not even know I was there. I was trying to stay under the radar, remember? This meant that I didn't play loud music on my laptop, and I rarely socialized with others on the lot. I didn't want to give Walmart employees, patrons or fellow campers any reason to remember my name, face or vehicle. I wanted to blend. *Greetings, random citizens! I am but one more camper on a cross-country trip, and I'll be leaving in the morning (yeah, right).*

I knew that if enough people noticed *me* specifically, there would eventually be some busybody who would complain about a homeless person living on the lot— assholes like this exist in every community. We all know them, don't we? They're the next-door neighbors who sit waiting for you to park your car just an inch too far from the curb, or for your hedge to extend just an inch too far over their fence, or for your grass to grow just an inch too long before they file a complaint and sic the cops on you. They don't care about your circumstances; they don't care if you're clean-cut and quiet and respectful; they don't care if you mind your own business and never bother anybody. To them, the fact that you are homeless says everything about you. *How dare you continue to live an independent life, Brianna Karp, relying on yourself instead of on charity, trying to get back on your feet?* To them, the only place a person like me belongs is in a homeless shelter. People like this *will* pursue the issue, so I tried never to give them a reason to remember me. My motto became: Just. Blend. In.

The third karma-driven rule: I also gave Walmart my business. The company is controversial, and many people don't like Walmart. I can completely, 100 percent understand this. However, I also feel that anyone unwilling to at least occasionally buy supplies from Walmart, should then probably find somewhere else to park. You have to give the company credit for one thing: Stores that allow campers and the homeless to park there are doing them a huge service. I planned to take full advantage of this service, so it was only fair that I reciprocate by purchasing goods from them occasionally. Besides, it doesn't get much cheaper than Walmart, except for the 99 Cent Store. If you're among the earning homeless, and aren't yet relying on a soup kitchen, it's hard to find a more affordable place to shop.

The vast majority of my time—other than that spent taking Fezzik to the local tri-city park for exercise, thus thwarting the inevitable stir-craziness of a massive breed dog in an eight-foot-wide space—was spent in Starbucks, looking for work. Craigslist, Monster.com, CareerBuilder.com—I scoured them for hours, applying for anything that would pay more than unemployment. I wasn't proud. Although ads with the words *Executive Assistant* or *Secretary* were particularly attractive, due to my work experience, I was willing to do just about anything, short of nudity, that could help me get back on my feet. It was a recession, after all. As the media kept telling me, I couldn't afford to be picky.

Starbucks was, I quickly discovered, optimal for a homeless girl trying to blend in. For one thing, the stores were ubiquitous. You couldn't walk more than a block without finding one. There was, in fact, one right in the Walmart shopping center, so I rarely had to drive anywhere, conserving fuel that I really couldn't afford anyway. Starbucks was also air-conditioned, in possession of comfy couches and would allow me to remain all day, if I wished, as long as I purchased a cup of coffee. The purchase of a $5 Starbucks card allowed me unlimited internet access for an entire month. I would arrive at the shop early in the afternoon, in my comfy *Sweeney Todd* sweatshirt and snug plaid flannel pants, after spending a couple of hours exercising Fezzik in the park. Often, I had my pick of seating. Occasionally, the couches would be occupied, and I would buy my coffee quickly, then perch like a hawk with my laptop on a rickety chair, until the more cushy seats were vacated. Then I would swoop in, plug my laptop into the nearest outlet and spend the next ten hours or so applying for jobs, and occasionally refilling my coffee, until the Starbucks closed. The employees never asked me to leave, or even really seemed to notice me all that much. I must have seemed like any other local college student living out of a coffee shop all day long. One green-aproned hipster with chunky glasses like mine and a choppy blond haircut once walked up to me and asked if I was a writer or something. I laughed cheerfully, and decided to run a little social experiment.

"Oh, no, I'm homeless!" I responded, beaming. He looked uncomfortable.

"Oh…I'm sorry…I didn't realize…"

"Nah, it's OK, really. I use the Wi-Fi here to job-search. I don't know what I'd do without it!"

He backed away slowly and never approached or spoke to me again, except to take my order. But from then on, occasionally a regular employee would silently slip me a bag of leftover pastries or muffins at the end of the night, the ones they normally threw out.

· · ·

The downside to parking at Walmart or Sam's Club is that there are no electric/water hookups for RVs. This doesn't matter anyway to those living out of cars. But for those living out of a trailer, I found that I could get around the electricity thing relatively easily. The lots are well-lit, and parking under a light helped a bit. I also bought a high-powered flashlight (from Walmart, naturally) that stood on its end and reflected off the ceiling, lit the trailer bunk almost as well as a lamp and certainly well enough to read by late into the night. I only needed to replace the batteries once every month or two. I purchased foods that didn't need to be refrigerated (which meant I very quickly got tired of bologna sandwiches, chips and bagels, but, still, it worked).

I was always sure to charge my phone and laptop during the day at Starbucks. That way, I could use the laptop in the evening to watch DVDs. It was also incredibly important, I realized, for my phone to be active at all times in case of an emergency. The last thing I wanted was for my trailer to be set on fire or for someone crazy to try to break in, or something, and not be able to call 911.

Water was another dilemma, which I solved by picking up several large gallon jugs from Walmart. After that, I saved money by constantly refilling them via hoses or restroom sinks. I even used the stored jugs of water to cool down in the heat, or to wash in an emergency. I found out *very* quickly just what was important, and just what standards I was able to lower. (*Hint:* Most of them.)

Restrooms posed another problem, of course. The trailer had a toilet, but since there were no water hookups, it was useless to me. So, instead, I located an Arco gas station up the street that was open twenty-four hours a day. I tried to regulate my peeing schedule, but occasionally I would wake up in the middle of the night with an uncontrollable urge. In a pinch, I would hop into my car and cruise up the street to the Arco, which felt kind of ridiculous and silly—going so far for a piss—but that's one of the things that you take for granted until you find yourself homeless. Being female, it was more difficult to surreptitiously pee in the bushes or against a wall. You *notice* a woman squatting in the bushes, trying to keep her balance and avoid tipping over, and, next thing you know, you're prosecuted for indecent exposure and on the sex offender list. (That's something I always thought was one of the more absurd and unconscionable reasons to brand someone as a sex offender for life. I mean, seriously? A homeless person peeing against a wall because he must indulge a basic biological necessity is *not* equivalent to a creep in a trench coat exposing himself to a child in a park.) Besides being illegal, peeing outdoors can end up being pretty gross and unsanitary for a woman. It's not like being a guy, where you just "point and shoot." I've tried peeing in the woods before, on camping trips, and have always been an abysmal failure at it. There is absolutely no directional control. Women *spray*. Ladies, you know what I'm talking about.

For showers, I found various options. There's always the possibility of a cheap gym membership, of course, which I eventually found. I also learned that most gyms offer free one-week passes to entice new members. You can print these out at a library or FedEx Office, use it for a week, then move on to the next gym in the area. A 25-cent printout for a free week of showers. Yes, please! Also, an online website assured me that you can often start a month-to-month membership and have your sign-up fees waived just by asking. It never hurts to ask. The worst that they can say is no, right? Smaller, mom-and-pop gyms and community centers are your friend. Their fees are waaaaaay lower than superchains like Bally's, 24-Hour Fitness, Curves and the like. Some colleges also have showers on campus, and if you have the brass to walk in and shower as if you're a student there, usually nobody will assume otherwise, unless you look scared. And again, in a pinch, there's always Arco, and the ever popular strip-and-stand-and-sponge-yourself-off-body-part-by-body-part-in-a-public-restroom. This won't get you as clean as, say, a public shower, but it will help ease the sweaty, stinky feeling a bit.

The most irritating thing, I found, is when people question "luxury" items like phones, laptops or vehicles. "I just saw a homeless person with a *cell phone!* Guess he's not *really* homeless." "Wait a second, how do you *blog* if you're homeless?" "Why don't you sell your phone and laptop and car and buy food or rent an apartment?" There was even a huge uproar in 2009 when a *Los Angeles Times* writer took umbrage with a possibly homeless person using a Black-Berry to snap a photo of Michelle Obama volunteering at a soup kitchen.

Or, as my online friend Matthew Mazenauer sarcastically put it, "Gee, if you can afford a $40-a-month cell phone plan, then you can afford a $40-a-month house!" I don't begrudge homeless people access to useful technology, or even "splurges" with their own income on whatever the hell they want. Since when is it my business to judge how someone else spends his income, or judge his priorities? It's not my place to say what anybody can or should spend his own money on, homeless or not.

I can understand potentially taking issue with government money being misspent—if a homeless individual is receiving housing funds for a very specific, designated purpose from an assistance program, and spending them elsewhere. But personal income? It's yours, you've earned it, and if you want to use it to buy a cell phone or a laptop or a book or a necklace or even a goddamn pack of cigarettes because you feel that any of the above will improve the quality of your life or just plain make you feel a little happier or more humanized for a short while, then good for you. I will never be the one to demand to know how much it cost you or look at you askance and mutter about how you wouldn't be homeless if only you didn't buy A, B or C. It's basic respect, and I don't think that basic respect and the right to privacy end when you lose your home.

I feel very strongly that the impetus behind such financial "curiosity" is purely for the purposes of judgment, and thus the motives behind such queries are impure ones. If it's none of your business when a person is housed, then it's *still* none of your business when she's not. Unless a homeless person volunteers financial information of her own accord, I won't ask her about it. Again, with the occasional exception of adventurous or experimental types taking a conscious leap off the grid, almost nobody chooses to be homeless. Whenever I meet a homeless person, I assume that if she were financially or mentally capable of affording and maintaining a home, then she would be in one, regardless of any "luxury" items I see in her possession. It's that clear-cut for me.

Sustainability is the key to any lifestyle. Sure, I could sell my phone and my laptop for the price of a few hamburgers. But, then, the hamburgers would soon be gone, and so would my phone and laptop. I would have absolutely no phone, so an employer could contact me. And without a laptop, I would only be able to search and apply for work

online during the hours that the public library was open.
I wasn't always homeless, of course, and neither were most
of the homeless people out there, whether they're the more
visible ones you see in the doorway of a 7-Eleven begging
for spare change or they're able to blend in a bit better,
as I do. To me, it's the most basic thing in the world to
use your resources wisely when you become homeless. In
today's society, a phone and internet access are no longer
"luxury" items. They're practically necessities. These are
tools that by themselves aren't worth enough to get you
a deposit on an apartment (and even if they were, they
certainly wouldn't continue to pay rent for you ad infini-
tum), but they *do* hold out the potential in the long term
for getting you a job. Why on earth should anyone be
dumb enough to give up such an important resource for
a couple of meals? As for true "luxury" items, I challenge
the notion that homeless individuals "do not deserve" to
own anything that may bring a small amount of happiness
and pleasure into their lives, which are generally otherwise
uncertain and bleak.

The other thing that irked so many people about the
Michelle Obama/soup kitchen/cell phone fiasco was that
the *Los Angeles Times* writer simply *assumed* that the man in
the photograph was homeless. He could have been anyone.
He could have been homeless, sure. He could also have
been another soup kitchen volunteer. He could have been
a random citizen wandering past, who said, "Oh, crap!
That's Michelle Obama! I'm gonna get a picture of her!"
But too many people saw the photo of a black man in
sweats and a ski cap, snapping a picture with a BlackBerry,
and the assumption was made. That's the way dangerous
stereotypes work. And the next thing you know, an article
comes out in the *Los Angeles Times,* demanding to know

how, if a homeless man is too poor to buy himself food, he can afford to own a cell phone. Many commentators on the article even insinuated that such a nice phone *must* have been stolen. Because, after all, homeless people are all criminals, right?

The article made me want to scream. If indeed the man *was* homeless, then what exactly was he supposed to do— sell off any and all useful possessions upon losing his home, so that he could fit into an ignorant journalist's definition of poverty? Would readers feel more comfortable believing he was a "real" homeless person if he was sans phone and dirtier, hungrier, perhaps mumbling to himself or pushing a shopping cart full of random odds and ends down the street? Did any of these readers consider that there are several state and federal programs that hand out cell phones with free plans to homeless people, so that they are able to look for work and call 911 in case of an emergency, since living on the streets is dangerous?

Nope. Very few people who have never been homeless consider the importance of hoarding available resources, or the thought and planning that goes into using them to maximum effect. Resources are the absolute most important thing when you're homeless. You learn to make the most of *everything* you have. I was lucky; I had retained more assets than many—a vehicle, a trailer, a laptop, a phone, a little bit of money, a decent résumé. Many homeless people have one or more of these things. Many have none. The only resource that *all* of us have is ourselves.

My body and my mind were and are my most important assets. As long as I was alive and healthy and physically/mentally capable of coming up with a plan and executing it, I knew I'd be OK. I didn't need to utilize resources that could and should be allocated to homeless people in more dire circumstances than me—perhaps people struggling with mental illness, drug addiction or some other challenges. State and federal programs can be limited, as it is, in who they're able to provide for. I'd rather people without the advantages that I had get first crack at those. The only benefit I accepted or even applied for was unemployment, during the periods when I was looking for work. After all, I had spent over a decade paying into the system, so that was only right and fair.

I occasionally saw the other homeless people in the lot during the daytime, as I would leave to take Fezzik out for a walk or head to Starbucks. I tried to enter and exit the trailer mainly early in the morning, before Walmart customers began to show up, or late in the evening, after 10:00 p.m., when the store closed. We didn't interact that much, but we were all well aware of one another, and would occasionally exchange little nods of mutual acknowledgment. One day, I ran into a group of them conversing in the parking lot, and chatted with them for a few minutes. One of them was Pete, who owned the trailer next to mine. He'd been here the longest; homeless for a year and on the lot for a few months, and was the self-proclaimed "mayor of the Walmart parking lot." He used to be a limo driver, owned seven neatly pressed tuxedos and was regarded with deference and respect by the others. There was also a former doctor, who spoke four languages, living out of another trailer, who was considering taking a job in India teaching English as a second language—free accommodations and a decent salary. Then there was another man living with his wife out of their car—they had owned two homes before the recession had forced them into the parking lot. At any given time, the lot had between eight and twelve permanent residents, in addition to those passing through who would only stay for a night or two before moving on, or those who would rotate between three or four different parking lots—either for a change of scenery or because they were afraid of wearing out their welcome.

I was as under the radar as they come: My dog was quiet and I found a small chain gym in Anaheim, called Planet Fitness, that charged only $10 a month for a membership. I became known there as the girl who would show up every three to four days, around 7:00 a.m., take a shower and leave. Planet Fitness was eight miles away from the Walmart, which was an incredible waste of fuel just to bathe, so I had to make each shower count.

There are times when a general air of innocence and naïveté can serve you well. One of them, I discovered, is when dealing with the police—try to remain calm and sound appreciative, even if you're not.

I blended in well enough that I only occasionally came to the attention of police officers. This usually occurred when Starbucks would close, and I would continue to loaf in the Starbucks parking lot in my car, catching the wireless signal for another hour or two until my laptop battery died and I had to wrap the extension cord around it and head back to the trailer for the night.

Tap. Tap. Tap.

I would roll the window down, placing my hands on the windowsill and putting on the most innocent, bland face I could muster, peering up through my lashes with wide, doelike eyes. A baby couldn't have had a more angelic face.

"Good evening, officer! Can I help you?"

I have to admit, I was pretty good. I was never ticketed, and was clearly charming enough, because they would generally give me goofy grins and speak to me in patronizing *What're-you-doing-out-here-alone-at-midnight-little-lady?* tones.

I avoided the word *homeless.* I was aware of the sort of response the word triggered in law enforcement, though of course it was pretty obvious what must have been going on—I had a back seat piled high with emergency changes of clothing, after all.

"I'm sorry, officer, my *[boyfriend/mother/father/roommate]* and I had a little tiff, and I didn't have anywhere to go tonight. I'm going to be calling my sister in the morning and going to stay with her. She's out of town until tomorrow, though, so I just picked a parking lot. I apologize if I shouldn't be here; I didn't realize! *[shocked expression]* I'll be on my way, if it's not all right for me to stay here…"

I would trail off, and the cop would invariably smile at the poor, confused little girl, her eyes verging on tears (I completely lack the ability to cry on cue, but I *can* throw a little waver into my voice that would make any man swear that my dry eyes are red and brimming with tears), and hastily assure me that he understood—we'd just keep it between us, and I could go ahead and park here for the night. I would shake his hand gratefully and firmly (none of that dead-fish grip here!), and thank him profusely for his kindness.

This patter, of course, likely wouldn't have worked if I'd been a man (or, I'm sad to say, an ineloquent woman). If I'd been a man, I'd probably have been asked to move on, or worse. Orange County, in particular, is overwhelmingly conservative, white suburbia—keen on appearances and hasty to drive out all appearances of homelessness. That's what LA is for, they figure. To be homeless in Orange County, you have to not be seen.

I did get the impression from the police I encountered, that they were trying in their way to take the recession into account, to go easier on the rapidly rising number of homeless people. I don't believe that most of them would be intentionally cruel to a homeless person. More that it was just an unfortunate, inevitable side effect of asking them to move on. Did it sadden me that perhaps a man, or someone sleeping on a park bench, or someone who was mentally ill would be treated worse than me in a police encounter? Absolutely. It's horrific, when you think about it. The more "visible" homeless individuals out there needed compassion far more than I did. They were the ones who really needed the cops to be flexible on the rules, to leave them in peace to sleep or at least to point them in the direction of a shelter or a program that could help them.

Still, that didn't stop me from taking advantage of the natural, built-in benefits of femininity. My gender is viewed as a hindrance in many other life situations—may always be. It was about damn time it came in handy for something, and I intended to make full use of it.

Job hunting was another pain in the ass. Nobody was hiring, or even bothering to call back. So many people were out of work that every job posting must have prompted hundreds or even thousands of résumés in response—an inbox-shattering wall of cover letters, a jumble of the qualified, the unqualified, the overqualified and the utterly hopeless. Everyone was desperate and willing to apply for *any* open position, however slim the chances were. I'd be lucky if a hiring manager ever even opened my email, much less read my résumé. The interviews that I *did* get were uncommonly dismal.

"What do you think about this recession we're going through?" asked a large, puffy interviewer behind the desk at a stainless-steel bathroom accessory factory. He stared at me in my business suit, freshly showered and primped at the gym, looking just like any other job applicant. He looked at me with saggy eyes behind round, dinner-plate, owl glasses.

I told him the truth—that it made me sad to see everyone having such a tough time, struggling, losing their homes, wondering where their next meal would come from. I said that I hoped the economy would right itself quickly and that things would be back on the up-and-up soon.

"No!" he slammed his hands on his desk dramatically and leaned over, into my personal space. "This economy is *excellent* for us, and do you know why?"

I wasn't sure how he wanted me to respond. I was having a hard time thinking of anything positive to say about the recession. I kept my mouth shut and raised my eyebrows, smiling slightly at him as though he'd asked a rhetorical question.

"It's because," he crowed, "now we, as a company, have our pick of the litter. We can hire people like you for dirt cheap. You've got great experience and credentials!" He waved my résumé in the air. "If everyone's out of work and desperate for a job, we can choose who we want. The best of the best. I couldn't do that a year ago. Somebody like you would never have come in to interview at a place like this."

I couldn't quite believe this conversation. It stunned me that anybody would be so tactless and rude as to say such a thing in a job interview, much less rub a potential hire's face in it, even if his company *were* profiting from the recession. Not only did it show a lack of professionalism, but it reflected utter crudeness of the lowest sort. He made me sick. I resisted the urge to grab a flabby cheek in each hand and bang his head on his mahogany desk.

Then he offered me the job, at a wage lower than entry-level. Lower than even unemployment. Bare minimum wage. I politely declined, when what I really wanted to tell him was to get stuffed. I'm a damn hard worker, but I'm nobody's slave.

Chapter Eight

Between job searching, I was updating the blog with random musings I was still positive nobody would ever read. Brandon, who called to check up on me every now and again, suggested that I start a Twitter account. I had vaguely heard of this Twitter crap, and thought it was ridiculous. Microblogging? One hundred forty characters? Why? What was the point? I simply didn't get it.

"No, really, Bri. It's, like, the wave of the future for self-promotion and advertising. You can make all sorts of connections on Twitter!" Brandon had a Twitter account himself, with about nine followers. I thought he was completely full of it. Still, I did it, to make him happy. "The Girl's Guide to Homelessness" wouldn't fit within the username limit, so I became "tGGtH." Feeling like an idiot, I punched a single tweet out into the internet ether:

www.girlsguidetohomelessness.blogspot.com. Tips for surviving homelessness.

It was March 2, 2009. My twenty-fourth birthday was four days away. I had no way of knowing how much that

single tweet would rock my entire world to its foundation.
I had no way of knowing the chain series of events it would
set in motion, changing my life—and me—forever.

All I knew was that within an hour, I had my first follower, @w0lfh0und, from across the Atlantic. His name
was Matt Barnes, and he was formerly a homeless activist
from England. After spending several months homeless, he
had recently been placed in a government-subsidized flat
in Scotland, and ran a website called HomelessTales.com, a
forum where homeless and formerly homeless writers could
publish articles about their experiences, as well as engage
in commenting and constructive debate. More than that,
it was a place to come together, propose solutions, create
friendships and form a support network.

Matt monitored keywords on Twitter. Any time the
word *homeless* or *homelessness* was tweeted, his Google
Reader picked up on it. He was sifting through that day, at
the exact same moment I grumpily sent out my first tweet,
and amid the myriad daily offerings of "If a turtle has no
shell, is it homeless?" and "Oh my god, I just saw a homeless guy with a cell phone! How is that possible?!" he saw
my tweet. After reading the few blog entries I had already
posted, he began following me, and I gratefully returned
the favor, feeling slightly less dumb now that I had my first
Twitter pal.

"I read your work, and I really enjoyed it. I'd like to
have you do a guest post or two on my site, if you're willing, one of these days," he wrote.

It was something to do, in between looking for work,
and if he thought it could do anybody any good, I was
happy to oblige. His site looked pretty great, too. I respected the concept of the work he was doing. The single

photo of him on his profile page was a bit shadowy, but I saw that he was kind of cute, in a sad-eyed, resigned sort of way.

Matt and I exchanged email addresses so that we could correspond without the inconvenience of a 140-character limit. Although I eventually told him my real name, once we'd emailed enough to the point where I trusted him, he set up an anonymous bio for me at HomelessTales.com. He would soon publish my first piece for the site—an essay about bad choices versus just plain rotten luck when you're homeless. It was mainly about how nobody is impervious to homelessness, how you don't know a person's backstory by looking at her or why she became homeless and the importance of withholding judgment as to which homeless people are "deserving" of help and which aren't, including those who use drugs or may have made poor life choices previously.

The piece was far from Shakespeare. It was plenty flawed, and perhaps more than a little naïve in parts. But I felt there was much truth in it. And I did seem to make something of a splash among the more established authors on the site, who debated my ideas more fiercely than I'd expected. Some agreed with certain points I'd made; to others I was an inexperienced girl born with a silver spoon in my mouth, merely playing at homelessness. I hadn't yet paid my dues. I knew *nothing* about the seamier side of things.

I think what they hadn't expected was that I would agree with them. "You're right. I *am* new at it. I have *no* idea *what* I'm doing. I'm figuring it out as I go along, and I *do* have a lot of assets and advantages that many homeless people don't have. But, then, isn't that the point? We all have different pasts, but for whatever reason, we're all homeless. There are as many perspectives on homelessness as there are people who are homeless. Mine is just another viewpoint on it, reflecting a particular set of circumstances. I'm here to make friends, learn from you and your stories, and contribute however I can."

I meant it, too. I think my earnestness disarmed them. I figured out pretty quickly that I could hold my own there, and even befriended the ones who had been the most suspicious of me at the start.

Matt, I noticed, was normally very reserved and restrained when commenting on discussions and debates. He clearly considered himself a moderator first, and strove to remain as neutral and above the fray as possible. He always considered his words carefully and refrained from betraying emotion on his site. It wasn't lost on me, then, that he was rather quick to jump to my defense when I was criticized. Occasionally I would consider for about a second and a half that he might be interested in me. But then I would laugh it off. It was a stupid premise. Clearly, he was just being kind and protective of the youngest writer on the site, the baby who couldn't defend herself. It was sweet.

I'm still not quite sure how it started. Soon we were exchanging three to four emails a day, and suddenly, I was yearning for the next morsel of correspondence. If I only received three in a day from him, rather than four, I was disappointed. We connected over shared loves of architecture, literature, film…and also over our mutual traumas. I opened up bit by bit about my past, and so did he. He marveled at it.

"American girls aren't supposed to be like you. You're all supposed to be airheads over there. You're not supposed to be interested in any of this stuff." I would laugh, and tease him about his misconceptions.

He was thirty-six years old and divorced. He and his wife, Victoria, had been together for five years, and married for less than two, when he came home early from work one day, on the second anniversary of his proposing to her in Prague, and she announced that she wanted a divorce. It wasn't him, it was her. He hadn't done anything wrong, but she just felt as if she had married too young and had missed out on too many life experiences, so she'd like to get off the ride now, please. It was, he said, completely out of the blue and had set off the chain of events that made him homeless. She had moved out immediately, but sentimentally refused to consent to sell their house. He couldn't afford to continue paying the mortgage on a single salary, and the bank soon started foreclosure proceedings.

He had fought to save the marriage, he said, but she refused to be moved. He didn't handle the separation well at all. He would have breakdowns or sometimes even tantrums at work. His company soon put him on an extended leave of absence until he could pull himself together. He was diagnosed by a doctor with abnormally low serotonin levels, he explained to me, which not only wreaked havoc on his sleep schedule, but caused him to behave irrationally (basically, my trusty Google explained to me, it causes bipolar disorder symptoms), explaining the uncontrollable outbursts at work. The doctor put him on medication that gradually worked to even out the serotonin levels, but it would take a month before he was stabilized.

Out of his mind with grief and illness, Matt gave away almost all of his possessions to charity the week before the bank was set to evict him from his home. He packed a suitcase with an old laptop and a few other belongings, and walked out the door. For several months, he slept in the woods on some nights, in hostels on others.

A girl named Lori, whom he had met in the months between the breakup of his marriage and his becoming homeless, and who had a major crush on him, contacted him out of the blue to see how he was doing, and he explained some of the particulars of his situation. She was moving back to Peterhead, Scotland with her stepfather and offered for him to stay with them. He had nowhere to go, and he accepted. He stayed there for three weeks or so, and even halfheartedly began a romance with her, which she had hoped for all along. Still, he explained, he just wasn't happy with her. He couldn't bring himself to love her. She was incredibly dull and he couldn't hold any kind of a serious conversation with her. It was like being in a relationship with a ten-year-old, he said. The house was also in a condemnable state, and he didn't like her stepfather. After the three weeks were up, he told Lori he was sorry, but he just couldn't see a future with her, and he felt that he needed to move on. He moved into temporary hostel accommodations before the local council offered him permanent housing in the small rural village of Huntly, fifty miles away. He accepted, and had been there for a month or two when we met.

March 6, my twenty-fourth birthday, I spent the day with Brandon at Disneyland—it was local and they had a "get in free on your birthday" program, which I intended to take full advantage of. Standing in line at the entry, I checked my email on my phone. Matt had emailed me a Happy Birthday wish, and a jpeg of a morning glory—my favorite flower. He signed it "Matt xx." I spent the rest of the day on Splash Mountain and Space Mountain and the Matterhorn and Indiana Jones, trying to figure out what he meant by those two xs. It was the first time I'd allowed myself to seriously consider that, despite the secret schoolgirl crush I harbored on him, perhaps he might be interested in me as more than a contributor on his site. I was petrified. I was also too much of a wimp to ask him straight out. So I did what any wimp would do—continued our email correspondence as before, without referencing those two enigmatic electronic kisses.

Many people have questioned my responsibility and/or sanity for keeping an animal while homeless, especially a giant dog like Fezzik. There were several reasons, though, that I wanted to at least try to keep Fezzik. First of all, I had a source of income. I was on extended unemployment for at least eight months, or until I found work, so I was, thus far, fully able to pay for my dog's food, treats, toys and even vet bills, should the need arise. Second, I had shelter. Living out of a thirty-foot trailer is a luxury that many homeless people do not have. I did not keep Fezzik cramped up in a car, or on the side of the road on a leash. He had a crate as his den and a nice wide trailer to stretch his legs in. Third, the Brea Walmart is within walking distance of a tri-city park, a large, green expanse with a lake, where Fez and I would go walking every day. There were eight acres of trees and grass for him to sniff, ducks for him to look at and nice fishermen and children to pat his head.

"What a big, beautiful boy!" they exclaimed, and I beamed with pride.

I always knew, though, that were my situation ever to

deteriorate and become more dire, I would contact the
rescue from which I adopted Fezzik and make arrangements to return him. I love my dog. He is a source of
companionship and comfort, and he is *definitely* a means of
protection for a woman in a vulnerable state (people give
me a wide berth on the sidewalk—you don't want to mess
with a dog that looks like Fez). But when it came down
to it, I realized that I should and would send him back in
a heartbeat if I couldn't provide for his needs. So far, he
had not had to endure a single day without food, water,
exercise and love. I hoped that would always be the case.

The topic of homeless people and their pets is such a
hot-button one that Matt asked me to write a column at
HomelessTales.com about it. It was another controversial
column and inspired a lot of discussion, which was what
Matt had intended. For all my confidence, however, I
knew that summer was rapidly approaching, and that in
the deadly California heat, there would be no way I could
continue leaving Fezzik alone in the trailer, especially all
day while I worked. He would broil to death. I had a short
reprieve, but I needed to get a job and get out of that parking lot fast, or else find somewhere else for my dog.

Around this time, I came home one night to a notice
taped to the window of my trailer threatening to "evict"
me:

**WALMART DOES NOT ALLOW OVERNIGHT PARKING!!!
MOVE OR YOU WILL BE TOWED!!!**

It turned out that a newer moron on the lot did some
really stupid things, such as running his noisy generator
around 1:00 a.m., littering all around his trailer and un-
hooking his trailer from his vehicle and leaving it in the

parking lot while driving around in his truck, thereby technically "abandoning" a vehicle. Not only did he do all this, but he did it while Walmart corporate executives were visiting the store, and they took notice.

Five or six RVs fled that night in search of greener pastures, with no idea where to go. A few other trailer dwellers and I stuck around, and two of us (myself and Pete, the "mayor" of the Walmart parking lot, who had lived there for four months and counting) went into Walmart in the morning to speak to the manager. I showered and put on a business suit before going in. Pete wore one of his limousine driver tuxedos, which I thought was a tad over the top, but he definitely didn't "look" stereotypically homeless, that's for sure.

The manager was the same woman I had spoken to over the phone in the first place, and she was nice enough. "Oh, wow. You don't *look* homeless."

That was kind of the point. "Corporate visited yesterday, that's all. When they visit, they always send someone out to post those flyers on the RVs. Luckily they don't even bother leaving notices for the homeless living out of cars and vans—just the trailers. It doesn't mean much, we never *actually* tow anybody."

For good measure, Pete showed the lady all the Walmart receipts he had accrued, demonstrating just how much business the store got from allowing him to stay. I explained that we were quiet and kept to ourselves, never littered and so on. I explained that I was not a "bum," and that I, too, bought supplies from Walmart. I just needed a place to park while I transitioned out of this, and that was why I had called ahead to make sure that would be OK.

She told us that we seemed nice and respectful, and recommended that we just stay in the parking lot. She reiterated that the store managers would not call the police on us or have us towed—they didn't want to have to pay hefty fees to tow giant RVs out, plus, they really had no problem with our being there as long as we didn't draw attention to ourselves. It was just the corporate office's beef, and they had left already. She said that if someone filed a complaint with the police, or the police came by of their own accord to speak to us, they would most likely only ask us to move, not ticket or tow us. She said that if that happened, she would recommend moving to another Walmart a few cities over, or to Sam's Club, for a night or two. Then we could come back.

So we stayed, and there were no further problems or requests to leave. I felt terrible for the people they scared out of there with those mean flyers, though. I wondered where they went.

Sadly, the Lord of the Generator was not one of the ones that left. You'd think he could take a hint.

In early March, I was offered a position as an executive assistant at a small web design company of five people. The pay was nothing near what I had been making at KBB—the hiring manager blamed it on the recession, of course—but I didn't care. I needed a job, and I was humble enough to take anything that paid more than unemployment.

I stopped filing for unemployment benefits as soon as I was hired, but I had yet to receive any of the checks for the previous several months for which I had filed claims— there were so many "unavoidable delays" and it was nearly impossible to get through via telephone with the swarms of unemployed people in California bogging down the lines. The Employee Development Department (EDD) also didn't have an answering machine, or a Hold line: If you called while all the lines were busy, which they always were, they would ask you to hang up and please try again. After spending several hours straight hitting the Redial button and hoping for good luck, I gave up and resorted to contacting them via email about the problem, which often resulted in a canned response, bearing little to no relation to my problem, or no response at all.

I sighed it off. I would continue pursuing the EDD for all my back checks, but in the meantime, I had something. I had a job. There would be options for me very soon, in the future. Matt was the first person I emailed to share the news.

Brandon and my best female friend, Sonia, were the only two people in my life aware that I was living in a parking lot. Nobody else knew, not even my own family, who hadn't given any further thought to where I was going next, after watching me trailer off bumpily into the sunset. Brandon and Sonia agreed that I could mention them in my blog, and I offered them their choice of pseudonym. Brandon chose "Dwight."

"What, like Dwight from *The Office?*" I asked incredulously. He seemed wounded.

"No, like Dwight from *Sin City!*"

"Ah." Brandon didn't remotely resemble Clive Owen, even if Clive Owen had been Asian, but OK. Dwight it was.

Sonia couldn't think up a pseudonym.

"Just call me whatever," she said. She was too busy working on becoming the first Bangladeshi soldier in the U.S. Army to focus on trifling things like pseudonyms. We had known one another since junior high school, when her family had immigrated to California. Sonia is a tiny, delicate girl with lovely huge eyes and the longest, curliest, blackest hair you've ever seen. She looks like some kind of fairy-tale princess. I was scared to death for her, and begged her not to go into the military. I just knew they'd somehow break her in half with all that boot camp stuff. But she was bound and determined, and there was nothing I could do to stop her. She would be leaving for boot camp in May, so I had less than two months to spend with her. I decided to rechristen her on the blog after one of her favorite actresses, Aishwarya Rai.

"Oh my gosh, really? Stop insulting Aishwarya. I don't look anything like her. Pick something more low key" is all she would say, eternally humble and self-disparaging.

On a whim, Sonia and I drove out to Hollywood one night to see the movie *Sunshine Cleaners* at the only California theater in which it was currently playing before going into wide release. The movie was great—touching and funny. I knew going in that it was a dramedy about sisters who start a crime scene cleanup business, and I figured that parts of it might remind me of recent events, but I hadn't expected the opening sequence, in which a man walks into a sporting goods store, asks to see a .20 gauge shotgun, and promptly sticks it under his chin and blows his brains out right there. I suppose it hit a little bit too close to home for me.

Also hitting close to home was Amy Adams in a role that just wrenched my gut. At one point, she says, "I'm good at getting men to want me...not date me or marry me...but want me." I wanted to start bawling right there. It was one of the rare public bouts of self-pity that I indulged in, and I went to Starbucks the next morning and wrote an in-depth blog about just how crummy it felt to wonder if it would ever be possible for anyone to love me.

Matt wrote me that evening, as usual.

"I read your latest blog post. It almost brought me to tears. It saddens me to know that you suffer such feelings. I can empathize to some extent, knowing what it feels like not to be loved back. Impossible to fully comprehend though what it must be like to endure it repetitively and exclusively. I know it sounds somewhat trite, but it really will happen for you someday. I realize I don't know you that well, but I've seen enough to know that you have a great deal to offer and I have no doubt that sooner or later (and probably sooner) someone will discover your true worth."

I got a little misty, reading his email. I responded in as upbeat and positive a manner I could, to reassure him. Then I asked, "Hey, wanna see what I look like?" and attached a photo of Sonia and me that I had snapped that night with my phone's camera. It was the first time he would see my face, and he told me that I was beautiful. It was the first time I'd ever believed it.

Meanwhile, I was continuing to work full time and the blog was garnering a bit of attention. I was contacted by a reality TV show, MTV's *True Life*. They were interested in finding out more about my situation and potentially shadowing me for an upcoming episode on homelessness. It was a surreal feeling; my blog still had very few readers and I was keen on remaining anonymous. I expressed my misgivings to the producer who contacted me, but told her more about my story. She backtracked rather rapidly. I don't think I quite fit the "downtrodden" mold they were going for. That evening, I passed on the news to Matt.

"They said that since I'm educated, resourceful, don't utilize shelters and now have a job, they don't believe that I am representative of the general homeless population. I told them that I don't necessarily know if anybody is 'representative' of the issue. If anything, I'm trying to buck the commonly held myths and stereotypes about the homeless—pointing out their resourcefulness, their value, their ability to contribute to society, their desire to work and continue leading normal lives and their drive to create a sustainable lifestyle while they try to reverse their circumstances.

"But, I understand and I'm not offended or anything. If anything, I can see how a story about a LGBT kid kicked out for being 'different' or a kid on drugs or a kid living in a cardboard box would make for much more compelling TV than me; when it comes down to it, I can't compare to that level of interest or drama. And those kids are probably the ones more in need of the help (and money!) that such focus will provide them. In the end, they're trying to put the issue out there, which is great."

Matt was decidedly more upset at the news than I was. "I could feel my blood starting to boil as I was reading. That really irks me. Not representative? Of course you are, and that's the point. You are the reality of modern-day homelessness. One of the missions on Twitter mentioned today that 50 percent of their clients are employed full time. They just want someone who will fit their comfortable, narrow-minded image of homelessness, and that is exactly how stereotypes continue to be reinforced. I would have torn them to shreds if I were you. No wonder they work for MTV. Raaaaaaa!!!!

"OK, rant over. I'm going to be helping a friend highlight a problem concerning homeless deaths. Her mother had alcohol problems and mental health issues and was believed to have been homeless for years. She searched for her for years, was in contact with the local authorities on a weekly basis and posted stuff all over the internet. Unfortunately, a few weeks ago she discovered that her mother had passed on a couple of years before. The problem is that despite the ease with which the family could have been notified, nobody ever did and, as a result, she has been buried in a pauper's grave. She cannot even place a headstone for her. She wants to bring her home."

Just when I thought I couldn't have any more of a crush on him, there he went, being all noble and self-sacrificing like that. I loved that he cared so much about helping others. When was the last time I'd cared about helping anybody? This was a man I respected and wanted to emulate. Plus, this was the first time I'd seen him go on a rant. It was surprisingly sexy. Beneath all that stoic English-ness, there was passion and protectiveness, too. It made me want to bury my face into this near-stranger's chest and feel safe. So, clearly, I was nuts. *He'd never think about me that way. Not in a million years.*

Around the same time, I was contacted by another homeless activist, who was gaining notoriety for his video interviews with homeless men and women throughout the SoCal area. He wanted to do a video interview with me in my trailer, in the Walmart parking lot. He seemed a little bit pompous and pushy, and I was still very keen on anonymity, so I balked and asked Matt, who knew the man, for his opinion as to what I should do. If there was anybody whose opinion I respected, it was Matt's.

"I have no doubt of the value of his work," he said. "If you do it, though, you should definitely let him know that you don't want your name or location revealed, for safety reasons. You're justified in wanting to stay anonymous. Rarely does a day go by that I don't read about some poor homeless person set on fire in the news. There are some very sick, prejudiced people out there."

I hadn't known him long enough to realize that he was choosing his words very carefully. I thought he was just being British and polite. It turned out that, while Matt truly did believe that there was value to the man's work—that of putting faces and stories to homelessness—he didn't always approve of his personality, methods or ethics. The man would later go on to do a month-long sponsored road trip across the nation. He would draw criticism for leaving his rent unpaid during the trip; running out of money nearly immediately, due to poor planning, and subsequently sponging off sponsors and demanding freebie stays from hotels; and begging for donations from his Twitter followers. Most of all, he was criticized for sneakily filming children and domestic violence survivors in shelters, against the express instructions of staff, and posting their unblurred faces online, endangering their safety and privacy. He has since publicly attacked homeless individuals who have expressed reluctance to meet with him and put their names and faces on film, calling them the "fake" homeless and asserting that a *real* homeless person would never turn down an opportunity for "help." I have since made it clear that I am not in any way affiliated with this activist, and refused to engage when he publicly attempted to castigate me for distancing myself from his version of "help."

Of course, none of this had yet occurred, and I trusted Matt's judgment. If he thought that my speaking on camera would be of value, then I would do it. The activist promised that a pseudonym would be used, and that my location would not be revealed. He came to my trailer a few days later (over two hours late), stayed and filmed me answering his questions for twenty to thirty minutes. Then he asked me for a hug and prayed aloud to Jesus for me, which made me incredibly uncomfortable. There's really no polite way to interrupt a praying Christian and explain that you're an atheist, and ask if he could possibly do his praying for you in his quiet private time, is there? I was relieved when he left.

A few days later, the video was posted on the activist's website. I was shocked to see that my correct first name and my location were used. Panicked, and sure that there had been some mistake, I contacted the man and requested that my name and location be removed immediately, reminding him of our agreement.

"Oops," he laughed. "Well, it's too late now. Somebody else hosts the site for me, and I don't think he'll want to change it. Besides, all the *other* people I've taped have used their own names, and they've been fine. Don't worry— this video is going to do great things for you and get more people interested in your blog. You shouldn't be ashamed of it. Embrace it."

I wasn't ashamed. I was simply concerned for my safety. Matt, too, was angered by the man's refusal to back down, and refused to communicate with him or promote any more of his work. After a few days stewing, I decided to shrug it off and let it go. The video did indeed send several viewers to my site, which was fine, but I would never again like or trust that man. The whole thing served only to make me more guarded about the people I was willing to speak to.

I didn't know it at the time, but Matt spent hours painstakingly downloading the video interview on his incredibly slow, rural internet connection. I would later learn that he watched it over and over again, learning my mannerisms, the inflections of my voice, my nervous laugh. It made me all the more real to him. He noted that, at one point, I mentioned writing for his site, and when I spoke his name, an uncontrollable smile spread across my face. It was true. I couldn't help myself. There was so little to be happy about in my current predicament. His friendship and support were among the few rays of light that kept me going.

One night I received a text message from Pete in the Walmart lot. Some kids apparently were teasing Fezzik through the trailer window while I was at work and he started going insane barking (thus breaking that cardinal rule of "Ye must not attract any attention"). So, the other RVers asked me to move for a while, and I understood, of course. I felt terrible.

I moved the trailer to Sam's Club a few miles away and texted Sonia, who told me to call her in the morning and she'd take me back to Walmart to pick up my car.

Big mistake.

First of all, the lot at Sam's Club, while pretty much completely deserted at night (unlike Walmart), is located in a much crummier part of town. And it's situated right by train tracks. This loud train came through honking its horn, all night long...waking me up about every hour and a half. Then, around 4:00 a.m., Fezzik started barking nonstop and I couldn't figure out why, because he's never been much of a barker unless he thinks that a strange man might hurt me.

I finally got up, stepped outside and found myself facing about fifty Mexican immigrants gathered around my trailer, cooking breakfast on a portable grill and appraising me confusedly. Apparently, I had chosen to camp out in the spot where they stand around all day waiting for under-the-table work.

Well, fuck.

So Fezzik was, of course, going nuts because he didn't like all the strange men hanging around my trailer. But then, the only other option was going back to Walmart, and I figured I couldn't show my face back there for a while, until I found somewhere else for Fezzik.

I decided that I had no choice but to board Fezzik. I didn't want to stay in the Sam's Club parking lot. Pete mentioned that he had sent another RVer out there to drive by and see if I made it OK, and he had seen all the day workers hanging around my trailer and was concerned. Walmart was a much safer option, and I was touched to learn that the other members of my little RV community cared enough to drive by Sam's Club and watch out for me.

Brandon fronted me the money for one month of boarding, until I got my paycheck from work. It would stretch my finances a bit, I knew, and probably even prolong my homelessness, but Fezzik has always been worth every bit of it.

Matt talked me through my despair over the Fezzik situation. He had to give up his two cats when he lost his home and he mourned their loss. He recognized that I would give up Fezzik if I absolutely had to, and became unable to care for him, but I wanted at all costs to exhaust every option before that was necessary. I still hoped that I wouldn't be homeless for too much longer, even with the added expense.

I wasn't much of a fan of the boarding facility. They didn't allow the dogs to play together, they said, so I told them I wanted to come and take Fezzik out to the dog park on weekends.

"You *can,*" said the nebbishy lady at the desk reluctantly, "but we discourage it. It'll just depress him. They get all excited and happy about seeing you, and then they get sad again when you bring 'em back."

I was seriously starting to doubt how much better this boarding thing could possibly be for Fezzik. It sounded to me like he'd be getting less exercise and absolutely no interaction with other animals. Plegh.

She slipped a flimsy little string lead over his neck to take him back to the room. I offered the woman his Halti nose lead, since he was used to it and it kept him awesomely under control. Just a little tug and he's putty in your hands, since, like all dogs, he follows the direction of his nose. She said no, took it off, gave it to me and led him to the back room.

I signed the last form and turned to leave. All of a sudden, commotion, and then Fezzik came hurtling madly out from the back room, dragging the hapless receptionist behind him.

She silently took the Halti from me with as much wounded dignity as she could muster, and this time he went along meekly. I didn't know whether to laugh or cry.

It was around this time that Matt and I finally got down to brass tacks and figured out just how much we meant to one another. For some reason, a Hotmail glitch randomly and suddenly prevented his account from receiving my emails and stuck my IP address on the "automatic spam" list. Likewise, his emails to me vanished in a cyberspace vapor, never arriving in my inbox. I became alarmed when he didn't respond to any of my emails for several days, although he was still posting articles on Homeless Tales. Perhaps he was just busy, I rationalized. Too busy to talk to me. Or perhaps our increasingly flirtatious emails had scared him off. Perhaps he realized that my feelings for him were starting to become rather strong, and I was mistaken in thinking he could feel the same way.

A week went by with nothing from him. I was devastated. I had somehow scared off my friend. I later learned that on the other side of the world, he was an equally nervous wreck. He couldn't figure out why I was ignoring his emails. He had never believed that he could love anybody again after his wife left him, and now foolishly he had allowed himself to hope. He was angry with himself, and as hurt as I was.

We finally figured out what had happened when I had an instant message conversation with a mutual friend and homeless activist, Jon, also known as "Beat on the Street" in homeless circles. Jon was from Ireland and as crazy as... well, an Irishman. He was also hilariously good-natured and proactive, and Matt's best friend these days, although they had never met in person. They were currently working together on a "homeless hike" in the UK, planned for September, in which they would camp wherever they could find for two weeks or so across Scotland, from Inverness to Edinburgh. The hike would be sponsored and filmed to raise awareness of homelessness, and the proceeds would benefit homeless charities in Scotland and Ireland.

As Jon and I chatted, he explained that he was also chatting with Matt, who was online on gtalk.

"Oh?" I spoke cautiously, probing. "Is he very busy? I haven't heard from him in a week, I guess he hasn't had a lot of time to answer any of my emails...."

Jon pinged Matt.

"Hey, bro, I've got our friend, Bri, in another window. She's wondering about you."

Matt responded in a decidedly dejected manner.

"If she wanted to talk to me, she'd answer my emails." Jon was confused.

"I dunno. She says she hasn't heard from you in a week. She really does seem like she wants to talk to you. Just send her a chat invite already!"

In that way, Matt and I connected via gtalk, and soon figured out the Hotmail glitch. He had to do some digging around to determine what had happened, and change a few settings to begin getting my emails again. But that one horrible week had made both of us realize just how much we meant to one another. I found myself repressing hysterical sobs in the middle of Starbucks as I typed.

"We could have never figured it out. We could have gone on forever thinking that we hated each other for some reason. It's so scary." He agreed, shakily. The shock of how close we had come to losing whatever it was that we had sent us reeling to our cores, and seemingly before we knew it, we were spending every day after I got off work at the web design company, and all day on the weekends, chatting together. We were spending upwards of ten hours a day with each other, and we both realized very quickly what it had become. And it terrified the hell out of both of us.

Love.

Chapter Nine

A few months after I started blogging, a web developer named Adam wrote in and offered to buy me my own web domain and host my site for free. So, I became *www.girlsguidetohomelessness.com,* and I was no longer simply a free blog, but a true-blue *website.*

I tried to focus on my happiness about the dot-com development, but I was too busy missing Fezzik. I missed having his huge oafish self around to hug and cuddle, and I also missed how protective he was of me. Every time I entered my trailer late at night, I was now superparanoid about opening the door; there was always the possibility that somebody had broken in and was lying in wait. I always held my keys in a fist, pointy ends poking out through my knuckles, just in case.

Working for the web design company was starting to wear on my moral compass as well. I hadn't realized, when I'd taken the job, the nature of our clientele.

There were only five employees, including me. The life of an executive assistant isn't particularly glamorous or exciting. It mainly involves being at the computer for long stretches of time, drafting correspondence of Excel spreadsheets, Human Resources paperwork, fiddling with accounting and payroll, and occasionally picking up lunch and coffee for the boss. Boring stuff. Essential, but boring. So I focused more on the administrative side of things. I was managing the money coming in, but it took a couple of months before I realized exactly where it was coming from, what kind of websites we were selling and building—loan modification websites, for mortgage scammers masquerading as legitimate foreclosure assistance programs.

It first clicked when, within the span of a week, several of our clients across the United States were arrested and shut down by the government. It was apparently rather publicly handled, and our company started receiving a lot of hate mail for being willing to work with that kind of scum. I was in charge of sorting incoming emails, so I was perplexed at the sudden onslaught of threatening letters. When I asked one of the web designers about it, he laughed.

"I hate to be the one to tell you this, but nearly all of our clients are scam artists. They're our bread and butter. There are so many loan mod companies springing up now, offering to help homeowners in foreclosure, for a fee, and the government's going through a major crackdown right now on it."

"That's not allowed?"

"Yeah. They're not allowed to charge for their services. There are government programs that offer the same assistance for free. These homeowners are so desperate and ignorant, they'll fork over hundreds or thousands of dollars to our clients, in exchange for a promise that they'll talk to the homeowner's bank and arrange a payment plan. Then they usually take the money and run."

I was horrified.

"But…but we're *helping* them!"

He shrugged.

"It's not illegal to make a website. Sure, we know what it's for, but *they're* the ones actually running the scams. If you want to blame anyone, blame the dumbass home-owners who don't do a little research and learn to protect themselves from being scammed."

I couldn't bring myself to accept it, though. The com-pany I worked for was making money by helping scam artists fleece people who were about to lose their homes, like me. There were plenty of other, reputable industries out there that we could have focused on, but the com-pany marketed its web design services to loan modifica-tion companies specifically. We were profiting, and not particularly indirectly, off others' misery.

I wigged out and told Matt everything. I didn't have another job lined up, but I didn't want to stay. He was creeped out by the entire thing, too, but encouraged me to keep the job until I could find work elsewhere.

"It's shady, but you can't get in trouble with the law for it, and if you leave now, you'll be out the paycheck, and you need it."

Besides, he reminded me, I wasn't doing any of the web design work myself. I was just the coffee-getter, the girl who submitted employees' paperwork for their choice be-tween Kaiser Permanente or Blue Cross health insurance and the one who tallied up and crunched the numbers at the end of the week.

It was true, but I still felt dirty.

. . .

Matt and I were still coming to terms with our burgeoning romance. We decided that maybe I'd travel to Scotland in September, if I could save up the money, and go on the homeless hike with him and Jon. Though we eventually let Jon in on the secret, after a few weeks, we decided not to make our relationship public yet. We knew we were in love, but we danced around the word—speaking in euphemisms for it. It didn't feel right to say it to each other over a computer. We wanted to meet in person, to make sure everything we were feeling across a couple of computer screens was as real and powerful as we suspected.

As the weeks went by, we realized that there was no way we were going to last until September. It was crazy and rash and irrational, but we had to meet. Being apart was too difficult. I began scraping together whatever I could spare from my paychecks, and he from his benefit checks. Perhaps in a month or two we could make something happen.

Fezzik was not looking well. He was always very happy to see me, but he was also depressed and lethargic, and he'd lost a lot of weight, which was really bothering me. I asked the kennel to ramp up his feeding.

"Oh…so, you're saying that you would rather we give him two feedings a day instead of one?" My brain promptly exploded in a series of cartoonish destruction flashes. *"How much have you been feeding him?"*

I pressed the unenthusiastic kennel drone until she finally admitted…

"One cup a day." That was *all* that Fezzik had been getting.

Just for reference, adult Neapolitan Mastiffs should be eating eight to ten cups of food each day. It was no wonder that Fezzik was rapidly skeletonizing, practically in front of my eyes. My dog was starving.

What kind of fucking morons *were* these people? And now they wanted to charge me extra for extra feeding—an extra dollar per cup. Wasn't that why I was *already* paying so much more to board him than I would for a smaller dog?!

I pumped the pimply teenager at the desk for info like she was a terror suspect, tied to a chair and interrogated under a lightbulb. I learned that (contrary to what I had been told when checking Fezzik in) he was not being exercised daily. Apparently that would cost me extra, too, even though the other receptionist had told me when I first boarded him that it was included.

Fezzik was spending every day in a four-by-twelve-foot dog run, and his nights in a four-by-four-foot cage. At least with me, he had a thirty-foot trailer to roam in— more than twice the space he now had. He'd lost a ton of weight, was blowing coat and his nose was raw from rubbing it on his kennel door.

I cried for hours that evening. It made me so angry to see my dog rapidly decline like this. He was *so* much better off with me, and yet I was paying for them to starve him.

I didn't want to make a scene, but I was livid. Ruefully, I forked over nearly all the cash I had on me for the extra feeding, and then immediately began looking for somewhere else to move Fezzik. Again.

Several of my blog followers put out a Twitter call for help for Fezzik. Eventually, a friend of a friend of a friend came up with a solution. I was on the verge of having a breakdown when the message arrived in my inbox. There was a woman who could board Fezzik for next to nothing. Her name was Maryse-Noelle Sage, though everybody called her just plain "Sage." She was a warm, tiny, hippie-esque, New Age-y woman with waist-long blond hair. She was perhaps in her forties but looked much younger, due to her natural diet and the exercise that inevitably comes with constant dog/horse rescue. Sage ran her own photography and ad agency—sagency.net—lived on a quasi-rural lot in Riverside and would end up playing a very important role in Matt's and my lives.

I didn't realize this at the time, though. What I did learn on that first visit was that Fezzik *will* chase chickens. And horses (but only if they run). You'd think a few well-aimed kicks in the general region of his head would dissuade him, but nooooooo. He came running to me whining for about a second and a half before deciding to see if his next attempt would go any better.

Idiot dog. I love him so.

I filed the previous year's tax return with H&R Block, rather than doing it myself and waiting eight weeks to receive my refund in the mail, for the simple reason of *sheer fucking immediacy.* I needed money *now,* and I'd rather H&R Block take a ridiculously high chunk of it and hand over the rest within twenty-four hours, than try to figure out how to survive on peanuts until my next paycheck. Part of the tax return money went into the "get together with Matt for sex" fund. Yes, it's completely shallow, but along with being in love and all, I really wanted to get laid. Our increasingly frequent "frisky" gchats only made both of us hornier. There, I said it.

We had started speaking over the phone as well, when we could scrape up enough minutes. He'd heard my voice before, in the video interview, but I'd never heard his until now. He sounded younger than I had expected, and occasionally I had to struggle to understand him— the distortion of the phone connection, in addition to his Portsmouth accent, induced frequent and recurring exclamations of "I'm sorry, what?!" from me. We would then laugh nervously and he would repeat himself. The first phone conversation was the hardest and the most tense. We'd already spent upwards of a hundred hours in one another's company online, but neither of us were "phone people." I think we both also wondered whether the magic connection would hold up as well in person, and the phone was a precursor of that, a harbinger of things to come.

We were both so terrified at first. The conversation lasted for about ten minutes (I was on a break at work) and concluded with him saying quickly, "Well, it was nice to speak with you. Good bye." It sounded so formal, and I briefly worried that that was it—he was having second thoughts. I hurried back to my work computer, where a gtalk message was waiting for me.

"Oh, my god, did I really just say, 'Nice to speak with you?' I'm so sorry, I feel like such an ass. I was just so nervous. I'm *really* not a phone person! I adore you. Get back to work! Talk tonight at Starbucks!"

I laughed, and everything went back to the way it had been before the phone call. Over time, we became just as comfortable over the phone as in person. Depending on our finances at any given moment, we could talk for an hour or longer before grudgingly hanging up the phone.

"I don't want to go. I want you to stay."

"Me, too. When can I talk to you every day, without having to hang up? This sucks."

"It does suck."

It felt fantastic. If the two most antiphone people in the world could handle this, then there was no stopping us.

I was very good at keeping my homelessness a secret from people at work. I had opened a P.O. box and was using the post office address as my physical address for job-related paperwork, with the box number as my "apartment number." The mail was delivered to the box just the same.

I had my routine down pat. Wake up early, shower at Planet Fitness, make it to work long before everybody else so that my hair had a chance to dry, do my job and head home. I kept my work life and my personal life very separate and didn't usually bother making friends at work. At the end of the day, I wanted to switch off that part of my life. I wasn't the type to go out for drinks after work with coworkers. There was only one occasion when I can remember my two lives bleeding into each other.

It was an employee's birthday, so my boss took the staff out to a local Persian restaurant for some congratulatory falafel. Since the recession was such a popular topic at the time, the conversation soon took that turn. Before I knew what was happening, my boss's partner exclaimed, "I just don't get it! There's absolutely no reason for *anybody*, even in this economy, to be homeless. I have *lots* of friends who've been laid off. *They're* not homeless yet. They're looking for new jobs. The only reason for *anybody* to be homeless, *ever*, is because they're lazy."

He leaned back in his chair and crossed his arms smugly. I felt my blood begin to boil.

I cleared my throat. "*I'm* homeless. Do you think that *I'm* lazy?"

A hush swept across the table. Fuck, I was in for it now. But I didn't care. Let them fire me. I couldn't keep quiet while someone was slandering homeless people. Lazy? Why would a lazy person ever choose this life? You couldn't be both lazy and homeless. You wouldn't survive a week. I knew far lazier people who lived in mansions and thought *work* meant sitting in your office and playing solitaire while ripping off the ideas of younger, poorer, more talented underlings.

The pause seemed interminable. Then, the girl next to me, a coworker I'd spoken to maybe twice since starting, piped up, "My boyfriend and I lived out of our car for several months last year."

The boss and his partner seemed shaken.

"You never told us that."

"Of course not. Who hires a homeless person?"

"Right," I agreed. "There's such a stigma about it. You had such great things to say about my résumé and my cover letter when you called me in. You told me that I was far more coherent and articulate than hundreds of other applicants for the position, and that was why you wanted to hire me. But would you still have wanted to hire me if I came branded with the word *homeless?*"

I didn't lose my job that day, as I'd feared. But it did set everyone at that table to thinking, and I was glad that I could at least do that. And they all wanted answers to the usual questions—how I came to work looking clean, looking *normal.* I'd allowed my coworkers to learn a little more about me, and I guess at least I was able to challenge the preconceived notions of a small group of people, made them question their initial perceptions.

. . .

Matt and I were also learning more and more about each other, opening up the darker sides of ourselves. We wanted each other to know all our flaws and weaknesses. I had plenty of skeletons in my closet, obviously. Besides "Oh, hey, I was a sexually and physically abused cult member for the first eighteen years of my life," I also had to open up to him about the other traumatic events in my past.

I had been date-raped at nineteen, I explained to him when I felt ready. I thought back to the event. I had met the guy—little more than a kid—out swing-dancing with a friend in my performing swing troupe. The friend was blonde and gorgeous, used to soaking up attention from men everywhere she went. For some reason, though, this boy had kept coming back to me for more and more dances. I couldn't fathom why he took an interest in me, but I agreed to go on a casual date with him the following week. We saw *Spider-Man 2,* and ended the evening with a chaste peck on the cheek and a handshake.

I didn't expect to hear from him again, and was surprised when he texted me and invited me out to lunch at a nearby rib joint. I agreed, but over the meal explained that I didn't feel ready for a relationship at the time, and hoped we could just be friends who hung out. He amiably agreed, and then invited me back to his apartment to watch a baseball game with his roommate. When we arrived at the apartment, the roommate was nowhere to be found. We watched the baseball game, and I stood up to go afterward. He stood up with me, grabbing me and roughly kissing me. I started to protest frantically and push him away. He was stronger, a former athlete in high school, and I found myself dragged into his room and pushed facedown onto the carpet as he pulled off my jeans and ran his fingers up the back of my legs, the softness of his caress in direct contrast to the other hand holding me down by the back of the neck in an iron grip. I began to cry, and he ripped off my purple lace underwear with pink edging. It was a cheap, ninety-nine-cent thong and the strings snapped like they were candy floss. I would never wear thongs again. He threw his entire weight onto me, thrusting roughly into me, and I began to scream, begging him to please stop.

The screaming rattled him, I think. He pulled out hastily, mumbling apologies and running into the bathroom, presumably to finish himself off. I scrambled to my feet, snot pouring from my face, and pulled my jeans on, stumbling toward the door. I bolted, jumping in the Honda Magna that I drove at the time and speeding away, never hearing from the guy again. I drove home, changed my clothes and then went to a swing dancing lesson with my performing troupe in the park, pushing the day's occurrences deep down into some far corner of myself. We had a show coming up in a month and it was important that I be at practice and not let them down.

For months, I convinced myself that it was my fault. I didn't go to the police because I had doubts as to whether what had happened even counted as rape, or was it just a matter of a dumb kid losing control and making a mistake? I had somehow led him on. Because of me, he had gotten carried away. He hadn't *meant* to rape me; it had just happened. It was a holdover from the old Jehovah's Witness implication that the woman is always asking for it. If a Jehovah's Witness woman is raped and doesn't scream, then the elders at the judicial committee must not count it as rape, but adultery, and the woman is considered to have consented. She is then held to be at fault just as much as if she had chosen the path of fornication, and she's punished accordingly. I *had* screamed, true, but the dubious mentality still held. I was unsure as to whether I had screamed loud enough, or if putting myself in the situation of being alone with a "worldly" boy was, in itself, enough to condemn me. By the same token, I was afraid of condemning *him,* of being a female accuser pitting her word against a man's. The submissive-to-all-males mind-set was—*is*—more deeply ingrained than I'd ever realized.

The other part of my past that I wanted Matt to know about, because it was something I was ashamed of—and I wanted him to know everything about me, to make sure he could really love me warts and all—was a threesome I had taken part in when I was twenty-one. I had spent a year and a half in North Carolina, desperately trying to escape my past. While there, I befriended a couple who, I later learned, were looking to experiment with their first ménage-à-trois. When they made the proposal to me, I laughed it off. Despite no longer being a virgin, I still held onto many vestiges of JW morality, plus there was no way I wanted to put myself into a can-of-worms situation like that. Besides, I had never been attracted to women, and the "girl-on-girl" scene just wasn't my cup of tea. I was slowly overcoming the antihomosexual prejudices that the Watchtower Society had embedded in me from birth—even had a few gay friends—but the idea of the act itself was still repugnant and would take a couple more years to get over completely.

The couple did what any self-respecting couple would do, I guess. They smiled and said that they totally understood, no biggie, we could still hang out and be friends. Then, a few weeks later, I went through a bout of depression (rural North Carolina was absolutely the most isolating place I have ever lived, and it was taking its toll on my psyche). They invited me over to watch movies. We put on *Cinema Paradiso* and they plied me with Smirnoff Ice wine coolers. After four or five of them, I was feeling pretty happy. Before I realized fully what was happening, the man was grazing up against me, kissing my neck, stroking my body. The girl joined in, and I guess you could say the whole thing just sort of happened. I was lonely, I was isolated, I was unloved and suddenly there was some sort of human contact. No matter how much I objected to the form that human contact took, when it came down to it, I was simply incapable of refusing it at the time. I'm not proud of the frame of mind that led me to that point, but there you go. At the same time, I'm no longer ashamed of it. It was what it was—a lost kid experimenting a little. Hardly unique or earth-shattering.

A week later, the couple, who had been together for two years, broke up. I was miserable. I was sure that it was somehow all my fault. I felt I tainted everybody I came into contact with. I moved back to California soon afterward.

Now I was in therapy dealing with all the crap in my past as best I could. The clinic provided services on a sliding scale. I'd been seeing my therapist, Lindsay, since before I became homeless, but once I began living in a parking lot, my therapy sessions went from $20 an hour to free! Lindsay was remarkably nonjudgmental. I had been skeptical of therapy, but slowly I came out of my shell with her. I credit her with helping to mold me into a far better, stronger person. I'm in no way perfect, but I made tremendous strides under her guidance, and became far less of a blubbering, nervous wreck than when I had first entered counseling.

Matt handled most of this in stride, but the threesome threw him a bit.

"I just can't imagine you as that sort of person," he said. "That's not how I imagine you. I believe that true intimacy can only be experienced between two people."

I knew polyamorous people would disagree with him there. But I understood what he meant. I, too, felt most comfortable experiencing intimacy within a monogamous relationship. But this hadn't been about intimacy, I tried to explain. It was about sex. I wished I could somehow make him understand how isolated I'd felt, how much I'd craved some kind of contact.

"I do understand what led to it. I don't blame you. I went through a similar situation, right after my marriage ended, and I slept with a lot of people at work—my boss, some coworkers—it wasn't pretty, and I'm not proud of the place that I was in. It's not something I ever want to do again."

I was a different person now than I was then, but I was still afraid that that was how he would perceive me forever. I was terrified that I'd blown it. But my fears were unfounded. He understood; he loved me for who I was. The past was the past. He quelled my doubts by assuring me that now that he'd found me, he had no intention of ever letting me go.

Chapter Ten

I was on Craigslist perusing the job listings when I stumbled across an ad seeking writers and fashionistas to participate in an advice columnist competition. Specifically, they said, they were looking for "the Next Carrie Bradshaw."

OK, I have to admit, at that point, I'd never seen a single episode of *Sex and the City*. Yes, I'm a traitor to my gender. You may sling your Manolos at me now.

In any case, I figured I'd send in a quick letter anyway with my story, and see what happened. I didn't see myself as a writer, as much as a blogger, but I have always loved writing, and I love fashion, or at least I love vintage clothing. I could out-cute Sarah Jessica Parker and her super-overpaid stylist any day.

It was a shot in the dark and I was quite certain I'd never hear back from them.

And then I did.

I had no idea, until the phone call, just who these people were. What I thought might be a dinky little unknown show, which might present me with some small opportunity to escape the dreary world of executive assistant for a few weeks, turned out to be a show by Fremantle Media. The *American Idol* guys. The guys with all the clout. With millions of viewers.

The casting director told me more about the show being cast, and I learned that the winner of the competition, if the show was picked up, would receive an internship with E. Jean Carroll, the advice columnist for *ELLE* magazine. I was stunned. I had read her column for nine years, and admired her verve and practical advice, mixed with glamorous, over-the-top Old Hollywood–style wit.

Knowing how big this could be made me incredibly nervous. A swarm of random actors sat in the lobby of the Fremantle Media office, waiting to try out for a different project (a TV sitcom or something). I wore the most adorable, bright grapefruit–hued vintage '50s dress I could dig up. I got a lot of funny looks. A tall, rail-skinny chick stood in the corner, gesticulating and mouthing lines. I was the only one there for the advice columnist show, so I started to fill out my application and waited for the casting director to come get me.

This scary actor lady came into the lobby and sat next to me. She was a bit older, in her forties or fifties. She was like Carol Brady on *crack*. It looked like her plastic surgeon had had a field day with her—her eyes were open too wide and her smile was frozen in place. She talked *way* too loud. In the quiet lobby, her voice reverberated and echoed and people started staring at her.

"OH AREN'T YOU ADORABLE! WHAT A PRETTY DRESS! EVERYONE LIKES TO GO OVER THEIR LINES WHILE THEY'RE WAITING, BUT I'VE FOUND THAT IT'S BETTER TO JUST STAY

MYSELF AND INTERACT WITH THE OTHER ACTORS!"

I mumbled that I wasn't an actor, hoping she'd go away, or at least take the hint and talk at the room level, which was at about a whisper. After interrogating me about what I was there trying out for, and making sure the entire room knew that I was (a) a "reality girl" and (b) *not* an actor—never acted in anything besides a high school play—she *grabbed my half-completed application* and started reading the questions aloud.

"LET'S SEE…'WHEN WAS THE LAST TIME YOU CRIED?'"

She looked at me with great anticipation, and I realized that she was actually expecting me to answer. I drily informed her that I was crying on the inside, right now. In a way, it was more true than she could have realized, but she laughed and took it as a joke.

"OK, HOW ABOUT THIS ONE: 'WHAT ARE THREE THINGS ABOUT YOURSELF THAT YOU *NEVER* REVEAL TO SOMEONE YOU'VE JUST MET?!'"

I slouched a little further into my chair and tried to imagine myself far away, in some place really beautiful and inspiring and, most important, *not with this chick*. Maybe in Czechoslovakia or Italy. "'NAME A TIME WHEN YOU GAVE BAD ADVICE.'"

At this point, I was thoroughly psyched out and ready to either break down in tears or else kill this woman with a smile on my face. Luckily, I was saved by Peter, the casting director, who came out and called me back.

"OH MY GOD, I LOVE HER! SHE IS JUST SO CUTE! SHE JUST TOLD ME SHE'S CRYING ON THE INSIDE RIGHT NOW!" she informed him as I walked through the door.

I could have died.

Peter was very nice, sat me down in a chair and turned on a camera and a spotlight—which was a tad intimidating and very "Tell me where you were on the evening of March 6." He asked me a few questions, which I struggled to answer. My mind kept blanking; I was so completely freaked out. He was very sweet about trying to gently guide me into showing more of my personality, but I just sort of shut down. Later on, I would obsess over all the better answers I could have given, or ways I could have let my personality out more, but in the moment I was just completely stone-cold petrified.

I totally bombed. I mean, how could I not? I was so overwhelmed and nervous just realizing the magnitude of even getting called in to screen-test with such a company.

Poor dude. He was clearly regretting wasting his time calling the homeless chick in. In any case, after it was over he told me if I heard anything from them in two weeks to two months, that would be good news.

"It all depends on the executives, you know? Don't worry, though. You did well."

(He *had* to say that to everyone, I was pretty sure.)

"Anyway," he continued, "I tend to look for interesting people over model types. Not that you're not beautiful or anything. You're very pretty."

OK, so he was completely bullshitting me, but still, yay for nice casting directors! *Even though I bombed, at least I can still feel good about it now.* Thank God I wasn't in a room with a nasty Simon Cowell wannabe or anything. I think I would have completely crumbled.

I went into the lobby and pushed the Down button to call the elevator. Insane Carol Brady Doppelgänger cornered me.

"DID YOU JUST GET DONE?! I JUST GOT
DONE! I'LL TAKE THE ELEVATOR DOWN WITH
YOU...YOU DIDN'T WEAR YOUR GLASSES FOR
THE SCREEN TEST, DID YOU? YOU TOOK THEM
OFF, RIGHT?!"

Ouch. A tiny dart of sadness pricked me in the eye.
I *like* my glasses. They're a *part* of me.

After the abominably disastrous screen test, I went back
to work and laughed it off that evening with Matt. I never
got a phone call from Fremantle, and I hadn't expected to,
after the showing that I put on.

But a couple of days later, on a whim, I fired off an
email to E. Jean Carroll through her personal website. I
gave a brief rundown on my situation, and joked about the
screen test I had botched. I didn't suppose that she could
use her goddesslike influence to pull a couple of strings
and get me a second shot, could she?

I hit the Send button, fully expecting nobody to ever
read the email, and never to hear back. But, hey, it was an
opportunity, right? A whim, a joke. You just never knew. I
didn't even mention it to Matt. It was one of those random
little things you do but never think anything will come of
it, like dialing the radio station on the off chance that you
might be caller #9 and win the Evanescence tickets.

A few days later, I would face a much more serious issue.
During my lunch hour at work, I logged onto gtalk to see
if Matt was around. This had become our regular routine, stealing time together wherever we could—during
lunch, breaks and the six to eight hours between closing
time at work and the two hours after closing time at the
local Starbucks, when my laptop would finally die and I

would drive back to the trailer, which I had restored to the Walmart parking lot upon boarding Fezzik, and fall into a restless sleep for five or six hours before I had to be back up and get ready for work again. I barely felt tired at all, though. I was in love. Nothing could bog me down.

"Hey, sexy!" I typed exuberantly at seeing the little green circle icon next to Matt's username. "I'm on lunch, are you busy?"

"Hey, beautiful. Listen, something has happened, and I need to talk to you about something serious tonight."

Uh-oh. This did not sound good. Had I done something wrong? Was he leaving me before he'd even met me? Everything had seemed wonderful the previous night: There had been online kisses and cuddles and proclamations of eternal adoration and rhapsodizing about finally getting the chance to meet each other, once my damn retroactive unemployment checks finally arrived in the P.O. box.

"What's wrong, darling?"

"I don't think we should talk about it on your lunch break. It's pretty serious. It's going to take a lot longer than an hour to discuss."

"Well, now you've got me worried. You can't just leave me hanging here for four more hours! Please, at least just tell me what it's about. Please. Are you breaking up with me? What's wrong? Please don't make me suffer for the rest of the workday worrying."

There was a pause. The longest pause of my life.

"I don't want to break up with you. The thing is... there's talk, apparently, that I may soon be a father."

I immediately masked the violent hurricane that had just taken up residence in my gut.

"Ah. I see." Pause. "Who is she?"

"It's Lori. I swear, I had no idea until today. Her brother just showed up to tell me. I haven't seen her since we broke up. She's a couple of months along. She didn't know how to tell me, so she sent him to do it."

I took this all in and proceeded to freak out, tears of panic streaming down my face, though I continued to phrase my words carefully, sending messages as calmly and placidly as I could.

"I see. You guys were only dating for a few weeks, weren't you? I was under the impression that you used birth control." We had had discussions about potentially marrying and starting a family down the road. Birth control was important to both of us in the meantime, though. I had already started the weeks-long process to obtain an appointment with Planned Parenthood and get an IUD put in. When I had a kid, I wanted it to be on my terms, and definitely not while I was living in a trailer.

"I was. I was using condoms. She wasn't using anything. One night, about a week before we broke up, the condom broke. She said that she'd take care of it and get the morning-after pill."

I could feel the hysteria rising in me, clawing its way up my throat. I fought it back down.

"I see. Babe, I'm not trying to judge you, but did it occur to you to take her to the pharmacy yourself?"

He had. 't. He'd trusted her to take care of it. The poor guy was clearly miserable, and I felt awful. I wasn't making the situation any better—what was done was done, there was no going back. I didn't want to hurt him, so I tried to refocus on how much he must be freaking out at the moment.

He was mostly numb, he said, but he needed to meet with her soon. The baby was his and he took responsibility for it. I dreaded what that would mean for us, but he told me that was entirely up to me. I was the most important thing in his life and he didn't want to lose me. He was terrified that I'd walk out, and he understood if that was what I opted to do. But he hoped that I wouldn't. He wanted me to stay; he wanted us to be together.

My heart broke for him.

I decided to stay.

It wasn't as though he had cheated on me; it was just one of those unexpected things that happens. Just another obstacle we'd have to work around.

My most pervasive fear was that he'd eventually feel as if he needed to leave me and go back to Lori once the baby was born. He loved me now, but would that change? Tears spilled from the corner of my eyes as I imagined how much more painful it would be to keep nurturing our relationship, become so much more attached and in love, only to have it end inevitably a few months later when he decided to be with Lori for the baby's sake.

He was vehement and defiant, though, when I suggested that.

"That will NEVER happen, whether you decide to walk away or not. I left her because I didn't love her. I could never love her. There was no future with us. When I meet with her, I'm going to make it clear that my responsibility lies with the child and the child only. *You're* the one I'm going to marry and spend the rest of my life with. Nothing could ever change what I feel for you."

He was adamant. If I stayed, he could promise me that I'd never again have to wonder whether I was loved—not even once.

And, just like that, I trusted him with my life. It was that simple. He'd never once lied to me, and his complete, naked honesty even now, under the most strenuous of circumstances, made me realize just how much I wanted to share my life with this man.

"OK then. Let's do this."

I gasped with joy as I opened my P.O. box. A beaming, glowing ray of light fell on the envelope from California EDD. The angelic chorus sounded. For a brief moment, the world was eminently lovely. Finally, *finally* after hours of fruitless phone calls trying to get through, several emails begging for a response, with only maddeningly robotic (and clearly deceptive) "We will get back to you within forty-eight hours" automatons to appease me...*finally!*

My claim forms for my retroactive unemployment benefits had arrived. I'd waited a long time, and the back benefits I was owed would make a world of difference. With trembling hands, I ripped open the envelope to find...a (second) "approval" notice, letting me know that, yes, I *was* eligible for extended unemployment benefits (well, *duh,* it was the same exact notice I'd already received waaaaaaaay back when this crap saga started)....

There were no claims forms included.

None.

Zilch.

I knew the EDD was backed up because, besides Michigan, California was the current poster child among states for insanely skyrocketing unemployment rates. But seriously, *what did a girl have to do to get paid?*

Following several angry, lawsuit-threatening emails to the EDD, my wish finally came true two weeks later. My benefits were in the mail.

When the P.O. box suddenly bloomed with envelopes, I was ecstatic. I had to budget the money wisely, of course.

But I also had to see Matt. The UK homeless hike in September had been postponed indefinitely. Lori was due to give birth in late November, but we didn't want to take any chances on a potential preemie.

Matt met with Lori two days after he found out about the impending baby. He was blunt with her: He was seeing a girl in the States, he was going to be there much of the time and he would eventually be moving there. He would always take responsibility for the child—financial and otherwise—but they needed to decide on shared custody arrangements. He wanted equal time in the child's life.

"How'd she take it?" I asked when he filled me in.

Not very well, he told me. She got very quiet and wouldn't say anything for a while. It was hard for him to tell exactly what she was thinking, but he got the impression that she might have been hoping for him to come back to her. He made it very clear to her that that wasn't an option.

Clearly, she hadn't counted on this unexpected wrench thrown into her plans when she set out to trap her former boyfriend into rekindling their relationship by means of her pregnancy. I can't say I felt particularly sorry for her—after all, she'd pretty much complicated our lives beyond belief by sneakily skipping a morning-after pill—but I did feel sorry for the baby, and for Matt. But, hey, we'd make it work. Somehow.

We hastily made plans for Matt to fly to California. Because I was working, it had to be that way. I couldn't take time off from a relatively new job to go to Scotland.

Matt was allowed to stay for up to ninety days on a visa waiver program before returning home. It was May, so we assumed that he would stay until August. He let Lori know that he would be out of the country until then, and she threw a wrench of her own into the works—only the first of many.

"She wants me to attend the next ultrasound scan in a month. I can only stay in California until June. Then I have to go back for the scan. It'll only be for a week or so, and then I can fly back."

I was frustrated and upset, though I tried to be reasonable. This was my money, after all, that we were spending for him to fly him here—his benefits didn't cover anywhere near that much—and I felt, perhaps unfairly, that he was treating it in an awfully cavalier manner. An extra plane ticket so that he could be present during an ultrasound? Why? What could he possibly do besides sit there while she got her belly scanned?

"It's not for me, honey. I understand why it bothers you, but we need to try to keep her happy, right? I don't want to make her angry. What if she decides to start making it difficult for us in the future, fights me on custody? Shouldn't I try to be friendly with her? Besides, she's pretty much a chav."

"Chav?"

"It's an English slang term. Basically means a backwards idiot. What you guys might call a 'hick' or 'trailer-park trash.' She has no idea what kind of questions to ask the doctor. I need to be there so that I can ask those questions."

"So arrange to listen in on a conference call from California, or something. Or get written permission from her to contact the doctor with any questions. Yes, I understand you want to keep her happy, but I'm afraid this is going to give her hope. I'm not saying that you are, but, in *her* mind, this is you choosing her over your girlfriend. You do realize that, don't you?"

"Yes, I guess I do realize that. But *you* know that I'm not choosing her over you, right? I'm just trying to make it easier for all of us down the line."

But he *wasn't* making it easier for all of us down the line! I wanted to cry. He was letting her think that she could push and push and push until she got her way. And then it would only be harder in the future, when we were ready to get married. Please, please put your foot down now. Head off her bullshit at the pass. Do it for us.

I wanted to scream it all at the top of my lungs. But that would be crazy. After all, it was *my* fault that I was upset, not his. *I* was being unsupportive. This was his first child. He was already losing out on the whole prebirth bonding process. The listening to the baby via belly headphones, the feeling of a fluttering kick from the womb against his hand. This was all going to be hard enough for him, especially once the child was born. Just let go. Give in. Be the supportive girlfriend, the supportive *future wife*. Do this for him.

So I did. He was right. The two of us would need to be the adults in this situation; we would have to make compromises.

We booked the trip. He would stay in California for one month. On May 20, 2009, I would meet my future husband at LAX Airport in Los Angeles. The butterflies began. It was all about to become so very real.

Chapter Eleven

H e spotted me first, across the swarm of arrivals criss-crossing paths, knocking into one another with their rolling suitcases.

I wore a green-and-black dress, and was shaking as though it were freezing, though the California spring was out in full force. He was tall and lanky, weedier in person, and his face slightly more creased, a minuscule tad older than the photos had shown. I would later learn that this was because he was exhausted; he hadn't slept a wink in the two hours he'd spent on the train to Aberdeen Airport, and then the sixteen-hour flight. Later, after he got a full night's sleep, his face would relax into the smoother, youthful one I knew from the past few months. He had the faintest flecks of gray just beginning to crop up around his temples. I found that distinguished-looking.

I think we had both imagined an airport meeting in which we rushed into each other's arms and kissed like we were in a Meg Ryan/Tom Hanks romantic comedy. Reality won out, however. We were both too afraid of what the other was thinking. We walked quickly toward each other, blocking the flow of traffic. I stared up at him. I couldn't tell what he was thinking. He'd seen me in photos and video, but what if now, in person, he was thinking he had made a mistake? I couldn't read anything, but his eyes were kind.

"How was your flight?"

"Oh, it was…you know…long. I'm feeling pretty tired."

"Right. Of course. Right. Let's get you back to the motel. You must be exhausted." I had rented a motel for a week or two with some of my EDD money. It didn't seem right for me to bring my future husband back to a Walmart parking lot right off the bat.

We had spoken about what our first meeting would be like, of course. Would I take him to a secluded spot on Laguna Beach and make love on the sand under a blanket, as waves crashed around us?

Nope. This was real life. He was clearly about to drop from exhaustion. We walked briskly to the parking structure and piled into my car. Then, we just sat and chatted for a while. I can't tell you exactly what we said for the next ten minutes. Mindless prattle, mostly. Something to fill the void. Just when I was positive that this was all a big mistake and that he was quickly figuring out that he couldn't stand me, that going on a first date *to California* that you couldn't get out of by simply having a friend pretend to call with an emergency was the dumbest idea of his life, he kissed me.

And it was perfect. We stayed like that for a while, just kissing softly and easing ourselves into this.

He pulled back after a few minutes. I was trembling.

"Are you OK?" he asked.

"Yes. You?"

"Yeah."

"I was starting to get worried that you were disappointed by me," I said.

"No. *God,* no. You're beautiful. Just taking my time. You seemed awfully nervous."

"I am. I mean, I was."

"Me, too. But everything's going to be OK now. Right?" he said.

"Right."

"OK. Let's go." He squeezed my hand, and we drove back to the Orange County Motel, him stroking my elbow as though it were the most natural thing in the world and we'd known each other all our lives.

Once at the motel, we checked his bags and got settled, flopping on the bed, propping our heads up and chatting some more. We both knew what was coming, what had been coming for months, but we instinctively knew that some lead-in was required. We just needed to get to know each other in person some more, settle into a new kind of energy, before we took that step. Also, I realized, he was so very tired that he would probably need some sleep before we…

He reached out and pulled me close, drawing me to him tenderly. I did what I'd wanted to do forever, burying my nose into his chest so that he wouldn't see my eyes well up with tears of relief and happiness. We took our time, exploring each other's bodies very slowly, before finally making love.

I'd never made love before, chiefly because no man had ever loved me. When Matthew Barnes looked into my eyes, his own moistening up, tears running down into the cracks on the side of his nose and plinking softly onto my face, it was the first time any man had ever said those words to me, and I wouldn't have had it any other way.

"I love you."

"I love you, too."

He came inside me, and then held me for hours upon hours, finally drifting off into the soundest of sleep together. He meant it, and so did I. It wasn't what we had imagined our first meeting would be like in the preceding months, but its essence was everything we could have hoped for and more. We awoke several times throughout the night and made love again and again. It was nothing short of miraculous to us. What we'd felt did carry across the ocean. It was real.

The following month was wonderful, in every sense of the word. Sure, we were switching between motels and the Walmart parking lot, but every day there was something new for me to share with Matt. He even found ways to share new things with *me*.

One day, Matt insisted that we take a walk. He spent all day alone in the motel while I was working, and would go wandering around Tustin to keep himself occupied. I was tired from work.

"Nooooo, I just wanna toss myself on the bed and rest, maybe read a book or watch TV or have sex. Pleeeeease?" The last thing I wanted to do was walk.

"Come on. There's something I want to show you. You'll love this."

Grumbling, I pulled on a pair of jeans and took his hand. He pulled me down the residential back streets of Olde Town Tustin. We walked and walked and suddenly, looming before me, there was an old-fashioned Victorian mansion, framed with giant, luscious oak trees. I gaped.

"I knew you'd like it. But wait, there's more."

We explored the twisty, winding roads, marveling at houses so beautiful, so old, so anachronistic to their surroundings. I could never have imagined homes like these in SoCal, home of the cookie-cutter Craftsman Bungalow and the Stucco Ranch House, much less in Tustin. Finally, he stopped me at a street corner and pointed.

"Oh, my god! It has *turrets!*" It was like my dream house come to life. He stood behind me, wrapping his arms around my waist and whispering in my ear.

"I knew this one would be your favorite. I saved it for last. We're going to have something like that house, one day. There will only ever be the best for you, I promise."

We had known that we couldn't rent motels forever, but it was nerve-racking bringing Matt back to the trailer. I still felt an element of shame about it, even though intellectually I knew that was ridiculous (after all, he too knew what it was like to be homeless), but he put me at ease, cuddling me on the stale mattress and having long talks with me about quantum physics, philosophy and similar high concepts that I'd never quite understood, but that he made elementary. By the time he'd explained it to me, it all seemed within my grasp. He, on the other hand, was astonished and grateful that I could keep up with him, and even hold my own in a debate—often winning, as a matter of fact.

"I used to try to talk about this stuff with my wife, and she'd just look at me blankly. 'Use four-year-old language, please!' she'd say. And there was no point even trying with Lori, of course. Every day you surprise me more and more. You have no idea what it's like to finally be with somebody so tailor-made for you, someone with *intelligence.*"

"Yes, I do."

We made love on the stale mattress, until I had to go to work in the morning and he would walk to what he considered the greatest American treasure of all—Denny's—for a Grand Slam, which he declared positively rivaled any British food ever invented in scrumptiousness. Then he'd trot over to the local Starbucks, buy a coffee and run Homeless Tales from the Starbucks couch, until I could escape work and rush back to him, and we'd twine our fingers absentmindedly and dream about the house on the East Coast—where it was beautiful and full of nature and history and architecture and far, far away from my family and my past—that we'd buy, once we were married and I'd saved up enough from work to make a down payment. Then we'd make love until we slept, and then do the entire thing all over again. It was the first time I'd ever known what true, ongoing happiness was.

After a few weeks, we couldn't contain it any longer. Both of us wanted to shout it from the rooftops, and we decided to announce our happy news to my readers, and to Matt's community at HomelessTales.com. Just writing about it made me a little misty-eyed, and my heart felt kind of weighted, like it was going to throb open. But it was so, *so* superbeautiful, finally getting to share it with the people following my life.

The one thing Matt didn't want to talk about publicly yet was Lori's pregnancy. In fact, he didn't even like talking about it much privately, with me. I thought that we should start making plans ahead of time, get things all ironed out before the birth. I figured it was important to talk to Lori about a mutual custody agreement before the baby was born; to get things in writing so that later on there were no problems, no "he said, she said."

But I didn't understand what it was like trying to talk with her, he exclaimed irritably. If he ever tried to talk to her about *anything* serious, she either spaced out or started to cry and said that they should talk about it later. She seemed to understand about him moving to the States to live with me, and accept that there was no future for them. He had tentatively proposed sharing custody, a rotation maybe every three or six months, but he couldn't seem to pin her down to putting anything into writing.

That was all the more reason to deal with it now, I pressed. It would only be harder for her to be objective about sharing custody after the baby was born, and what if she decided to make things hard for Matt later on?

If he thought she was going to be reasonable, then that was awesome. But get it in writing. I needed him to trust me on this. I had seen a lot of single new moms turn into total ogres after the baby was born, and try to take the father to court, or keep him from seeing the baby, after promising everything would be amicable. I watched an otherwise delightful former friend of mine do just that. It's one of the reasons we're no longer friends. I watched her go absolutely nuts after the birth of her baby, and do her utmost to destroy a very good man, and a good father, because she changed her mind about their *verbal* custody agreement.

Maybe he didn't *think* Lori would pull a stunt like that, and maybe she wouldn't. I had never met her. I didn't know. Maybe she was a completely rational person and had no intention of ever taking Matt to court. *But we had no way of knowing that.* For his protection—and hers—I urged him to make arrangements and get them in writing *now,* so that we wouldn't have to worry about the possibility of misunderstandings or court actions later on. I spoke as lovingly as I could, and from the heart, but it only seemed to make him touchier.

"Look, I'm not like you, OK? I trust people!" he snapped.

Ouch. I didn't know what the hell that was supposed to mean.

"Sure, you have *reason* not to trust people," he continued. "I mean, look what your family and the Jehovah's Witnesses and everything put you through. But that doesn't mean everyone's like that! In the UK, things are different. *People* are different. You can *trust* people, OK? She's not the brightest girl, but I believe she's fundamentally decent!"

I was stung.

"I *do* try to trust people. I *do* try not to be cynical or overly suspicious. Believe me, I would love to live in that kind of world, Matt! But that's not the world we live in. I'm not saying grill the poor kid or anything. I swear I'm not. If you think she's a good person, I'm sure she is. But look—pregnant women are hormonal. New mothers are protective. And people forget their promises sometimes. Hell, half the time I can't remember conversations I had a week ago. I'm just saying, for the protection of everybody involved—so that *neither* of you forget later what you agreed on—sit down and hash this out when you go out there for the ultrasound. Look, I even found a binding UK legal form for it." I pushed it toward him.

"All you guys have to do is sit down together and come to an agreement on issues like how often each of you gets to watch the baby, how you'll handle issues like school and religion and all that hairy stuff. Then you fill it all out on this form, get it notarized and boom! You both have it there to refer to later, if there's any dispute over what you agreed to. Explain to her that this is for *her protection* just as much as yours, Matt. If she's as decent as you think, then why would there be any problem with such a basic agreement?"

He sighed. "I guess you're right. I'll give it a try when I get back there." He broke down in tears and sobbed, pulling me close on the trailer mattress. "I just don't understand. I wish it was *you*. I want it to be *you* having our baby. It *should* have been you."

Right around this time, Matt became somewhat obsessed with the idea of *us* having children of our own.

I'd just gone through the very unpleasant process of having a Paragard IUD put in. I had to deal with a rude, unsympathetic Planned Parenthood nurse who treated me like dirt when she read the descriptor "homeless" on my chart. She kept pushing me to accept hormonal birth control, which I'd already learned via trial and error turned me into a miserable, raging bear of a person—an experience I did not wish to repeat. I politely declined, explaining my reasons, and requested the IUD again. The nurse angrily jammed a speculum into my cervix without preamble and opened it all at once, like an umbrella, then refused to place the IUD when I cried out, saying, "Well, if you can't handle pain like that, you won't be able to handle the cramping of having an IUD placed inside you." I'd had my annual Pap smear faithfully, up until this point, always with a gentle gynecologist who'd open the speculum slowly, notch by notch, always careful not to hurt me. Never before had I felt pain during an ob-gyn exam. This woman had very deliberately *hurt* me. I felt seriously violated. I left the room in shock, arriving at the front counter in tears and shaking all over. The receptionists took pity on me.

"She's always like that...don't worry, it's not just you. We can make an appointment for you at the Anaheim office. They'll put in an IUD for you." I thanked them through my tears. I'd had to wait three more weeks to get the IUD placed. The nurse at the Anaheim office was about my age, very kind and very gentle. There was some minor cramping and wincing, but I didn't make a peep, and in five minutes it was over. It certainly came nowhere near approaching the level of pain that the other nurse had inflicted on me.

I'd gone through all that *not* to get pregnant. I couldn't understand why Matt would even consider something so irrational. I was *homeless*. We were living in a *parking lot*. What was I supposed to do—raise a kid in a thirty-by-eight-foot box?

"Do you even know how much it costs to *have* a kid here? It's $10K just for the birth at the hospital! And that's if there are no complications! That's what it costs just to get the baby *out of me,* before you even have to start paying to raise it!"

He looked at me blankly. "In the UK, all that's covered under Universal Health Care. Everything's free. I'll never understand your American system. Do you realize that in the UK, *everybody* gets free health care, homeless people go on a short waiting list and get a free flat—and you can live there the rest of your life if you want to, never even have to get a job or anything if you don't want to. That's why I was only homeless for a short time. It's all cradle to grave there. We *care* about our people there."

That was all beside the point, though. For one thing, it would be completely selfish of me to have a child before we had a proper home. For another, I was terrified. Terrified of the painful birthing process; terrified of taking care of a tiny, dependent human being that puked and pooped and screamed; and terrified of becoming someone like my mother, of morphing into the kind of person who could abuse and fuck up a child beyond all belief. They say we all become our mothers, right?

Matt was casually dismissive. "That won't happen to you. I know you and I love you. You don't have to become your mom. You'll be a fabulous stepmother, and a fabulous mother. You can give *our* children all the things that Lori can't. I'm not saying I don't think she'll be a good mom—I think she'll love and take care of our kid—but she's not exactly the nurturing type, you know? There's not much she'll be able to do for the baby by way of education, culture, that sort of stuff. And don't worry about the birthing process. Women wouldn't keep doing it if it was so unbearable."

Easy for him to say. Did *he* feel like pushing a cantaloupe out of his nostril any time soon? I didn't want to believe that I'd become my mom, either. But I was scared. I just needed him to understand *why* I was scared and let me wait until I was ready. Until *we* were ready. Once we had a home together and got married and spent a couple of years building a life, maybe then. I wasn't averse to having a child with him. I *loved* the idea of eventually being the mother of his children. Or maybe we could even adopt a child—there were so many who needed homes.

"I don't think I'd ever want to adopt."

"For heaven's sake, why not?"

"I'm afraid I could never love an adopted child as much as my own, and that wouldn't be fair to it."

"What?! That's ridiculous! You're the most loving person I know. Of course you could!"

He protested that he was just being honest; that he was even afraid about this baby on the way. What if he couldn't bond with it? What if he couldn't love it because it wasn't *mine?* What if he wasn't able to make any kind of connection with it at all?

My stomach tightened and I felt a pang on his behalf.

Of course he'd love it, I reassured him. It was a natural fear to have, but they say fathers fall in love with their babies the moment they hold them. That may seem like a strange assertion coming from someone with a father like mine, but I truly believed that Matt would hold that baby and look into its eyes and he'd adore it instantly. He'd feel completely idiotic that he could ever have thought otherwise. I'd had friends with loving, kind parents, so I knew that they existed—in fact, that was one of the reasons I'd begun to realize in my teens that my home life wasn't normal and that not all children were as miserable as me. I wasn't crazy to feel like so much about my family was all wrong. I knew Matt would never be a sick, twisted father like Bob. He had the greatest capacity for love and generosity of anybody I'd ever met, so *of course* he'd be a fantastic father. There wasn't a doubt in my mind.

"You'll adore that baby more than you could ever love me, even." I forced a laugh, though I was only half-joking.

"Not possible. I love you more than I've ever loved anything in the world, and more than I ever could love anything in the world. One day, you will be the center of our children's universe. We're going to wake up in our beautiful old Victorian house with four kids climbing all over us, clamoring for us to come down and open the Christmas

presents! Our kids are going to look at you like you're perfect. They'll all love you as much as I love you."

"I believe you." I whispered. It would be exactly that
way, one day. But, for now, we needed to focus on the
immediate—the child who was already coming. I knew
that maybe he was hoping to fill the void that he'd feel
while the baby was in Scotland with Lori. But getting me
pregnant right now with another child as filler wasn't the
answer. And both of us knew it.

We nicknamed the upcoming kid "Sproglet," since we'd
have no idea of the gender until it was born (in the UK,
nurses are not allowed to let you know the gender during
ultrasounds; you can go to a private practitioner and pay a
ton for a private gender scan, but few people could afford
it and the NHS wouldn't tell you for legal reasons). Occasionally, I'd try to initiate more discussions about prepa-
rations we should make for Sproglet's arrival, but I was
stonewalled.

"Please, sweetie! I know you're trying to help, but I just
want to talk about anything *but* the baby! I don't want to
think about it. I already know I'm going to have to think
about it soon enough when I go back for the ultrasound.
Please can we talk about something else?"

Hurt, but trying to hide it, I assured him that I understood and quickly changed the subject. And I *did* understand
why it was all stressing him out so much. There were no
easy answers, and he just needed a break from thinking
about it for a while.

I took him to a sports bar that evening—Matt was going
nuts from not being able to see his beloved "football"
(soccer, to me). There was an important game that evening
(the World Cup Qualifiers, I believe), and I didn't want
him to miss it. The bartender gave us a funny look when

we asked him to put the soccer game on one of the TVs. Matt had outfitted me in one of his prized soccer jerseys and I recognized what an incredible honor he felt it was for his girlfriend to wear it. Not surprisingly, there weren't any other British soccer fans there, so it was just the two of us, cheering at the screen and downing pizza and drinks. Matt's team lost, and when I saw how frustrated he was, I was frustrated, too. I wished his team had won, if only to make him feel better. On the way home, P!nk's "So What" came on the radio and I cranked it up to 11, head banging as I screamed out the words, and drumming the steering wheel in time with the beat. I looked over and turned red, realizing that Matt was cocking his head to the side, watching me quizzically and grinning.

"What's the matter?" I was embarrassed.

"Nothing. I've just never known anybody so absolutely perfect. Don't feel self-conscious. Go ahead and sing. I just want to watch you. You're the most adorable thing I've ever seen."

Two nights before Matt's flight back to the UK, he published an article on HomelessTales.com called *Twitter's Transatlantic Homeless Love Match*. He'd been secretly writing it as a surprise for me. It was the first time I'd gotten to read about our story from his point of view, so it was particularly sweet and heartwarming.

Matt was very well known in the social media world. He'd spent nearly a year building up contacts with the most influential people in the business, and was very active in promoting the work of others, especially on Digg. If you could make the front page of Digg, your website's article would get masses and masses of traffic. It was all supposed to be based on a user voting system, but Matt explained that 90 percent of the stuff that hit the front page of Digg came from about only 2 percent of actual Digg users, the top tier—including himself and all his social media friends. He'd already had a few Homeless Tales articles hit the front page.

"It's all in who you know," he explained. "Sometimes I need to work all day promoting, and you also need to know the type of content, and just what attention-grabbing headline will catch readers' eyes."

He thought that the article about us stood a good chance of making front page, if he spent a few hours on it. We drove to an all-night local coffee shop that charged $1 for Wi-Fi, and camped out as he busily contacted all his social media friends and got them to spread the word. I loved to watch him work. It seems like it would be such a dull thing, sitting at the computer for hours at a time, but he got very intense and focused on what he was doing, which I found supersexy. Again and again I refilled our coffee cups and snuggled with him on the shop's old purple velvet Victorian couch, leaning my head against his shoulder, getting excited every time he refreshed the Digg page and saw the votes first creeping up, then rocketing up.

Around 3:00 a.m., we launched ourselves off the couch and began jumping up and down, hugging each other. The story had rolled over to the front page. Because it was so early in the morning, it would likely stay there for quite a while, perhaps even for hours.

Sure enough, Homeless Tales saw masses of traffic from the story—perhaps forty thousand or fifty thousand hits that day, and even raised more ad dollars than usual. I even saw quite a spike in my traffic, from people who had searched out my blog, intrigued by the story. Nowhere near Matt's volume of traffic, of course, but maybe four thousand or five thousand hits, and several supportive comments. It was quite the rush, and I understood the thrill Matt got out of his work. I was experiencing it, too, vicariously.

Dropping Matt off at the airport was difficult. We'd rented a motel for our last couple of nights before his departure. Sometimes we just needed to feel human, and summer was nigh, so the trailer was often stifling, even at night. A couple of evenings with air-conditioning, a working stove and microwave and a TV (for him to watch his soccer matches and for me to watch *The Daily Show* and *The Colbert Report*) did us an indescribable world of good.

We sat hunched on the floor, backs against a window, and cuddled at LAX for the two hours before he had to head through security. It was so strange, how having had one another in our lives for such a relatively short period, neither of us wanted to imagine life without the other.

When it was time for him to go, I tried to put on a brave face, but as he handed his passport to the security guard, I burst into jagged, red-faced, snot-running sobs. They let him through, and he ran up to the barrier, leaning over and kissing me for a long time, weeping himself. It was oddly reassuring to see him cry, too. I finally watched him head up the escalator toward the boarding area, until I lost sight of him. He turned around many times to catch my eye and wave.

I tried to keep myself occupied with random tasks, like updating my blog, surfing the internet, catching up on *So You Think You Can Dance* online, making dinner (ramen noodles again!), reading books—anything to keep my mind off the gaping hole in my life. It was hard enough being without Matt before he ever showed up in

California, but now that he had been here, it was much worse. I wasn't only longing for something I'd never had, I was now missing something that had been here, filled my life and was now absent.

The passenger seat of my car felt empty. My hand felt empty without his to hold. The mattress felt empty without him to cuddle with. Everything felt kind of sepia-colored and a weight rested on my chest. Occasionally, I thought I was all cried out, but something like a half-finished carton of grape juice or a bag of Doritos he left behind would start me off again. My pillow smelled like him. There was still sand on the floor that we'd tracked in from our day at Newport Beach the previous weekend (he'd wanted to see the Pacific Ocean). I knew I'd feel a little better once his flight landed and he had arrived safely home in one piece. But I wouldn't be top-notch until he also returned to me safely in two weeks' time. Then, things would be well on their way to as perfect as imperfect, unpredictable life could ever possibly be for two crazy kids madly in love with each other.

Chapter Twelve

I woke up the next morning to a flood of emails and blog comments, all from people who had read Matt's article—currently homeless people, formerly homeless people, people who had never been homeless but "just wanted to say, 'You go, sister!,'" people who wanted to wish Matt and me well, and share their own crazy love stories. I was confused. I'd thought the hype had died down over the previous two days, and I didn't understand where the revival was coming from. I had to read several of the emails before I figured it out. I kept reading, "I found you on the BBC," and "I found you through AOL." Huh?

Some quick searching pointed me in the right direction. A website called Urlesque.com had picked up the story in its "Today's Cry" column, and it got so many comments that AOL linked to the article on its front page. The BBC Web Monitor had also picked it up. Matt and I were the human interest story of the week. I spent hours frantically trying to get hold of Matt, who, by my calculations, would have just gotten home on the train from the airport, and would probably be conked out for the next eighteen hours, recovering from jet lag.

Matt loves the BBC with a passion. Much of his visit to California was spent lamenting that American news stations don't cover as much international news and topics as the BBC. I think a little part of him died every time he saw a major news channel run something along the vein of "*Twiggy the Water-Skiing Squirrel*" when he was thirsting for more information on Iran, North Korea and Pakistan.

"What is this crap?!" he would yell, sitting on the edge of the motel bed and gesticulating wildly at the TV as I sauntered in the door from work.

"What are you watching?" I jumped behind him and locked my legs around his waist.

"This! Where's all the *real* news? What's *wrong* with these people? They're idiots!" I leaned over his shoulder, then laughed.

"Baby, you can't watch this. This is Fox News. It's not *real* news. No wonder." *Duh.* I grabbed the remote from his hand before he could hurl it at Nancy Grace's monologuing face. "How about we try a little CNN? That should be a bit more to your taste."

Matt was thrilled with the response to his article. He'd never expected quite this much interest in the events surrounding our relationship, and we'd even been contacted by a *Newsweek* reporter taken by the story.

Meanwhile, Matt attended the ultrasound scan with Lori. The doctor said everything was fine—the baby was healthy so far and developing normally—but Lori was extremely underweight. She wasn't eating enough for her and the baby, and except for the basketball stomach, was looking increasingly frail and skeletal.

"She looks really rough," Matt told me over the phone. "I mean…just really haggard. She's looking *awful*." I expressed concern for her, though my concern was more for the baby. It was perhaps a mean-spirited thought, but I was secretly glad that he found me prettier than Lori.

Most births in the UK are facilitated by midwives. Hospital births are only for emergencies or complications. Lori had selected a local midwife, but the doctor sternly told her that unless she'd gained more weight by the next scan, she would have to have a Cesarean section in the hospital, as it would be far too dangerous for her to give birth naturally. Matt was nervous, but confident that she understood the seriousness of the situation, and that she would step up to the plate and start eating.

I knew he must have been pretty preoccupied with the scan and talking to Lori about her health, but hoped he'd at least gotten a chance to mention the custody stuff to her. He had tried. They talked about what they agreed on, and he explained to her that we were moving to New York together and getting married. She seemed agreeable to sharing custody, he said—the baby in New York with us every three months, and in Scotland with her every three months. Later, when the baby was old enough for school, we could switch to the school year in one country, vacations in the other.

"Oh my gosh, that's so great! I'm so glad that she's being reasonable about it! Tell her if she wants, we'll even pay for her to fly out with the baby, put her up for a week in New York or something; she can have a mini-vacation while she's at it!" My words bubbled and tripped over themselves. I was so happy that things seemed to be going smoothly.

He liked the idea—thought it would go a long way as an olive branch. He also said that he'd sign over his council

flat in Huntly to her once we were married, since her stepfather's house, where she was currently living, was disgusting—
no place for a baby. I suggested going the extra mile, and
that perhaps we could offer to pay her utilities on the flat,
too, in addition to the child support. So that she could use
her benefit money on important purchases—clothes and
food and such for her and the baby.

It was *we* all the way in my mind—how could it ever be
anything else? I wanted nothing more than an amicable
relationship between the three of us adults, for all of our
sakes, and for the baby's sake. "I thought about that, too.
I was going to bring it up with you. I'm so pleased we're
on the same page about all of this!" He really did sound
happy, too. Maybe none of this would be so bad, after all. I
mean, sure, we'd be paying for an international plane ticket
every three months, but I was working and we'd swing it,
somehow, especially if he kept up his social media work
online and expanded it a bit, and once we were married
and he had his green card, he would be allowed to work in
the United States and bring in a regular income in addition
to mine. He didn't bring in much at the moment from his
social media work, freelance article writing and ads from
the Homeless Tales' site—maybe a couple hundred dollars
a month in addition to his disability benefits—but it was
a start. We could save up enough for an apartment or a
mortgage, whichever we could manage first, by the time
we were ready to get married and move him here per-
manently. I wouldn't be living in a parking lot for much
longer—I just knew it.

"Perfect! So is everything in writing?" I trilled. Life was
looking up!

"Er..." My heart sank. "Well, I pulled out the form, but
she said she didn't want to sign anything right now, and
that we could do it later."

"Later? *When?* You're coming back here in a week and a half, and you won't be back in Scotland until just before the baby's born! Please, do it all now before the third trimester crazy hormones kick in!"

His good mood vanished as abruptly as it had come on. "Look, do you know what she's going through? Her stepfather is a disgusting pig, all her brothers and sisters were taken away from her neglectful mother, who just kept pumping out babies one after the other from different men, even after they started taking them away, and her mother and aunts are now trying to convince her that I'm going to try to take the baby away from her! They've got her paranoid!" He didn't want to spook her.

But...but that was the whole point. A written agreement wasn't just for him—it protected both of their rights. A written agreement ensured that he *wouldn't* take the baby away from her, just as it ensured that she wouldn't take it away from him. I couldn't understand why he would willingly make the situation any more precarious than it already was. Even if it was hard to get her to focus, couldn't he at least *try* to sit her down and *make* her understand the importance of an amicable custody agreement?

I got nowhere with him on this one, though. She wasn't going to be pushed and that was that. He'd try again later, in three months, when he went back to Scotland for the birth. It was one of the rare times that I wondered why he bothered asking my advice at all. Did he think that, because he was twelve years older than me, I was dumber or less experienced than he was? That I just didn't know how the world worked?

I had never minded or even noticed our age gap before. If anything, it had unexpectedly ended up being preferable for me. My experience dating men my age had been abysmal. Most were still stuck in the noncommittal, loud, immature "frat boy" stage, and I found myself rolling my eyes far too often with them.

I'd spent my formative years crushing on Alan Rickman while my sister and all of my school friends pined over Leonardo DiCaprio and Jonathan Taylor Thomas. I didn't want to swoon, I didn't want somebody young and impulsive. I wanted literate. Cultured. Refined. Witty. Honorable. A conversationalist with the mind of a steel trap. Alan Rickman meets Atticus Finch meets Eddie Izzard meets Oscar Wilde (minus the gay part) is my ideal man. Or, you know, not. I'd be willing to settle, as long as the frat boy could at least wax philosophical about art or classic films while crushing the beer can against his forehead.

One of the things I adored about Matt was that we were on the same level, at the same stage in our lives, and looking for nearly all the same things. Normally, I could tell how intelligent he thought I was. Normally, he was so sweet and careful about taking my feelings and input into consideration. But on this matter, it was as though he listened to everything I said, nodded his head, said, "Yes, dear," and then went right ahead and did exactly what he was going to do anyway.

And yet, I was afraid to push too hard, afraid to keep begging him to trust me, because then I would have been unsupportive. The last thing I wanted was to drive him away, to be a nagging shrew like my mother. So, again, I let it go. Eventually, I calmed down and my fears were allayed when he returned two weeks later. Our disagreements were rare and, when I let them go, I realized, he was apt to be more relaxed and more trusting. In hindsight, it was the right decision to back down and trust him to do the right thing. Trying so hard to be a strong woman all the time, and to set a good example for readers, occasionally made me feel tired and burned out. In every action Matt took, I knew that he sought to protect me, and it was freeing to occasionally hand over the reins every now and then to somebody else, so that I could finally allow my tensed muscles, eternally poised for fight-or-flight, to relax.

Matt and I had picked out an engagement ring for me. It was beautiful, my dream ring, an antique, circa 1900. It straddled three of my favorite eras—Victorian, Edwardian and art nouveau. Two graceful arms set with tiny diamonds swirled around one another, meeting in the middle. We weren't at a point where we could afford an engagement ring, but a sympathetic seller on the antiques website RubyLane.com, who was enamored of our story, offered us the pick of her shop for next to nothing. It was such a kind gesture that I wanted to weep at how good some people were.

We weren't required to pay anything for the ring except shipping, but I felt we should send the woman at least what we could, a small amount of money, the equivalent of four to five days' work for me, as compensation for it. It didn't seem like too much of a financial hit in exchange, and while I would have married Matt with a ring from a Cracker Jack box, or no ring at all, it was a nice feeling for us to have something official and traditional. I paid Victoria for the ring, since Matt wasn't able to. I didn't feel mooched or sponged off at all. He needed to save up for the baby and, besides, we were a team now. He was pulling his weight by helping other homeless people and promoting our sites. We'd also fallen in love with an old, Victorian fixer-upper in upstate New York that we saw online. We longed to try to purchase it one day, and if we ever got the house, we knew he'd probably be watching the kids and doing a ton of fix-it stuff while I went to work and pulled in the cash. That's just how it is—you each bring your strengths to a relationship, and if it works for you, then fine. Sure, most people would consider it odd that I was the homeless one, yet I was the one contributing the biggest paycheck, but we found it funny. This wasn't like Britney Spears buying her own engagement ring. This was just each of us doing what we could, doing what worked. Neither of us ever gave it a second thought.

Matt told me to hold onto the ring and give it to him when he arrived in California. He'd keep it in its box until he was ready to ask me, officially, to marry him.

There were a ton of paparazzi hanging around the international arrivals gate at LAX on the day that Matt came back to California—David Beckham was supposedly arriving on the same flight as Matt, one of the photographers told me, and I also saw Eric Dane (from *Grey's Anatomy*) and Rebecca Gayheart (from *Dead Like Me*) get off while I was waiting. It was surreal, later, to see myself in the background of a tabloid paparazzi photo, but at the moment I was too excited to see Matt again to care about crossing paths with quasi-celebrities.

I saw him first this time, and he looked up in panic to see a blurry ball of redhead bouncing at him. I screeched to a halt just before knocking him over at full speed, and then hurled myself into his arms. It was so much better now. The first time around, I had been too nervous about whether he'd like me as much in person, or whether I'd be invading his personal space. But this time, we both knew all signs were go, so we could sink into each other and kiss for what felt like hours, as the airport ground to a halt and faded around us.

. . .

Matt and I sat in my car in the LAX parking garage, where we'd had our very first kiss before. He asked me if I had the ring box, and I pulled it out of the glove compartment and handed it to him. Unexpectedly, he opened the box and I watched, as if hovering far above us, as he slid it onto my finger. He didn't want us to wait. He knew I was what he wanted. It was beautiful and, more important, *he* was beautiful and he loved me.

The ring itself was lovely, but didn't matter so much; it was the love obvious in the gesture that stuck with me. I was so completely certain that this was the man I wanted to spend my entire life with. I'd made plenty of fuckups in my life, but somehow I must have atoned for them, because I'd inexplicably gained *this man* in the end.

I wanted a small wedding, and he was relieved by this. He'd had the grand two-hundred-person bash with his first wife and found himself swept away in the exorbitant cost and Bridezilla-ness of the entire thing. Before he'd realized what happened, he was knee-deep in about £40,000 (about $65,000) worth of debt. When I suggested that we have ten or so of our closest friends come and stand under a pretty tree somewhere while we exchanged vows, and then go have pizza and ice cream or something, he stared at me with wonder in his eyes.

"I just can't believe it. I don't understand why I was lucky enough to find you. You're amazing. I can just picture it—it'll be beautiful. A gorgeous leafy spring day, you there in a simple dress, no frills. Just simple and perfect. All the excess junk stripped away."

"Well, yeah. I mean, we don't need any of that crazy, expensive stuff. I never got the point of it all. I don't care about having chair covers, or linens to match the chair covers, or a DJ and an open bar and dancing and tons of people we barely know there. At the end of the day, all that stuff is gone and you're still married. Isn't that the important thing? Isn't that what it's all about? I just want to marry *you*, and to hell with the rest of it." I meant it, too. He stared at me for so long and with so much love in his eyes that I actually felt a bit uncomfortable, blushed and looked down at my lap. He stroked my cheek and wrapped his hand around the back of my neck, pulling my head in to his chest. He held me there for a while, repeating over and over how wonderful I was, swearing that he would make me the happiest woman on earth for the rest of our lives.

One prevalent attitude I've noticed toward the homeless: Many people expect them to give up every last indulgence and every last shred of fun. We should spend all our time looking for work (never mind if we already *do* work, or *are* looking for work), or perhaps standing on a freeway off-ramp begging for change, or sitting in a government aid office, hoping against hope for assistance. We should spend *all* our time doing this. After all, if we take any light-hearted time to ourselves at all, we must not *really* want to rehouse ourselves.

I should either be working, searching for work or otherwise appropriately ragged, depressed and undignified, befitting my station, is that it? I should give up absolutely everything to prove just how much I deserve a home, and just how sorry I am for whatever I have done "wrong" that "made" me homeless in the first place.

While I agree that it certainly behooves homeless people to spend their time and resources wisely, and set goals and priorities for themselves, there is an inherent human need for recreation, for relaxation, for fun. Everyone needs time to unwind, and that goes double for a homeless person, because there is little more stressful than this life. Priorities are individual, and I do not believe that the occasional bit of fun should be at the bottom of the heap for anybody, much less that homeless people should be judged harshly if they sometimes choose it.

My fiancé was home again and I was thrilled, so I dragged him to a local Renaissance Faire for a day. Admission was cheap, and the proceeds benefited equine rescue, the local humane society and a nonprofit theater troupe— all causes I cared about. I got to gnaw on a freakishly large turkey leg and watch men in tights and armor joust on some lovely Percherons (rescued, of course). I also got to enjoy the supreme pleasure of watching Matt unwind and enjoy himself. He stifled his laughter at the overexaggerated British accents, but his (real) English accent clearly didn't register with nearly anybody, and certainly didn't seem to impress them.

We were living practically on top of each other, and summer was in full force, but Matt and I were as much in love as ever. The heat occasionally made us testier with each other, but even on the rare occasions where we argued, we always fought fair. There was no hitting below the belt, we resolved things quickly and we understood each other, or at least strove to. Our fights were pretty constructive, never nasty. There was never even the slightest hint or suggestion between us of throwing in the towel. We understood that we loved each other, we were in it for the long haul and, dammit, we both wanted to make it work.

One particularly excruciatingly hot day, we were both at our breaking point. We were stripped down to our underwear, lying spread-eagle on the mattress, sweating profusely and trying not to touch each other, lest our shared body heat turn into the straw that broke the camel's back. Suddenly, I just couldn't stand it anymore. I loved Matt so much, but hated the rest of it, hated not being able to take us straight from a trailer into at least a tiny apartment with working air-conditioning. I couldn't bear to lie in the heat for a single second longer. If I stayed in this trailer, on this lot, for another second, I would scream until I collapsed.

Without a word, I stood up and threw on the lightest clothes I could find.

"Where are you going?"

"I'm going to Starbucks. You can come, or you can stay, but I can't handle this anymore. I hate it here. I hate it! I hate it!" I began to cry, and grabbed my laptop, running out of the trailer and jumping into the car. He followed.

At Starbucks, it was so different. We picked out cushy chairs next to each other, and held hands affectionately as we continued working, until the sun went down and it was cool enough to return to the trailer.

"I think we both needed that," he said as he held me that night. "I feel just the way you do, you know. I'm so grateful that we have somewhere to go, but I can't wait until we're out of here and have someplace of our own. We can't do this forever, can we?"

From then on, whenever we were too hot or tired or stressed to deal with the trailer for another second, one of us would shout, "Starbucks break!" It was one of the very few ways that we could pretend that life was normal (and air-conditioned) for a little longer.

writer with the local newspaper had heard about my story and expressed an interest in doing a piece on me. I met with her but declined to be interviewed for the piece when she made it clear that her editor would only run the article if she was allowed to use my full name. Matt didn't mind one way or the other, but he was curious about my upbringing, and just why I was so determined to keep the blog anonymous and to avoid going public.

It was hard for me to explain everything to him. I didn't know where to begin. My family had no idea as to my whereabouts or my blog, and I still couldn't bring myself to hurt them, even after all that they'd done to me. I just wasn't ready to come out yet, I explained to Matt tearfully. I didn't want to hurt *anybody,* and that would be inevitable if my name were made public.

Blog readers had also started asking why I didn't write more in-depth pieces about my past, why I was so vague about it all. I didn't *want* to write about rape or molestation or my mother beating me. I did everything I could *not* to think about these things when I didn't have to—therapy had been going so well and done so much to get me thinking more positively. I didn't want to go back to that ugly place.

He held me and ran his fingers through my hair soothingly until my strangled sobs subsided into tiny hiccups. He understood. If I didn't believe I was up to going public about it, then by George, I shouldn't, and that was all there was to it. It was another of those moments when I realized just how lucky I was. There had been times when I thought perhaps Matt couldn't understand my more difficult issues, but at times like this, I was so glad to be proven wrong.

For instance, I had tried to explain, in vain, why I was afraid of demons, even though I no longer believed they existed. Since childhood, I'd been taught that Satan and his demons were real—as real as any person walking down the street—and they were always watching me, even when I was naked in the shower, trying to trip me up. If I did anything occult-ish to invite them into my life, like use a Ouija board or even read a demonic book or watch a demonic movie, they could infiltrate my home, hold me down in my bed at night and rape me, push me into walls and beat me up, lift up furniture like couches and beds with me on it, high into the air, spinning them as I screamed. It had happened to people my mother knew—she swore it. At the first audience screening of *The Exorcist,* the theater screen had burst into flames. It was a scientific *fact*.

The demons were so cagey, you could even pick one up without realizing it, by shopping at secondhand stores or garage sales. Demons *loved* to "attach themselves" to secondhand furniture or knickknacks, just waiting for a new, unsuspecting buyer to snap them up. There was no way of knowing what that item's previous owner had been into—she could have been a witch or an occultist! Satan worshippers were everywhere, hiding among us, dripping black candles and pentagrams and altars smothered in goat's blood in their basements.

So even though I now knew this was all ridiculous, I flipped out if Matt wanted us to watch *The Devil's Advocate* on YouTube. He just couldn't grasp why it would bother me, if I didn't believe in any of it anymore. It was completely irrational, of course. But I just wasn't ready.

Once, he asked me about the Jehovah's Witnesses' stand on refusing blood and blood transfusions. "But you eat meat. You *do* know that all meat has blood in it, right?"

"What are you talking about? Not meat that's properly bled before consumption." I recited the official JW line unconsciously, without thinking.

"Er...why do you think steak is red and juicy? That's blood. If there was no blood in meat, it would be gray and disgusting and inedible."

"No, they told us that's just meat juice. They inject food coloring into the meat so it looks nice and appetizing."

He started laughing at me, and I flushed red. "*Meat juice?* Oh, man. Now I've heard everything! You must realize that's complete bullshit, right? It's blood. It's impossible to remove all blood from meat."

I was horrified. I had never really thought about it before. I'd been eating blood all my life, in trace amounts, and had clung to some ridiculous, hypocritical, spoon-fed dogma flat-out denying it, without grasping even the most basic of concepts. And here Matt was probably wondering how the woman he loved could be both so smart and so stupid simultaneously. The same way I felt about my sister. It was rather mortifying.

But there was more that he wanted to know. If our child was dying, and the doctors said that a blood transfusion was necessary, would I allow it? I hesitated. I could tell that the hesitation deeply, deeply disturbed him.

"I want to say that yes, *of course* I would allow a blood transfusion. I'd do anything to save my child. I truly believe that I'd allow it, absolutely. I'm not hesitating because I'd take the Jehovah's Witness stand. I'm hesitating because all my life, it's been pounded into me that it's disgusting, revolting to transfuse blood. Even if my mind knows that it's just another medical procedure, my entire body is just going '*ew!*' I just have to get used to it, is all."

It was like the homosexuality thing. Jehovah's Witnesses believed it was a gross, disgusting sin—the epitome of nastiness. Even after I had close friends come out of the closet, and I realized that they were still exactly the same friends I'd always known, I loved them as much as ever and I had absolutely no interest in what they did in bed, it took a few more years of conscious effort to overcome the "ew" factor, the automatically triggered reaction that had been ingrained in me since childhood. I had finally gotten to the point where someone being gay didn't bug me at all—it was just another quality about that person. Not good, not bad, simply *that person*. Like blue eyes or being left-handed.

Racism has been similarly problematic for me. For instance, my mother does not consider herself racist. *After all,* she might say, *I have ethnic friends and don't use the volatile slurs* nigger *or* spic, *and I think the miniseries* Roots *was a moving and powerful cinematic experience.*

Invariably, though, my mother would home in on a Hispanic woman pushing a baby carriage down the street and scoff, "Pfft. Another Mexican pumping out welfare babies. Typical!" If the woman seemed young, then my mother would stage-whisper dramatically about how those slut Mexican girls couldn't keep their legs closed; all of them got pregnant at fourteen. The term *dirty Mexican* was applied liberally and with abandon—not only to Mexicans, but to Puerto Ricans, Costa Ricans, Cubans; anybody of Latino descent.

"*Mom!*" I said in horror, "*Stop* it! You're being *rude!*" She would roll her eyes and modulate her voice to clearly convey the absolute maximum amount of disgust and contempt with me.

"Shut up, Brianna. She can't hear me, anyway." This was sometimes true, and sometimes not, but that wasn't the *point,* I wanted to scream at her. Whether they can hear you or not, you *said* it! You *thought* it! At the time I couldn't fully articulate rebuttals like *You're tarring one ethnic group with the same stereotypical brush* or *How do you know that sixteen-year-old girl isn't babysitting her little brother?* or *Well, Samuel our landscaper is a Mexican immigrant, and a very kind, hard worker who labored for Grandpa for many years, and you don't seem to have any compunction now about employing him to do your gardening for dismally low wages....* I may not have been able to formulate these vague thoughts into coherent arguments, but I instinctively felt unclean when she came out with these bigoted comments. I knew her words were rude and cruel; I just couldn't put my finger on why.

She is one of those people who believes the statement, "I'm not racist, but..." immediately cancels out any and all ensuing bigotry.

"You know I'm not racist, and don't ever repeat this, but Brother Knight really is the quintessential pompous, arrogant black man," she would huff about a towering Southern congregation elder she disliked. "Thinks that he has to prove he's smarter and better and more articulate than the white people in the congregation. The way he gets all loud and forceful sometimes from the platform, or keeps reminding us that he's black, like a Baptist preacher or something." Knight was not the only elder my mother had locked horns with in the past but, then, she had never referred to any of the others as "arrogant white men." Why was the ubiquitous racial descriptor a necessity whenever Knight was discussed? I didn't much like him, either, but my feelings had more to do with the fact that I distrusted elders in general, rather than because I thought he was an "uppity Negro," who needed to be put in his place.

Which isn't to say that I didn't absorb some of these tendencies and thinking patterns myself. I did, though I didn't always recognize them as such. So did my sister. At twenty or twenty-one, Molly was pursued by Derrick, a gregarious, funny black man in the congregation. I met him a couple of times, and found him personable and charming. Moll clearly enjoyed his company, and considered him one of her best friends.

"He knows how to take a joke and laugh at himself," she told me. "We can rib him about liking watermelon and fried chicken, and he thinks it's funny, instead of getting all PC and offended and playing the racism card! He even jokes about being 'our nigga!'" However, she complained to me, she recognized that his interest in her was taking a turn for the romantic, and she wished that he would back off and just let them stay friends, "like brother and sister."

I was a bit confused, because Moll has always been hellbent on marriage and babies ASAP. I didn't think that she *should* settle for the first man who expressed an interest in her, but I must confess that, knowing her personality, I was a little surprised that she *wasn't* gung-ho about Derrick.

"I'm just curious, why *don't* you go on a date or two with him? You already know that you like his personality and sense of humor, and it's not like it could hurt, right? You never know: There could end up being a spark there. Besides, he's a real cutie. If you don't want him, can I have him?" I was being facetious about the last part, of course— there was nothing I wanted less than to date a Jehovah's Witness—but the guy *was* a looker, and I am not immune to fantasizing about eye candy.

She looked uncomfortable. "Jehovah says that we should only date to find a prospective marriage mate," she recited robotically. "Don't take this the wrong way—it's not that I'm racist or anything—but I just can't see myself marrying a black man. I've never found them physically attractive."

"Er...so you're saying it's not a racist thing, it's an *aesthetic* thing?" I was incredulous.

"Yes, exactly!" She beamed, relieved that I "understood."

"But, what if someone has everything that you're look-ing for, everything that you find important in a marriage mate, but then he just happens to be black?"

The discomfort was back. "Bri, can we just drop it? He's a great guy and I love him like a brother. Eventually, he'll move on to somebody more appropriate for him, and forget about me. It's not like I can *control* who I find attrac-tive, is it?"

I was seething with unexpressed frustration. *But people you don't initially find attractive can grow on you! Personality is what matters! And what's so unattractive about being black, anyway? Have you ever seen Denzel Washington?* At the time, I was dating a corpulently obese, heavily tattooed man three inches shorter than me with long, straggly hair and a micropenis. None of this jibed at all with my personal beauty ideals or my cravings for wildly experimental, flex-ible, swinging-from-the-chandeliers sex (we were limited to blow job, hand job, and girl-on-top, during which I could never tell if I was actually being penetrated or just giving a labial massage), but he was a relatively sweet man, good-natured and humorous, and an affectionate cuddler who was more than pleased to overcompensate for his physical shortcomings with admirable cunnilingus techniques. Within two dates, I was head-over-heels infatuated with him and never again gave his looks another thought. I just enjoyed being with him and that was that; to me he *was* handsome. So I was *not* in the mood to hear Molly complaining about her tall, dark, sexy and handsome would-be beau…especially when her only complaint was the "dark" part of it.

Thus spurned, Derrick did eventually move on and married one of Molly's friends, a Hispanic girl in the congregation named Elena. Moll was overtly and vocally relieved to be free of his chivalrous attentions, now directed toward a "more suitable" ethnic female. The happy couple, being young and unable to afford to rent a place of their own, moved in with Derrick's parents and Elena became pregnant almost immediately. My mother and sister congratulated them loudly and sweetly to their face, cooed over the adorable baby when it was born and (true to form) tsk-tsk-ed behind their backs the entire time.

"Derrick's a nice and funny guy," they confided to me. "We adore him to pieces, but he's being such a typical black—too lazy to get a better job and support his wife when he can just mooch off his parents forever. And getting Elena *knocked up right away!*" My mom shook her head piously, apparently forgetting her own reproductive history. "It's just so, so sad. But typical. It's a cultural thing. Aren't you glad you didn't marry him, Molly?"

Moll vigorously nodded. "Oh, yeah, I mean, just *think* about it! I feel so sorry for poor Elena. They're going to have such a rough time in the future, you can already tell.

And if I'd married him, that would have been *me!*" She shuddered, horrified at the vision of this alternate universe in which she married a black man.

It therefore follows that it's not been easy for me to adjust my filter on race and stereotyping. Even though I was by far the most PC of us, in that my family's bigotry repulsed me and I considered it rude to make similar remarks either publicly or privately, there's always been a silent war between what I believed and knew was right and how I was programmed to accept casual racism. In trying to disentangle my own cognitive dissonance, I noted that such thoughts cropped up in my brain far more often than I would have liked, even if only for a fraction of a second before I had to methodically and deliberately hit the Ignore button. Because that's what it is. It would be dishonest of me to say that I've eradicated such thinking patterns from my mental vocabulary, when what I actually do is overrule my own learned responses.

You throw a sponge into a sink full of dirty water and it'll soak up several times its weight and hold onto it. Throw something less porous, like a stone, into a sink full of dirty water, and it'll still get wet. Pull it out and it feels about the same, weighs about the same, but there's a slight change in texture, a film over it, and droplets of water are still settled into the minuscule pits and crevices of the stone. Even as a child, I recognized hypocrisy and prejudice at play, but I was also at my most impressionable and, inevitably, whether I liked it or not, I retained bits of it.

I have friends of all races, I rooted for Obama to win the 2008 election, I am a firm believer that any person of any background and any race can do and be anything that he aspires to do and be, I have never made a racial slur and I am no longer afraid to speak out against intolerance and hatred. It bothers me—hell, it *infuriates* me. So, the million-dollar question: Am I racist? Because clearly, all the preceding means that I'm not racist, right? Except... that I am.

I *am* racist, at least a little bit, in a knee-jerk fashion, and it's only one of many things that horrify me about myself. I would give anything to be able to instantaneously rewire my programming, root out even the briefest flickers of stereotyping lurking in those tiny mental fissures. Just because I choose not to act on them, however, doesn't mean that they're not there. They are, and though the stone is slowly drying out and their impact has lessened dramatically, on occasion I still recognize them. I wish that they were nonexistent; I hope that eventually I won't even *have* to overrule them; I hope that those microscopic synapses will simply one day refuse to fire, with no more fanfare or premeditation than a snuffed candle, just ceasing to exist.

But it's all such a damn process, isn't it? Such a damn, arduous, fucking, lifelong process.

So all of that, I tried to make Matt realize, was bouncing around in my brain day in and day out and I had to very consciously and deliberately make sense of it all, sorting out the difference between my ingrained responses and what I actually do or do not *believe*. But I hadn't gotten around to taking on the blood and demon issues as much yet. I was tackling my neuroses and my terrors one by one, and it was painstaking. I wished so much that he would just *understand* and back me up and hold my hand through it.

At moments like these, though, when he told me that he completely understood, that I could stay anonymous, that I didn't have to put my face and my screwups and my neuroses out there, naked in front of the entire world—I realized that he was doing exactly that. There was good reason for me to trust this man, and put my life in his hands.

few days later, on a Friday evening, I left work and
met Matt at Starbucks. We stayed until they closed,
so that he could get some social media work done,
and then we headed back to the trailer for some well-earned
sleep, hand in hand.

We realized, as we neared the lot, that something didn't
look right. It looked like the other trailers in the lot had left.
Everything was flat, open space. Where the hell was...?

The truck and trailer were gone.

Our home was gone.

All my belongings, except what I had in my car, were
gone.

Panic.

I frantically called the police department and was re-
directed to city towing. The dispatcher who answered
the phone informed me that it was now the weekend and
nobody could help me until Monday. We rented a hotel
room for the weekend, and were told on Monday that it
would cost in the vicinity of $1K to pick up the truck and

trailer (they counted them as two separate vehicles). In addition, I would be charged an additional $80 per day that the vehicles were not picked up, plus a $70 DMV lien placed on each vehicle—since they hadn't been picked up within seventy-two hours, despite the fact that I attempted to call over the weekend but was told there was nothing that could be done.

I was livid, and also coming to terms with the fact that I'd likely never see again the few belongings that I still retained. My books. My clothes. My dishes and glassware (which, I assumed, were likely smashed to pieces now, as the trailer was not prepared to be moved and I had not tied down my boxes). I had recently reopened a checking account with my local credit union, and Matt and I were trying to sock away as much of my earnings from work as we could in order to try to get ourselves into an apartment, or perhaps even a house, as soon as possible, but we had nowhere near enough to pay the impound fees, much less continue living life afterwards until the next paycheck. We were, for lack of a gentler term, royally fucked.

Sage, who was boarding Fezzik, invited us to come up to Riverside and stay on "the ranch," until we figured things out. We were grateful and took her up on the offer immediately—we had no other choice. We simply couldn't afford a motel long term.

And so we found ourselves coasting into the small area of Riverside called Pedley. Matt hadn't seen the ranch before, and he was as excited as a little kid. I tried to explain to him that it wasn't *that* kind of ranch, with the white picket fences and tall waving grasses and horses running free in paddocks, their manes waving in the wind. I don't think he heard me. As we exited the freeway, he saw men riding their horses right there on the sidewalk, more horses tied up outside a liquor store, horses everywhere you turned on the street. Most cities in SoCal weren't like this; he'd never seen horses on the streets here before. He bounced in his seat. "It's like Texas or something!"

"You've never seen Texas."

"I have in movies! They wear cowboy hats and ride horses down the streets, too!"

He was really disappointed, as I suspected he would be, when we arrived at the ranch. It was basically a three-acre dirt lot with a small stucco house, a bunch of sheds and trailers, and the little grass to be found was brown and dead. He scuffed at the dirt with one foot.

"You're right, it's not what I expected." He sounded sad, cheated of his green Texas ranch.

"Hey, it's not a parking lot! We'll have utility hookups!" I cried, and this seemed to perk him up a bit.

Sage met us out front. She was so excited to finally meet Matt, and he found himself pleasantly surprised by her. When I explained to him that a woman who barely knew us had offered to let us live on the same lot as her, he was immediately on the defensive and suspicious.

"Somebody you've only met once is willing to take in a couple of strangers? What if she's part of some freaky cult or something? What if it's like a compound where they'll try to brainwash us and get us to shave our heads and wear robes or something?"

It took a lot of convincing on my part to get him to acquiesce.

"Don't be silly. She's a very sweet, genuine lady who just likes to help others, and the man who owns the property, Thurman, rents out trailers on the lot to a bunch of other homeless people for $450 a month. It's even cheaper than a week at a motel, and unless you want to live out of the car, can you think of any better options? Besides, we'll get to be close to Fezzik. You'll finally get to meet him!"

He finally acceded to my coaxing.

Sage set us up in a trailer that had recently been vacated. The shower hardly worked, except for a trickle of water, and the swamp cooler was on its last legs and barely did anything at all to combat the heat, but we had lights and a sink and a working oven and microwave and stove! It was all the luxuries we'd never had in the Walmart parking lot, and thus a giant step up from what we'd gotten used to.

Fezzik was thrilled to see me, and launched his entire self at me like a bomb. He had put on a ton of weight, and finally looked like a Neo Mastiff should, following his disastrous stint at the kennel. He also took quite the shine to Matt immediately, which relieved me. He loved all women and children, but men could be touch and go when I first got him. Now, though, Sage had socialized him so well that I never saw him get nervous around a man again. In fact, he seemed to decide very quickly that he loved Matt even more than he loved me. It wasn't my imagination. I couldn't find it in my heart to be jealous, though. Fezzik was *our* dog now. This was the way it should be.

The following Monday, I was laid off from work. Again.

I was the only one of the five of us laid off. The boss called me into his office and told me sadly that he had overestimated his budget; that he couldn't afford an executive assistant. He asked if I'd be willing to stick around and work about ten hours a week, at a pay cut that would have brought my wages lower than unemployment. I suppose he thought he was doing me a favor. I declined, and tried to look at it as an unexpected bonus—escape from earning my paycheck shilling for a company that built websites for scam artists.

It did niggle a bit, though. I'd rather have quit on my own terms, with work at another company lined up. I couldn't understand why a company would bother hiring new people and then lay them off after a couple of months, due to "the recession." I figured that perhaps it was cheaper than paying a temp agency. But still, what a crappy thing to do to someone, after telling her that you were hiring her for a permanent position. Back to the drawing board.

It was especially bad timing with the trailer problem. Walmart was giving me the runaround, ignoring my emails and voice-mail messages to their corporate head-quarters, requesting an explanation and begging them to get my trailer out of impound, please. My supportive reader base was outraged, and many of them also wrote letters and phoned Walmart HQ, receiving only canned, stock reply emails in response. It was more than I had received. There was nothing but deafening silence from Walmart in response to my emails for the whole next month.

I began applying for jobs again, and even picked up a few interview calls within the first couple of days, so Matt and I were optimistic. We still had a small cushion of a few hundred dollars from my previous job and the retroactive UI benefit checks. Sure, we'd hoped to save enough to get a real roof over our heads, but at least we had something to get by on now, and that's what was important.

Then my car broke down.

As luck would have it, the turbocharger in my car de-cided to give out on the freeway on the way to a job inter-view. Karma dictated that the car would continue to run, albeit screeching in protest, until I got to the interview.

Afterwards, I rushed to the nearest auto body shop I could find and was advised that the car "should make it home," but not much further than that. The last seven miles of the way back, the car suddenly started making a grinding noise in addition to the high-pitched screaming whine of the shot turbocharger. By the time I arrived at my destination, blue smoke was billowing out of the exhaust pipe. I barely made it.

The car was only four years old and had just 56,000 miles on it. Nothing, but *nothing,* should go wrong with a car that new and with that few miles on it, I ranted to Matt. Why? Why me? Why did everything have to go wrong (again) *now?*

Thurman, who fixed up old cars himself, located a new turbocharger and offered to install it, as long as I paid him for labor. The part was very expensive, about $1,200, but still about half the cost the auto body shop wanted to charge. Matt and I had to make a decision between having the car repaired, or using our savings combined with my final paycheck, to try to get the trailer out of impound. We decided to go with the car. Without it, my options for potential work would be severely limited or curtailed completely.

Our cushion vanished practically overnight, and we were back to basic barebones.

We only managed to get by because my readers, vastly concerned for our welfare, took it upon themselves to donate nearly $300 to us via Matt's PayPal account on Homeless Tales. I had turned down offers of assistance for so long. I didn't want to be accused of sponging off anybody or e-panhandling. I cried at night, as Matt wrapped his arms around me and encouraged me to just let people help me, already, for once.

"You're strong and you're beautiful, but we need help right now and your readers *want* to do this for you. They're writing in to you every day *insisting* that you let them help you. So just learn that this is the moment to accept their help, and say 'Thank you.'"

"Fine. But I'm still not putting a donation button up on my site."

The $300 paid for nearly a month's rent at the ranch. I was so grateful, but I couldn't wait to get back to work so that I didn't have to feel like a mooch.

nd then came the event that changed everything. Monday, August 24, 2009. I was checking a new favorite site of mine, SaveTheAssistants.com. It was good for a laugh—the owner ran user-submitted horror stories that executive and personal assistants like me had to silently suffer through, plus there were job listings posted occasionally. It was the work I did, of course, so I wanted to leave no stone unturned.

SaveTheAssistants.com was featuring an E. Jean Carroll column that they had stumbled over from nearly a month earlier. The headline proclaimed E. Jean their "hero of the week." I perked up—*Hey, it's E. Jean! The one I wrote to all the way back, in April or May or something. How funny, what a coincidence!* I continued to scan the post…and found myself reading my own story (albeit edited and reworded a bit to sound far better than anything I ever could have written):

Dear E. Jean: I'm currently homeless and living in a Walmart parking lot. I'm educated, I have never done drugs and I am not mentally ill. I have a strong

employment history and am a career executive assis-
tant. The instability sucks, but I'm rocking it as best as
I can. Recently, I stumbled across a job notice (a reality
show casting call for executive assistants) and was in-
trigued enough to apply. It was a shot in the dark, and
I assumed I'd never hear back. Surprise! I was called in
this week! And I promptly bombed it. When I found out
who was involved in the show I got kind of starstruck
and completely froze up. My usual personality did not
radiate. My question: How does one get another shot
when one screws up a job interview?
—Homeless, but Not Hopeless

Miss Homeless, my dear: You don't get another shot.
You take it. Wear the new suit you get from Dress for Success (the fantastic organization that provides interview suits
and career development guidance to low-income women,
Dressforsuccess.org), find a company, a store, a business
you admire, and show up ready to work. When you speak
with the manager, don't ask for a job. Simply introduce
yourself, tell her why her company is brilliant, and give
her three ways you can help her succeed. Follow up with a
phone call, plus a visit the following week.

Of course, the cleverest way to land a good job (and get
an apartment) is to already have a good job/internship/
volunteer position. This strategy permits you to impress
the interviewers with the superhuman passion you have for
your current projects.

This is what you did with your letter: You knocked me
out with your courage and spirit. I am therefore, Miss Not
Hopeless, offering you a four-month internship. Of course,
it's the most hideously humdrum internship in America.
You'll be stuck with the tedious job of organizing research

for my book, transcribing interviews and analyzing data from 1,800,000 pages (not a misprint) of a college sex survey I did on Facebook. I looked you up and discovered that you're on the West Coast and that you write a highly entertaining blog. You possess a brain and access to a computer. Excellent! If you accept this internship, you'll telecommute to my East Coast mountain office one hour a day, six days a week. At the end of the four months, if you don't have a job and an awesome place to live, I will become *your* intern.

I began to scream and flail wildly. Matt, snoozing beside me, jerked awake in terror. Murder? Rape? Giant furry spiders??? "Baby, look! Looklooklooklooklook!"

I pushed my laptop toward him. He squinted at it blearily through sleep-filled eyes. He read it, but didn't comprehend.

"What is this?" He couldn't grasp why I'd woken him up and shown him an advice column.

"Read it again, honey! It's me! It's *me*. It's my letter! I've been offered an internship with the advice columnist of *ELLE* magazine!!! Can you imagine what this will look like on my résumé?!?"

I was still bouncing around, off and running, like a chicken with my head cut off, mind racing, and he was still blinking slowly, trying to clear the sleep fog from his mind, struggling to comprehend.

"I don't understand. When did you write this? You never told me anything about this. You wrote a letter? What?" More rapid, confused blinking.

I hadn't even thought to tell him. It was just a spur of the moment thing after I'd blown the Fremantle audition. I'd never dreamed she'd read it or care about it!

"Oh, my *god!*" I'd just realized that the column was nearly a month old. Nobody had contacted or emailed me with the offer, and I'd been so busy with all the craziness going on that it had never occurred to me to check *ELLE* to see if the letter had ever made it through. I'd assumed that they'd notify you or something, if they were going to publish your letter. What if I was too late? What if she assumed I'd rejected her offer? What if it was off the table? Noooooooooooo!

I jerked the laptop away from him and frantically started to type. I had to contact her and accept the internship, if I hadn't already lost it. Terror overcame me all of a sudden. What if a once-in-a-lifetime opportunity had slipped through my fingers? It would just be the cherry on my crummy week sundae.

Several hours of nail-biting later, E. Jean finally responded to me. Yes, the offer was still on the table, and my internship would start in a week, September 1. She gave me her direct phone number and told me to call her. I was shaking visibly as I dialed. Matt sat next to me, hand on my shoulder, trying to calm me.

"Hellooooo, darling?" She sounded in person exactly the way she wrote in her columns. Like Gloria Swanson or someone else similarly glamorous and over the top. Like she wore a silk turban and lounged in front of an art deco vanity in a supple, shimmering robe and fuck-me pumps. Completely at ease in her own skin and completely confident in her own larger-than-life persona.

Yet, surprisingly, completely easy to talk to—funny, charming and relatable.

Somehow, I managed to hold my own throughout the conversation without passing out from terror. I attribute it completely to her own conversational skills, by the way, not to mine. We spent twenty minutes or so getting to know each other, chatting about the internship and what would be expected of me, how I would telecommute... I can't get too specific here, because I barely remember the conversation over the pounding of my own heart. The doors to my future were opening wide before me.

Her cheery "Goodbyyyyye, darling!" still ringing in my ears, I turned to Matt.

"She's great. She's awesome. She's fantastic. She's just really, really sweet. This is gonna be great, right?"

He smiled and wrapped his arms around me. "You were no slouch yourself there on that telephone call. She's lucky to have you. Now, I'm going to make love to you, and then we're going to write an article about this."

"Really? You think you can spin it somehow?"

"Oh, yes," he murmured, his lips on my collarbone as he unhooked my bra with one hand. "This is exactly the sort of story that people love. I wouldn't be surprised if it got the same kind of attention as the article about us."

"Really?" I was surprised. "I dunno, isn't that sort of like lightning striking twice?"

"Leave it to me." He was nibbling my lobe, whispering darkly into my ear. "I know what I'm doing. You just keep being yourself and start your internship. I'll do all the rest. Now, come and fuck me. I need you."

"I need you, too."

Matt was as good as his word, and his article about the homeless girl getting the internship skyrocketed to the front page of Digg.

"Sweetie, the headline says that I won an internship with *ELLE* magazine. That's not strictly accurate, you know. It's with E. Jean. She's the advice columnist for *ELLE,* but she also runs her own website—AskEJean.com. In fact, most of what I'll be doing will probably focus on that."

"I know, honey, but you have to know what will catch the public's attention. I explain all that in the article, but the headline needs to grab them, and *ELLE* magazine is instantly recognizable. It's glamorous. It's that rags-to-riches story everyone's looking for." We laughed together at this, because, after all, we were still living in a trailer.

We both expected a bit of a hullaballoo like last time, but neither of us had any inkling of the kind of massive international interest this story would generate or how long it would run.

The following morning, my inbox was crammed with thousands of emails, and my cell phone was ringing off the hook. Blearily, I picked it up and slurred, "Hello?"

Pause.

"Oh, my gosh. Yeah, um, just one second, another line is ringing, I'll be right back...Hello? Er, wow...no, absolutely, I'm on another call, can I call you back? Sure, let me grab a pen...."

I clutched the phone to my chest. Matt stirred and looked up at me.

"Sweetie, I've got the *Today* show and a producer from *Ellen DeGeneres* on the line, and twelve voice mails yet to listen to." His eyes flew wide open. "I have no idea how these people all got my phone number, but I think I might need you to wake up and help me figure out some stuff. We should probably call E. Jean and find out what to do next."

The Associated Press picked up the story, and once the AP article came out, it seemed as if every last news outlet ran with it. I was getting interview requests from just about every continent, and E. Jean and *ELLE* were kindly facilitating which TV outlet would get an exclusive interview with me.

"I don't know what your boyfriend did, but tell him to keep doing it! This is unbelievable. I've never seen anything like it!" E. Jean crowed into the phone. Matt beamed. I was so proud of him, and so glad to see him getting recognition. I wanted to tell everyone who would listen, and did, that most of the credit for all this madness went to him, the love of my life. I was so afraid that he would feel left out or forgotten, as if I didn't fully appreciate him or realize how much hard work he had done to make this publicity happen, so that we could both bring attention to causes, solutions and stereotypes of homelessness—and also potentially climb out of it ourselves.

I was trying to answer all the emails from homeless people first. It was exhausting, but I wanted so much to help them—most were far worse off than I was. If I didn't know the answers to their questions, I asked around throughout the online homeless community until I found someone who could help them, or at least point them in the right direction.

After a while, I quit reading the news articles and comments about me. Ninety-eight percent of them were positive, congratulatory, constructive and encouraging. But I'm only human, and the remaining 2 percent were what I sometimes took to heart. More the ones that attacked Matt, actually. I was less concerned about the ones attacking me.

There were several people with ignorant gut reactions: "*Real* homeless people don't have cell phones or laptops!" "If you live in a trailer or a vehicle, you're not *really* homeless!" "Yeah, right, a homeless person who can afford airfare from another country—give me a break!" "*Real* homeless people don't work or look for work! If you're working, then there's no reason for you to be homeless!" "All homeless people are lazy bums, just trying to mooch off the system!" "Those panhandlers you see on the street *really* make $80,000 a year each! I saw it on TV!"

I was happy to respond to questions and disabuse people of misconceptions like these, if they were polite about it. I couldn't blame them for their instinctive responses. I'd been just as ignorant about homelessness less than a year ago. It was exciting to have conversations about homeless stereotypes versus the realities and statistics of homelessness. I was eager and optimistic about making some kind of difference in public perception, no matter how small.

There were the occasional low blows, however. One news website slammed me for talking about wanting to "put a human face to homelessness." The media coverage was so pervasive that I'd lost track of who was writing about the story, and Matt kindly tried to keep the article from me, but one of my blog readers indignantly forwarded it to me. It was something to the effect of: *"When she talks about putting a human face to homelessness, what she really means is the face of young, white privilege!"* the writer snarled. *"Nobody would care about this girl's story if she were black, would they? She's just another racist unaware of her own racism. She clearly believes that people like her, middle-class homeless affected by the recession, are the only ones who deserve help. She doesn't believe that the mentally ill or drug addicts on the street are as deserving as her!"*

Wow. I paced up and down the trailer, waving my arms in the air, as Matt sat on the couch quietly, his computer on his lap.

I had never said or implied anything like that. I don't care *whose* face is put on homelessness. I don't mean *my* face, I mean faces in general—black, white, green, whatever. I just wanted my readers to see that every single homeless person has a backstory, has a personality, is a human being. I'm just telling *my* story, and that's all I can do, right? Tell my story from my perspective, and let others tell theirs. I want solutions for *all* homeless people. Saying that the mentally ill and those with drug problems don't deserve help is ridiculous. All I've *ever* said from the very beginning is that I believe they are *most* in need of compassion and assistance—because, after all, I can pull myself up by my bootstraps, and they don't have any bootstraps to pull themselves up by in the first place.

It was so frustrating. These newspeople didn't know me, and I was well aware that most of them were picking up and summarizing the story from various other outlets; most hadn't even read any of my blog. If they did, I thought, they'd know that I haven't applied for any government benefits since becoming homeless, except for unemployment insurance, because I don't feel right taking already limited funds that could be helping people worse off than me. They'd know that I hadn't made a dime from my blog; didn't even run ads or have a Donate button, because I didn't want to be accused of e-panhandling. I wanted to prove that I could get out of this mess by myself.

"Honey, I've said from the very beginning that I have it better than so many; that I'm luckier than so many! What's the *matter* with these crazy people? GRAAAAAAAHHHHHH!!!!!"

He patted the couch, and I threw myself at him so hard, I nearly knocked him over. "It's OK, baby. It's OK. Nearly everyone else has good things to say. They're all so proud of you. Look at what we've accomplished. You've had so many people write in to you to say that you've changed their perceptions. You *are* making a difference. There will always be crazy or unreasonable people you can't please. But it's rare to see a media response so over-whelmingly positive, especially to a controversial issue like homelessness."

I shook my head violently. "I didn't accomplish this. You did. Barely anybody read my blog before. None of this would have happened if you hadn't made it happen."

He chuckled. "That's not entirely true. There's some-thing about you that people are connecting with."

"Maybe they're right. What if it is just because I'm a young, white girl? The 'face of privilege?' Even if it is molested, abused, raped, fucked-up-behind-closed-doors privilege. I'm female and white and I'm relatively educated and articulate, and I used to have a good job." My self-esteem was shot. I couldn't see myself as a writer of any particular talent, or even as a writer at all—definitely not someone who deserved any of this crazy attention.

"Even if that is part of the reason, so what? *You* know what you believe and what you want, and you believe that all homeless people should be treated with dignity and compassion, no matter what their race or background or social status. You want to break down barriers and stereo-types that have plagued the homeless for decades. Who cares *why* they're listening to you? You've got fifteen min-utes to make a difference and you're seizing it."

Negotiations were ongoing between *ELLE* and all the media outlets hoping for an exclusive. All I had to do was sit back, cross my fingers and secretly dream that Jon Stewart and Stephen Colbert had nothing more important to talk about than a homeless chick. Fat chance, but a girl could dream.

Of all the shows that had contacted me, *Ellen DeGeneres* was my first choice—she was awesome, and I was a big fan of hers. But nothing was that easy, it seemed. E. Jean explained to me that there were more factors than that. They had to put me on a show and a time that would get the story maximum exposure. They had already turned down the *Early Show* because the producers wanted to air the interview on a Saturday morning.

"Saturday morning! Ha! We don't *do* Saturday morning, darling. This is a major story," E. Jean sniffed. "Nobody's awake on Saturday morning." I had absolutely no idea about time slots, TV shows or media strategy, so I figured I'd take her word for it.

It turned out, in the end, that the *Today* show won out. I was excited, and also terrified. The producer informed me over the phone that I would be on the 10 o'clock hour with Kathie Lee Gifford and Hoda Kotb.

I assumed that they would fly Matt to New York with me. So did he. I mean, he was such a huge part of the story, and the reason that it had spread so far. Didn't these shows usually let you bring a guest with you, anyway? I'd be in New York City for less than twenty-four hours, but I was dying to run around with Matt and see the sights. I'd been there once, for a few days, with my family a couple of years back. They were visiting Bethel, the Jehovah's Witnesses headquarters in Brooklyn. But Matt had never been to the Big Apple. New York City was one of my favorite places on the planet, and I wanted so much to share that with him.

Nothing doing, though. They were only willing to fly me in, not Matt. My pleas and cajoling fell on deaf ears. Even E. Jean gave it a shot, to no avail. It frustrated me and depressed Matt.

"I don't want you to go alone. I should be with you. I'll miss you. I don't want to be without you."

"Baby, I'm trying. I can't convince them. I'll be back in thirty-six hours—you'll barely miss me. But if you want, I'll tell them no. Even if it makes everybody mad, I'll back out." I meant it, too. I hated seeing him depressed, or feeling as if I was leaving him behind. I didn't want him thinking I was getting an inflated ego, or that I'd ever step all over his feelings just to advance things for myself. We were a team, the *us* was what was most important to me.

"No, you can't do that. You need to go. It'll blow this story out of the water. But I'll miss you. And you shouldn't be talking to all those agents alone. I've heard about what they're like. They're vultures, and they'll try to take advantage of you. You're too sweet and innocent to fend them off."

I had resisted one earlier pitch from a literary agent to write a book because I was still anonymous at the time and I wasn't yet comfortable with the idea of telling my story. But now I'd had so many agents contact me since the story broke that I was losing count. My name was public now, after the Associated Press story, and my family was well aware of my blogger identity and the changes in my life. The bridges there had already been pretty much burned a few months earlier, when I introduced Molly to Matt via gtalk as my future husband. I had hoped that perhaps she would attend our wedding, be my bridesmaid. Despite everything, I wanted to somehow salvage a true "sisterly" bond before it was too late.

olly had grilled Matt as only a fundamentalist zealot knows how to grill. She was passive-aggressive and preachy, and I thought that, for the first time, he was realizing just how deep the nuttiness ran. I hadn't been exaggerating. He was polite to her, and chose his words carefully. She told him, as if she were trying to warn him, that "Brianna can be so *headstrong* and *independent*," as though those were dirty words.

"To tell you the truth, I'm glad she's marrying a man so much older than she is. She needs somebody who knows how to handle her and keep her in check." Horrified, Matt assured her that my independent spirit was just one of the many things that he loved about me, and that he looked forward to entering a marriage with me as his equal, and spending the rest of his life making me happy.

"Why do you love my sister?" Molly demanded.

"It's hard to explain love, isn't it? I guess the most honest answer I can give, even if it sounds corny, is that she makes my heart sing. She makes me glad I'm *me*."

Moll had expressed approval of this answer. Then she tried to convert him by offering to send him JW literature, a handbook on family life that would show him how to maintain his God-bestowed position as the head of the family in a proper Christian household.

"I'm not sure about *you,* but if I'm going to take *anybody's* advice on how to have a happy family life, it's going to be from the *creator* of life and the family unit—*Jehovah!*"

He hastily changed the subject, and after a little bit more chatter, told her he had to go, but it was so nice to speak with her, and she had no idea how much Brianna loved her, and how much it meant to me to have her attend the wedding.

After getting rid of her, he shuddered. "That woman is *never* allowed to be alone with our children."

I wholeheartedly agreed, although I felt sad saying it. Molly very (very) occasionally evidenced some cognitive dissonance that gave me hope for her escape from the cult. It was rare, but when it happened, it would amaze me. One day, just before she moved to Arizona, she had called me and, during what I had thought would be a routine phone conversation, brought up a childhood experience that even I hadn't thought of in many years.

"Bri, do you remember that one time, when we were playing in the pool, and we got in a fight and both called each other a bad word?"

"Um, not really."

"Mom made you drink soap."

"Oh. Right. Yeah, I remember that." How weird. I hadn't thought of that in years, and was surprised that Moll remembered it. I had been given the choice between eating an entire bar of soap or drinking an entire jumbo mug full of Dove dishwashing detergent. I chose the detergent, thinking it would be over quicker, since I wouldn't have to chew it. The actual consumption was over quicker, but

I then spent the next thirty-six hours retching and spitting up bubbles into a Tupperware container.

"Well, I never told you this, but after she made you drink the soap and sent you into the house, I knew it was going to be my turn, and I was afraid. But then she just gave me a stern lecture never to say dirty words again, and told me I could go back into the pool. I was confused; I didn't understand why we both said the exact same bad word, but you got the painful punishment, and suffered for days because of it. So I asked her why. She said that you and I were different people and learned in different ways. 'Brianna sometimes doesn't learn things just by being told. She questions things. She needs pain in order to learn, whereas a lecture is enough with you.'"

I barely realized it, but I had begun to tear up. My sister had never before acknowledged that there had been any difference in how we'd been treated. I had always known it was a survival mechanism—go with the flow, disappear into the wall, do what she was told, even if she knew it was wrong, and escape punishment. I tried not to fault her for it, but it stung all the same.

"It's something that really stuck with me," she continued. "Even then I knew that she was abusing you. I knew that drinking a mug of dish detergent might hurt or even kill you. And that day stuck with me up until now. *You've* already forgotten it because it was just another day that she hurt you, and it was something that you became used to. But *I* remembered it each and every time she hurt you, and I didn't speak up. I can never tell you how bad I feel about that, that I watched her hurt you for so long and never spoke out against it. You were the big sister who taught me to read when I was nine and all the teachers and Mom and Dad had given up, and even Hooked on Phonics didn't work because I got frustrated and threw it against the wall. You were the only one who kept trying, and in return I was afraid to say anything when I saw her beat you or humiliate you or tell you that you were worthless. Sometimes I even allowed myself to believe that it was true, that she was only hurting you because you were a worse child than me and you deserved it. But on that day I realized that it wasn't the case, because we'd done the exact same bad thing, and you were the only one who got a hateful punishment. For some reason, she hated you and hurt you and I let it happen. I hope you can forgive me."

Now *she* had started crying, and I wiped my eyes with the back of my hand and toughened up. Besides sadness, I felt an overwhelming wave of *relief.* So many years I'd worried that perhaps I was crazy or wrong, because nobody acknowledged or believed that what my mother was doing was abusive. Not even the people who lived with me could see it, I thought. And now I was hearing that Molly had known the whole time. I wasn't crazy. This was different than hearing it from my therapist. It was finally acknowledged by a firsthand eyewitness.

"Of course I forgive you. I understand why you did it. It wasn't your fault—you did what you had to do. You were a kid and you didn't want to get in trouble, too. Now, don't worry about it. We're adults and we're out of there and we're moving on to greater and better things."

It was the only time we'd ever spoken so honestly to each other, allowed ourselves to be that raw. It was also the only time I ever held out hope that perhaps she would one day figure out that she was too smart and strong for the cult she was raised in. I understood why, especially with how uncomfortable her conversion efforts made Matt and me, she would likely never be a significant part of our lives. And yet, I wished so much that there could be a Rewind button, that somehow we could one day be the kind of sisters who babysat each other's kids and braided each other's hair. That she could be the kind of sister I could recommend *Eternal Sunshine of the Spotless Mind* to, without her angrily calling me the next day, demanding to know how *dare* I tell her it's a good movie, when it had *seventeen F-words in it!* She knew, because she'd spent the entire movie counting. The subtext of the film itself was completely lost on her.

A few days after the introduction to Matt, a family friend who had secretly "faded" from the Jehovah's Witness cult, but was still considered in good standing among the congregation, contacted me. I got all the news on my family through this friend, since my parents didn't speak to me and my sister barely spoke to me. My friend filled me in.

As I'd suspected, Molly had wasted no time in circulating vicious rumors about the dastardly, *"worldly* man Brianna met on the internet!" Cue the gasps. Good Jehovah's Witnesses did *not* meet people on the internet. In fact, they were discouraged from using the internet much at all, as it was, they were assured, chock-full of apostates and demons. "This is nutty even for Brianna! I'm just so worried about her! She's really gone off the deep end this time. I think it's too late to save her, now." I was, it was agreed by all, a goner.

This was when I chose to cut ties with my sister completely, and spent the next several months reconciling the fact that I could never expect to have a reunion or a healthy relationship with my family. I was finally over the mental block against writing a book on my family and my childhood. I found it hard to care anymore. Once the Associated Press story went public, my friend told me, it got back to my family, who promptly spent hours reading my blog and denouncing me as an evil, demon-possessed apostate. I had blasphemed Jehovah and, for my own sake, I must be punished and shunned. Strangely, that didn't bother me as much as I might have anticipated. It was remarkably freeing. I no longer had to worry about pleasing somebody unpleasable.

I was still unsure as to whether I was *capable* of writing a book, of course, but Matt assured me that he believed in me, so I found myself believing in me, too. E. Jean and I had sifted through the agents and picked several of the biggest names to meet with immediately after the *Today* show. I'd be running nonstop while I was in New York. And now Matt was worried that I would be taken advantage of, without him there to take care of me. It was very sweet, but he needn't have worried.

"Matt, I'm not all that sweet and innocent. I can take care of myself. Besides, you know I'd never agree to anything without coming home and talking it over with you first."

"You mean that?"

"Of course I mean that, silly. You're going to be my husband."

"You know, I already consider myself your husband, and you my wife. We might as well be married already. I'm as committed to you and your happiness as any husband ever could be." It was true, I believed. He'd already long been referring to me as his "missus" and "wifey." Saccharine, perhaps, but I found it charming and lovable.

"I love you, and I consider myself your wife, too. So don't worry so much. Again, no decisions until we talk it out. Every decision from now on is together."

"I'm still going to miss you terribly. I always hated being

alone in the trailer without you, even when you were at work for eight hours and I knew I'd be seeing you again any minute."

"Take Fezzik for a few walks; chat with Sage. It's only thirty-six hours. Back before you realize I'm gone."

A couple of days before my flight to New York, a woman living in another of Thurman's trailers on his lot was evicted. She'd stayed for six months without paying a dime in rent, and Thurman had finally had it with her. He was a curmudgeonly man in his seventies, with a third-grade education and a penchant for fixing up old cars and complaining loudly in his twangy Southern drawl that everybody on this ranch wanted *something* from him, *all* the time, and he didn't have no *time* to be helpin' nobody no more; his time was *expensive,* dang it!

His gruff exterior hid a heart of gold, of course, but he hated for anybody to realize that, so he did his best to hide it. Matt went through stages of being mildly afraid of Thurman, but I liked him. Anybody who helped so many homeless people by allowing them to live cheaply on his lot, at the risk of getting in trouble with the law for it, was OK by me.

The woman trashed her trailer when she left (and broke into the communal coin-operated washer-and-dryer set that Thurman had brought in for everybody's laundry needs, I assume to abscond with $23 in quarters). Thurman spent a couple of days repairing the damage, putting in new carpet, and Matt and I were offered the option of switching over. It was a thrilling prospect—this trailer was slightly roomier, and even had running water in the shower and a better-working swamp cooler! Summer had been killing us; our mattress was soaked through with sweat, so we happily accepted. When we began to move our belongings over to the trailer, we realized that Sage had spent who knows how long decorating it to surprise us. She had made trips to the 99 Cent Store and brightened things up with hippie-esque drapes and pillowcases, a few sets of colorful plastic, reusable plates and cups, and a bathroom wall painted a cornea-searing tangerine orange. We were going to feel *cheerful,* dammit! We were both floored by the generosity and the time she had put into it all.

Matt hadn't showered in a couple of weeks. Sage kindly offered her bathroom for us to shower in, and I took her up on it—though I tried only to use it every three or four days, so as not to be a pest. Matt couldn't be convinced, though. He either couldn't or wouldn't explain to me why, but he wouldn't use her shower, or anybody else's but our own. When the trickle of water in the first trailer ground to a halt and showering became impossible, he simply went without. He was like a self-cleaning oven, greasy for so long that he eventually looked clean again, switching between the same three T-shirt and jean outfits he had brought with him from England. It didn't bother or repulse me, in any case—being homeless had lowered the standards for both of us, I guess, and a bit of grime was the last thing to worry about—but I couldn't understand why he wouldn't want to use a running hot shower fifty yards away from the trailer, and he got snippy when I asked him.

"I just *don't want to,* OK? Can't we just leave it at that?!" So I did. I figured he was experiencing the same feeling as I was, not wanting to accept charity or donations on my website, or maybe feeling uncomfortable borrowing somebody else's shower. It seemed to aggravate him when I pushed the issue, so I didn't. In any event, the overwhelming stench of livestock permeates the air in Norco and Riverside, so his being a bit stinky went relatively unnoticed. Our olfactory glands were obliterated. I shrugged it off, used Sage's shower and let Matt be.

Now, we had a working shower, though it didn't get hot water, only cold, and Matt was more than happy to use it as long as it belonged to us. Since it was a blazing-hot summer, the cold water didn't even matter yet—it was refreshing in the unbearable heat. We'd worry about hot water when winter rolled around, if it came to that. If we played our cards right, maybe we'd be out of here and on to upstate New York long before then.

The morning before my New York City flight, I got a cell phone call from CNN.

"Hi, this is Ted Rowlands."

"Um, wow, hi. I know who you are, yes."

They wanted to talk to me and Matt. I explained that I was packing to fly to New York very early the next morning, but I'd be back within two days, if we could schedule it for then.

"We were hoping to get something earlier. Can I come by now?"

"*Now?* Like, *right* now???"

"Well, yeah, maybe around 3:00?"

"Um, sure." I gave him directions to the lot and hung up. Then Matt and I called E. Jean to make sure it was OK, and wouldn't interfere with the *Today* show.

"Ted Rowlands? Do it!" she commanded. Okeydoke. Worked for us. Matt was particularly excited—to him, CNN was the American version of the BBC.

We spent two hours frantically tidying up the trailer and trying to make my greasy hair look presentable. Finally, I pulled it back into two fluffy buns and tossed on a news-boy cap and a vintage green cardigan. I looked as exhausted as I was, and makeup didn't seem to help, melting off in the heat as quickly as I put it on, so I eventually gave up. I was a mess, but it would have to do. All the media interviews and emails were beginning to blur together for me into one great big *Twilight Zone*-esque spiral. I could barely keep track of who I'd already spoken to, or what questions they'd asked. I was like a very sleepy shark for those few weeks; I only knew instinctively that I couldn't stop moving until it was all over.

Chapter Seventeen

The *Today* show had a car pick me up from the ranch and drive me to the airport. Upon landing in New York City, another car picked me up and drove me to my hotel, where E. Jean's niece (an *ELLE* intern), Lauren, met me. She ordered up room service and handed me a bag of clothes that *ELLE* had sent over.

In a panic, though, I realized that none of the clothes fit me. They were mainly slim, black sheath dresses from H&M. The labels bore my size, true, but it must have been one of those stores where the sizes run small, because I couldn't fit anything over my hips. I was used to wearing fun vintage clothing mined from thrift stores, and had never bought a designer brand in my life, so it hadn't occurred to me to worry about size differences. It was 11:00 at night and nothing was open.

"It's OK," Lauren assured me nervously. "We'll find… something. Somewhere. There's got to be *something* still open." She didn't look particularly convinced, but she was determined, I'll give her that.

Lauren and I frantically scoured the next several blocks

for an open store, *any* open store, that would carry something in my size, but it was futile. *I thought New York was the city that never sleeps!* I was due at the *Today* show studios in the morning around 9:00 for hair and makeup. There was no way that we'd find anything before then. Tears began to roll down my nose. Matt had started calling me Cinderella 2.0, but I didn't feel like a princess at all. I felt like a giant, fat whale of a slob who didn't belong on TV in New York. I wished I had brought some of my cuter vintage outfits from the trailer closet, but E. Jean said *ELLE* insisted that only they dress me for all TV appearances, from now on. It was clearly a great honor, and part of me had been looking forward to wearing girly, expensive stuff. I mean, when would I ever get the chance again, right? Vintage and affordable was my thing, and always would be, but the opportunity to dress up excited me.

Poor Lauren comforted me as I tried to smile and choke back my sobs. I had a gray vest and a pair of gray pants in my suitcase, in case I needed to change into something businesslike for the meetings with literary agents later. Perhaps *ELLE* had a loose silk shirt or something I could wear under the vest in the morning, I suggested.

"Don't worry. I'll figure it out. We'll get you something," she assured me before she left. "I'll be here at 8:30 a.m. with something for you to wear. I don't know what stores open that early, but I'll find something." She was so kind, and clearly the kind of intern who'd go the extra mile, or hundred miles. *ELLE* was lucky to have her, and I was so grateful for her help.

I should have tried to sleep, but I couldn't. I checked my laptop. Matt had emailed, saying that he missed me, and that Sage had lent him her phone, so that I could call him tonight if I wanted. It didn't matter how late, or if I woke him up. He missed me so much and needed to hear my voice.

So I called him, and we chatted for a couple of hours, Matt trying to assuage my nervousness, as I stared out the hotel window. St. Patrick's Cathedral was directly across the street, all dark, twisted, gothic stone spires and gargoyles. *He would have loved this.* I curled up in bed with the phone to my ear, wishing he was next to me to share it.

It was 8:45 a.m. and there was no sign of Lauren. I promptly began to freak out. I'd awakened early to shower, leaving my hair damp so they could style it at the *Today* studio. The studio was close, Lauren had said, only a couple of blocks away, but I had no idea where to go if she didn't show up at the hotel. She *had* said she was meeting me at the hotel, right? Oh my gosh, what if I'd misunderstood? What if she meant for me to meet her at the *Today* show set?

At 8:52 a.m., the concierge called my room, and asked if I would like to have a Miss Lauren Switzer buzzed up, Miss Karp?

Miss Karp. Tee-hee.

Lauren burst into the room with two shopping bags.

"I'm sorry I'm late! I found a department store that opens at 7:30. Here, try these on!" She flung dresses at me, and we settled on one with a vintage-esque feel to it; a black bodice with a flared tulip skirt. It was a bit shorter than I generally went, and I would need stockings, she decided. She thrust a pair of sharp, pointy stilettos at me. It wasn't the kind of heel I normally wore; I preferred retro, round-toed and peep toe, pinup-esque pumps. But this was no time to be picky! I slipped them on, and we dashed out the door. She would drop me at the *Today* show studio and then run out to a convenience store and grab some stockings.

The studio guard let us in, and pointed us toward the waiting room. I recognized E. Jean immediately. She didn't look nervous at all, waiting comfortably on a couch for me. She jumped up and we hugged, and she told me loudly how *fabulous* it was to meet me. She was every inch exactly what you'd expect. Somewhat wryly, I noticed that she had a perfect body and far more energy than me, even in her sixties. I tried to radiate confidence and enthusiasm; I wanted so much to gain her respect. Mostly, though, I think I just looked scared out of my wits and prepared to dive under the couch.

E. Jean and the producer sat me down and did their best to calm my nerves, running through the list of expected interview questions. I forced myself to pry my wringing hands apart and place them in my lap. *Scared? Me? Nah. Totally cool.* The CNN interview hadn't been as scary as I'd thought it would be, but that was because it was on my own turf, with nobody watching except Matt, and that had actually helped because he relaxed me and put me at ease. This was different, though. I was about to go out there live in front of millions of people. There was no editing to save me. No backsies. No rephrasing. Just two and a half minutes to try to fit in anything and everything about my story and about homelessness. No problem, right?

"Now," the producer explained, "these are the interview questions that we gave them to ask. But if you've ever watched the show before, you'll know that they, er, don't always stay on topic. Kathie Lee, especially, will sometimes go off and do or say her own thing. So don't be nervous, and if she asks a question we didn't go over with you, don't panic. Just try to keep on topic and do your best to steer it back to the questions we've just talked about. OK? OK. You'll do fine. And you've got E. Jean out there with you. She's an old pro at this."

Hair and makeup whipped me and E. Jean into shape. I noticed in the mirror that there was another waiting guest who kept staring at me. It was a little unnerving. I wondered if I maybe had a booger hanging out of my nose or something. Matt would later tell me that he was a famous tennis player, John McEnroe. I didn't know him, since I didn't really follow tennis. Plus, I didn't have my glasses on, so my vision was blurry. I kept trying to decide if he might be Billy Bob Thornton.

Lauren came back with three pairs of stockings in varying shades. E. Jean picked black, and I sprinted to the restroom to put them on. Then the three of us, E. Jean, Lauren and I, were ushered up some stairs and down a corridor. I could hear Kathie Lee and Hoda interviewing some star chef woman, and oh my God, Al Roker just hurried past me in the corridor! Al Roker just *smiled* at me! My life is complete. I can die happy.

We all stood watching as the cooking segment wrapped up, and the studio went to commercial. I now had five or six minutes before airtime. A bunch of techs jumped me and hooked me and E. Jean up to microphones, leading us to our chairs. Lauren stood back in the corner to watch the interview. Kathie Lee and Hoda came over and shook hands with us, settling into their chairs. We tried to make polite "Good morning, nice to meet you, how are you?" chitchat for the remaining few minutes.

I was breathing deeply to calm myself. This would all be fine. It was two and a half minutes and then it would be over, barely a blip in my life. As long as I didn't fuck up and say anything offensive on TV. Then, of course, I could never live it down. I tried to ignore the cameras pointing at me from every direction.

"Sixty seconds, ladies!" cried a tech.

Kathie Lee coolly nodded, then, I suppose attempting to make chitchat while waiting, turned her head and asked me, "So, do you really count as homeless? I mean, you live in a trailer and all. So do you really believe that you qualify?"

Everybody was looking at me, and they were counting down forty-five seconds. I launched, as smoothly as I could, into the automatic response that I gave whenever somebody emailed me to ask me this same question. It was a fair enough question, I supposed, but I was a bit unnerved, trying to answer it only moments before a live interview. I don't know if my voice shook audibly, but it sure felt like it to me.

"That's a common misconception. In fact, the legal definition of *homelessness* covers all people without a home, including vehicle dwellers and couch-surfers. Obviously, there are different levels of homelessness, and I've been very lucky to have a lot of advantages, but I believe it's important to debunk such stereotypes and misperceptions about what it means to be homeless." Or something to that effect. For all I know, that may have been what I *tried* to say, but it came out sounding like the "wah-wah-wah-wah-wah-wah" teacher in the *Peanuts* cartoons.

Fifteen seconds.

E. Jean patted my shoulder.

"Ready?"

"Ready."

5...4...3...

Hoda and Kathie Lee launched into their intro, reading off the teleprompter, and I tried my best to smile and refrain from hyperventilating. I really don't remember much of what was said. E. Jean did her share of the talking, of course, which I was grateful for, and I'm pretty sure that they asked me how I colored my hair while homeless. I gritted my teeth; I had hoped to focus on the more serious issues of homeless stereotypes and misperceptions and myths, and how Matt and I were hoping to combat them. But I'm sure to them this was pretty much a fluff piece, one of the multitude of "filler" human interest stories that they see every day, so they wanted to know about how a person dyes her hair and meets boys while homeless. In any event, as far as I can tell, they were very friendly and did their best to put me at ease.

I recounted a story about Mother's Day 2009, when I had snuck a bottle of hair dye into the deserted Planet Fitness gym bathroom and crouched in the corner of the handicapped stall, allowing the harsh chemicals of the color to set as I pawed through my copy of Kyria Abrahams's *I'm Perfect, You're Doomed: Tales from a Jehovah's Witness Upbringing* and holding my breath, squirming, when two lone women wandered through the bathroom and wondered aloud, "What's that smell?" referring to the noxious fumes.

It was a short segment, so there wasn't much time for anything else besides that. Before I knew it, it was over, they were pulling the microphone off me, and Kathie Lee was off her chair and headed down to a different studio for the next segment. Hoda stopped to shake my hand warmly and wish me good luck, then she, too, was gone. The techs amiably offered to snap photos of me, E. Jean and Lauren on set with Lauren's camera.

We headed back to the waiting room for our purses, and everyone there, watching the mounted TVs airing the show in progress, collectively looked up at me and burst into applause. My eyes filled with grateful tears. I didn't feel that I deserved anything of the sort, but it was such a kindly gesture. I turned red, ducked my head and tried to disappear into the wall. John McEnroe was on the TV screen above me, demonstrating Wii Fit Tennis with Kathie Lee and Hoda, who seemed to be having trouble grasping the concept.

"Come on, come on, hurry up!" John McEnroe prodded them irritably. "We don't have time to mess around. You've got another homeless blogger segment to do after this!"

Lauren had to get to work at *ELLE,* and E. Jean and I had back-to-back meetings with agents to get to. She pulled me out into the street and we bolted for a few blocks before I realized that I'd never make it in these shoes. I was used to walking some distance in heels, but these pointy toes were killing me, and I hadn't broken them in. I stopped, yanked them off, and took to the concrete in my laddering stockings. To hell with propriety. If we were ever going to make it on time, I needed my feet to be flat.

I noted that E. Jean slipped dollar bills to all the homeless people we passed on the streets, including a man surrounded by seven kittens. It was very sweet of her, I thought. A nice touch.

Matt was waiting up for my return from Ontario airport. It was nearly midnight, and he looked haggard, as though he'd barely slept since I left. He clung to me and said, "I thought I'd die without you."

"Ha. See? Nothing to it. Thirty-six hours. I'm back."

"The CNN interview aired around the same time as the *Today* show interview. It's been playing throughout the day. The traffic has been massive. *The Girl's Guide to Homelessness* was absolutely crushed by the traffic. Your server was down for a few hours. You were wonderful. I love you."

"I love you, too. I missed you. Let's go to bed. We can talk about everything that happened in the morning. I'm not even going to look at my email inbox. I don't want to know."

Chapter Eighteen

CNN invited me to be on again, this time on a segment called Young People Rock, with Nicole Lapin. That was in LA, so Matt could come, though he still didn't want to be on TV, no matter how much I coaxed.

I continued posting blogs, doing my internship, doing phone and email interviews and answering emails. A couple of days later, a Brazilian TV news show called and invited to fly me back to New York City for another segment. I was willing to do it, if they'd fly Matt there, too, but they demurred, so I turned it down. We didn't have much longer before he had to fly back to Scotland, and I wanted to spend every possible moment with him. I could tell that he was still a bit dejected about my trip to New York without him, even if he wasn't talking about it. I didn't want to give him anything else to take to heart.

Walmart finally returned my calls and emails for the first time, after an entire month of ignoring my plight. They swore up and down that signs had been posted the day prior to towing. They hadn't. There was no sign on my trailer. If there had been, I'd probably have moved it for a day or two to Sam's Club, as I had before. Besides, I pressed, *their own store manager* told me to ignore any MOVE YOUR TRAILER OR BE TOWED signs. I gave them her name again. The corporate guy said he'd call me right back.

Ten minutes later, we were on the phone again. "I'm sorry, Miss Karp, but there's simply nothing we can do. I apologize for any inconvenience. It's nothing personal. But it's not our fault or our responsibility."

I began to sob angrily.

"Look, don't tell me you're 'sorry for the inconvenience.' Maybe it's not personal to *you*. But it's personal to *me*. *You're* not the one who's just lost everything she owns in the world—I am. So save your apologies for somebody who cares!" I hung up the phone.

Meanwhile, two friends of mine were calling Walmart corporate right about then. One was Tommy Christopher, a Mediaite reporter I'd done an interview with, and who'd apparently been impressed enough with me to take it upon himself to call and see what he could do. He told them to do a quick internet search of my name, and said that he could hear the line grow silent as they realized that they had just stepped into more of a PR nightmare than they'd realized.

The other friend was Vicki Day, a follower of mine on Twitter who lived in London. I hadn't realized it, but Vicki was a big shot in London, and ran her own PR company. I just thought of her as one of those nice people who followed my blog. But she knew the head of Asda (Walmart's UK branch), and she was throwing all her weight into shaming him into calling up HQ and pulling some strings.

A few hours later, Walmart corporate called back and

told me that I could meet one of their managers at the impound lot the next day. He would bring the money to get my truck and trailer out. Over the month that it took to get any response from Walmart, the fee had ballooned to $3,500. Matt and I had no way of paying that fine, even early on, after my car had broken down. All our cushion money had gone into fixing it, so that I could keep going to job interviews. I was overjoyed.

Twenty-four hours later, I had the Dodge Ram and my trailer back. Thurman offered to buy it from me for $2,000, so that he could rent it out to more homeless people. I happily accepted, and moved my belongings out of it and into a storage shed. The same day, I received a call from a company I'd interviewed with a few months earlier. They offered me the job.

The position was as executive assistant and office manager at a motorcycle company. The company hadn't known that I was homeless when they hired me, and I did my best to keep it that way. I'd gotten the job on my own merits, and I was proud of that. It wasn't very high-paying at all; in fact, they paid far lower than industry standard. But I hoped that it would look good on my résumé, and any work was good work, right?

Unfortunately, it was also by far the most hellish place I'd ever worked. Though I didn't know about all of the staff hanky-panky going on with the owner at the time, I did stumble across a litany of labor law violations, health code violations, employee abuse, discrimination, harassment and illegal/shady/unethical financial manipulations. As I was hired to facilitate Human Resources, payroll and all the other business functions, I called attention to all these issues and was promptly fired for whistle-blowing (though I threatened to report them, and my termination notice was hastily exchanged for layoff paperwork). Matt was actually glad that I got out of there. The round-trip commute to and from work every day totaled over one hundred miles in rush-hour traffic, and they often required excessive—and illegal—amounts of overtime and he was barely seeing me anymore.

It didn't end up mattering much one way or the other. The day after I was fired, I was offered a book deal, and Matt and I decided to accept it.

I'd stayed up long nights with Matt agonizing over the book proposal and sample chapters. I begged him to help me, especially with the marketing and technical stuff, since he was so much more attuned to the analytical side of his brain than I was, but he insisted it had to come from me, and that I'd feel much better about myself for doing it on my own. He'd proofread it for me and give me some ideas and input, but it was important that it come from my own heart.

At one point, I remember drifting off as I typed, and awakening to Matt yelling at me. I was completely confused. I couldn't understand why he was angry. Matt never yelled at me. I *hated* people yelling at me—it sent me into freakout mode. In my mind, calm discussion was always better than angry confrontation. I sat up, wrapped my arms around my knees and reflexively started screaming back. *What's wrong? What did I do? Why are you yelling at me?*

He was startled. He'd seen that I was asleep and had tried to take the laptop from my hands and tuck me in, and then I'd started picking a fight with him, he said. He told me that my eyes were open and that I seemed completely lucid and awake, if a bit drowsy. He said I was acting nasty,

as he'd never seen me acting before, and I had even called
him names and insulted him. He had no idea why I had
suddenly started fighting with him, and his gut reaction
was to fight back.

I was horrified. I remembered none of it. It wasn't the
first time I'd held an entire conversation in my sleep with
a boyfriend. Dennis had related a similar experience to
me, when he hadn't realized I was still sleeping for a good
twenty minutes or so, until I completely stopped making
sense. Brandon, too, who occasionally let me crash at his
place for a movie and a change of scenery when both of his
roommates were out of town, once swore up and down
that I'd conversed with him at length, when I was actually conked out on his couch and blissfully unaware. I kept
shaking my head, trying to comprehend, and Matt eventually realized that I wasn't messing around: I had absolutely
no recollection of anything he was talking about. We held
each other and both of us trembled at the thought that it
could be so easy to fuck up a good thing over a little mis-
understanding. I thought, meanwhile, that maybe I should
go back to therapy. I'd been told that I had sleepwalked as
a child, and my mom even said that she heard me speaking
in French in my sleep in high school, when I had taken
French class, but this was an altogether different kind of
problem. I didn't want it to ever happen again.

It was time for Matt to go back to Scotland. The farewell
at the airport went tearfully, much as before, except that
this time I knew we'd be apart for much longer, and that
things would, one way or another, be irreversibly changed
by the time we saw each other again. There would be a
baby. I went back to the ranch and pressed my nose to the
grindstone in anticipation of the event, trying to put on

a happy face and subjugate my loneliness and fear; bury it beneath a smile and layers of bravado and confidence I couldn't yet feel.

Matt kept me well informed on the baby front. He and Lori went to another scan together. While he'd been in California, she'd somehow fallen in her kitchen and knocked out several teeth, so now she was wandering around with a creepy, gap-toothed grin, he said. It was also clear that she'd completely disregarded the doctor's instructions to put on weight. She had only gotten scrawnier and scrawnier. She was at a dangerously unhealthy weight, and the doctor told her that by no means could she be allowed to give birth naturally. They scheduled a C-section for her in Aberdeen on October 28, nearly a month premature. It was good that we'd decided to fly Matt home much earlier than the anticipated due date. Within weeks, the child would arrive.

He was frightened beyond belief, and it fell to me to give the pep talks, even if peppy was not what I was feeling. I was just as afraid as he was.

On the evening of October 27, I stayed up all night talking Matt through his bus trip to the hospital in Aberdeen. He was a wreck, and my heart broke for him. I would have given anything to be there for him, but all I could do was hope that my voice on the phone line would make a difference.

I was the first (and only, to my knowledge) person he called, an hour after the birth. It was a baby girl. *I wanted my first child to be a baby girl, and she beat me to it.* I tried not to get emotional. I was happy for him—really I was. I told him over and over again how proud I was of him. He sent me her first picture and her first video, shot on his camera phone. I watched the video over and over again. She was indeed beautiful, and obviously Matt's daughter. She looked exactly like him. True to my prediction, he was madly in love with her the moment she arrived.

"See? What were you so worried about, honey?"

"I don't even know anymore. You were right. She's absolutely perfect. I love her, and I love you."

Prior to the birth, Matt told Lori that Kelsey was a name that he really loved for a girl. It was his grandmother's name, he explained to me. He hoped he could honor her in this way. If it was a boy, he wanted it to be named after his favorite grandfather, John, with whom he'd been incredibly close. Lori had never come up with any ideas for names, he told me, so they named the baby Kelsey Barnes.

Lori had to recover from her C-section, and she wouldn't be able to take the baby home to Peterhead, Matt explained to me, since her stepfather's house was not fit for a child. He brought the baby home with him from the hospital a few days later. Lori only took the bus to visit him and Kelsey every few weeks, he told me.

In the UK, Social Services checks up on every newborn baby at its home for the first several months of its life. Lori, he told me, had listed her home address as *his,* so that they would do all the checkups at his home. I wasn't very fond of this idea.

"You mean, as far as they're concerned, you two live together. You're a couple."

"Well, I never really thought of it that way, but I suppose so, yes." I was silent. "Come on, Bri, this isn't for me. All three of us know the truth. She visits Kelsey, but she will never stay overnight in this flat, I promise you. It's just that if they see where she lives, they may take Kelsey away." I guess I did understand, but I was still protective. I didn't want to hate Lori, but in some corner of myself, I did. She had complicated our lives beyond belief, made demands upon Matt that had cost *me* exorbitant amounts of money, and put me in the position of having to make concession after concession in order to be a supportive wife to Matt. Now, in a manner of speaking, she was getting her way on another point—she was his girlfriend, too, if only on paper.

"How are you going to explain Lori's complete absence from your flat every time they do a welfare check?"

"Out at the store? Visiting family? Don't worry. They only do these checks for a little while. Besides, soon it *will* be her flat. I'm coming home to you for Christmas, right? I figured we'd get married on this next trip out…if you like. Then I can sign the flat over to her and she can move in with Kelsey."

All my fears were forgotten. I was ecstatic.

"Yes, *of course* I like, baby! Oh my gosh, I love you so much! I didn't realize it would be so soon! Let's do it."

"We will. I just need to keep her happy until next week. That's when we go down to the registrar's office and put both our names on Kelsey's birth certificate. If she only puts her own name on the certificate, then I don't have parental rights unless I go to court for them. But if we do it *together,* then she's automatically given me equal parental rights. So then, I won't even have to have her fill out that form you gave me."

"You still should, you know. Just because you have equal rights on the birth certificate doesn't prove the custody arrangements you agreed on for Kelsey—equal time in the United States and the UK, and once she's old enough for school, the school year in one country, vacations and holidays in the other."

"We'll worry about that afterwards. I need to keep her happy until my name is on that certificate. Then you and I are getting married and building our life together."

In a mere couple of months, I would be a wife, and there was so much for me to accomplish before then. I'd better get started.

Matt did indeed get his name on the birth certificate, and continued to care for Kelsey in the following months. He was a lot more exhausted than usual, obviously, with a new baby in the house. We still spoke over gtalk nearly every day, but our chats were constantly interrupted.

"Uh-oh...we have company! She's coming around."

You may think that this irritated me, but I wasn't usually bothered. If anything, it made me love him all the more, seeing how much he clearly adored his daughter. If I was going to eventually take on parenting (and stepparenting), I *wanted* my husband to be an excellent and attentive parent, and Matt was. Lori still didn't come around to visit her very much, he told me, so he was mostly on his own, and the rest of Lori's family had never met the baby once, or even expressed any interest in seeing her. They hadn't even come to the hospital when the baby was born, which made me feel a bit sorry for Lori—something I hadn't expected.

He often joked about getting Kelsey a passport, tucking her under his arm, and "making a run for it" to California with her. Lori would barely notice, he said. I would laugh and talk him out of it.

"I'm quite sure she would notice and mind very much if

you kidnapped her daughter, Matt. Besides, then you'd be leaving me with all the diaper changing, wouldn't you?"

"Well, that would finally be my chance to sleep."

"Ah, yes, there is that."

Right around this time, Matt seemed to begin developing unnerving fears about my becoming a public figure. It was a complete role reversal: I was gradually becoming more comfortable with the decision to ditch anonymity, and he was, seemingly out of nowhere, obsessing over whether he would be able to keep meeting my needs, or whether I would eventually leave him.

"Everyone leaves me," he would insist. "You'll leave me, too. What if I'm not able to support you, to take care of you? All you've ever done for me is be the one person in my life who's always there for me. What if I can't even do the same for you?"

I had no intention of going anywhere, and had never considered that there was any possibility under the sun he was anything other than exactly what I needed, and said so. I couldn't understand why this was coming out of the blue. He was working himself into an anguished lather.

"You just don't understand, Bri. No matter how much you say that it doesn't bother you, it's going to bother *me* from now on. You're going to leave me. The thought's in my head now and I'll just have to deal with it forever...."

Finally, it dawned on me. "Matt...you've been taking your medication, right?"

Pause.

"Sweetie?"

"I ran out the last week of my trip in California. I haven't gotten around to going to the doctor and picking up more yet."

I calculated quickly in my head. He'd been off his medication for *months*. What did this mean? I knew how my
mom acted off medication; she'd never been on it. But I
didn't know exactly what it meant for Matt. He'd once
told me that it was a place he never wanted to go back to.
He'd described his behavior off the meds as completely
irrational—outbursts of frustration or tantrums. Plus, *sans*
meds, he had trouble sleeping, and could be up for days,
no matter how tired he was, and he experienced terrible
memory problems.

"My wife could ask me to pick up milk from the store,
I'd say yes, and then, later that evening, I'd swear up and
down that the conversation had never taken place."

"So you'd forget to pick up milk? *That's* what would
cause huge arguments between you and your wife? You
didn't have anything more important to fight about? You
couldn't just laugh it off and one of you go get the milk?"

"Well, sort of. It's not just that I'd forget, but that instead of just realizing I'd forgotten, I'd never remember it
happening in the first place."

Forgetting the milk became an "in joke" between us, a
sort of code phrase for a massive overreaction to a petty
mistake. I understood what he was driving at, though. But
the problem was, he'd only *told* me about all this; I'd never
had to witness it myself, so it never had the opportunity to
become a deal breaker between us.

I understood mental illness, I figured. I'd known my fair
share of people who grappled with it. I also knew, from
firsthand experience, that it's perfectly possible and accept-
able to love someone with a mental illness. And Matt had
never seemed the type to lapse. He very much liked who
he was on medication, he had remained on it since he was
diagnosed and he had constantly claimed he didn't want to

return to the abject misery of being off it. I was always so proud of his bravery in admitting it up front; of baring the darkest side of himself to me and trusting me not to run.

"Besides," he continued, "you know it regulates my sleep schedule, and I'm watching Kelsey. I need to be up all the time! I can't allow myself to sleep for the normal eight hours anymore."

We just needed to figure something out for a couple more months. When we were married, we could share child-care duties during his visitation with Kelsey, and then he could get his full eight hours' sleep. I begged him to see the doctor, he promised to and the crisis was averted. He was still terrified, though, and nothing I could say soothed him.

"Maybe I'd better not talk to you about it. It'll just make you worry more. It's probably something I just need to deal with on my own. It's not your fault."

I was hurt. The last thing I wanted him to do was feel as if he had to internalize any grief or pain or fear he was feeling. We'd always been all about being completely open and honest with each other. And of course I understood irrational terror. *Remember those demons I'm still terrified of?*

"You know that I always want you to be able to talk about things with me, and this is important. I don't want this to be something that affects our relationship later, down the road. Please keep on talking to me about it. I'll keep reassuring you."

He went back to having upbeat chats with me from then on. Every time I asked him about his fears, he'd just say that they were still there, and that he was doing his best to overcome them, and no, he didn't feel like talking about it any more. I was happy that at least he was being honest with me. I'd reassure him that I loved him and would always be there for him, and he'd change the subject. "Hey, have you decided whether you're going to go by 'Brianna Karp' or 'Brianna Barnes?'"

"*Barnes,* of course."

"Aw, baby, really? Even though most of the world knows you as Brianna Karp?"

"Yup. I want nothing more than to take your last name. Who *wouldn't* want to be a Barnes instead of a Karp? Much more sophisticated!"

"I'm so glad. That's my girl."

"…even though Brianna Barnes kind of sounds like a porn name."

"What?! It does not!"

"Yes, it does. Haven't you ever heard of Brianna Banks?"

"Brianna Barnes is a lovely name. You'll only ever be *my* porn starlet."

Chapter Nineteen

While Matt learned to diaper a baby, back in the trailer I was dealing with an invasion of mice, spiders the size of a very small fist and giant crane flies—which Sage referred to as "mosquito eaters." Despite her assurances that they were completely harmless, they freaked me out by swooping around my face, and I would dart from one end of the trailer to the other, screaming as if Satan and his demons themselves were after me. Goddammit, if I had to deal with giant pests, I wanted them to be in the attic of my own nice old Victorian house. Here in the trailer, it was just adding insult to injury.

Right around now, Matt and I decided to make his daughter's birth public. We knew that we'd have to at some point, but he worried about losing his crew's respect, or the implication that perhaps he had cheated on me, or on Lori *with* me.

Also, not even his own family knew about the baby, or about me. He had been fully estranged from his father for a long time, and there was no hope of reconciliation there. His brothers and sisters lived all over the world, and weren't in touch. None of his family had ever even known that he'd been homeless. He still loved his mother, although they hadn't spoken for a couple of years, since he had been with his first wife. She was, he feared, in an abusive relationship with her second husband, and he felt guilty about that, as though he had abandoned her. He worried about his mother often, and talked about eventually calling her up or writing her a letter to let her know he was OK. I encouraged him to do it. He became deeply sad whenever he thought of her.

"But what am I supposed to do, Bri? Walk in there with you and Kelsey, and say, 'Hi, Mom. This is my wife, and this is my baby…from some *other* woman, *not* my wife?'"

"She loves you. Don't you think she'd understand that these things happen?" I was hurt. Was he *ashamed* of me?

"I'm not ashamed of you. I'm ashamed of *me*. I want her to see that I've succeeded, that I've done something right. Maybe I'll contact her later. Soon. But later. Once we're married."

I'd come to understand, by this point, that you just couldn't push Matt, so I let it go. I was getting good at letting things go.

He felt too embarrassed to write up his daughter's birth announcement for Homeless Tales on his own. He thought perhaps it would sound better coming from me. Perhaps if I wrote it, his crew would realize that everything was hunky-dory, I was onboard with the baby and nobody had cheated on anybody. So I wrote something up, he approved it and made a couple of minor alterations and additions of his own, and it was published on both of our websites. I tried to write it as delicately as possible, to take some of the inevitable heat and focus off Matt.

. . .

I was tight on funds since being laid off again, though I was picking up temp work. If I was careful budgeting my paychecks, perhaps I could bring Matt out to California for Christmas, as we'd planned, but it would be iffy from there, and we'd probably have to stay in the trailer. There would be no money for presents *and* a hotel or a similar rental for a couple of days over the holiday, especially if we wanted to eat. Matt didn't want to spend Christmas in a trailer. It would depress him, he said. He was already willing to leave his daughter with Lori for her first Christmas, so that he could come out here and marry me, but it was just too much for me to expect him to spend Christmas in the trailer *and* be away from his daughter. He wanted to rent a cabin in the mountains or something, to feel like it was a real holiday. I knew how important Christmas was to him—it was his favorite holiday and had always held a special meaning for him; it represented memories of better times for his family, in his childhood.

Granted, I'd never celebrated a Christmas before (my last attempt had, after all, resulted in Dennis breaking up with me two days before), so I didn't really comprehend the full magnitude of what was, after all, just another day. I mean, we were both atheists, and while there was definitely something to be said for tradition, and I *wanted* my first Christmas to be with Matt, I supposed I shouldn't make it an issue. I wouldn't be able to afford to give him a fairy-tale cabin in the snow for Christmas, so if he needed to spend it with Kelsey, then he should.

We agreed that he should stay in Scotland and celebrate with Kelsey while I continued to save up until we could afford to bring him back to California. I would have next year, and every year for the rest of our lives, after all.

I set out putting the extra temp money to good use instead, choosing Matt's Christmas presents carefully. For someone who was never allowed to celebrate birthdays or holidays, I've always prided myself on giving meaningful gifts.

We'd visited the Circle, a historic circular block lined with antiques shops and ice cream parlors, in the city of Orange on the second day of his very first visit. I wanted to show him something quaint and beautiful and quintessentially American apple pie, besides a Walmart. We'd spent hours wandering through the antiques shops, pointing out the things we'd buy to furnish our fixer-upper one day, when we'd have no worries in the world, least of all about money. He loved anything Georgian, and I adored Victorian stuff, but not fussy Victorian. I loved overstuffed, tufted leather gentleman's club chairs, dark woods like mahogany and cherry, chandeliers and rich, deep colors. We zeroed in on all the same things, and he could tell just by looking at a piece whether it was truly of the era, or a reproduction.

He pressed his palms and nose against a glass case, like a little boy, and homed in on a first edition of Jules Verne's *20,000 Leagues Under the Sea*. He dreamed of owning his own library, as did I, but he didn't want the books to read. That was for me. No, he wanted a wall of only beautiful, antique, leather-bound, gold-embossed books. He wanted them so that he could feel like a classy, well-bred, rich gentleman. He wanted that first edition simply to own it, to smell its ancient pages and binding and know that he was, in a very small way, part of something old and grand, from a more nostalgic time and place, if not a better one.

"I'll buy you that book, one day!" I insisted. He laughed at my ridiculousness—that book may as well have been the moon—but I repeated my assertion earnestly. And then we wrapped our arms around each others' waists and continued up the block, speculating in our most silly manner on the grand Victorian carriage we'd own one day, with a hefty Shire draft horse to pull it, and we'd let Matt drive it around in a top hat and a monocle, insisting that everyone in upstate New York address him by the title of "Lord Barnes," as though he were a Duke or something. And he'd have a grand study that looked like something out of *From Hell,* the Jack the Ripper movie, with a cabinet of curiosities and a biology lab and exotic old instruments. I'd have a phonograph with a huge morning glory horn and a four-poster canopy bed, and an art deco vanity with a giant round mirror and guilloche hairbrushes and empty perfume bottles, and a window seat with long, green velvet curtains, where the sun spread over the bench like butter. I'd play the piano badly and he'd sit in his study full of old books without reading them, and bouncing Kelsey on his knee. It would be perfect, even if it was all a dream for now. We had agreed together, it was a perfect day.

"We're going to be New Yawkuhs, baby!" I'd squeal, intentionally mispronouncing the word to sound like I had a tough New York accent.

"New Yokers." He failed miserably at the accent.

"No, honey. You sound more like a Southerner. New Yawk. *Yawwwk!*"

"New Yoke."

We collapsed into gales of laughter every time we did this bit. It never got old.

"Yawk."

"Yoke."

I went back to Orange and, with a lot of haggling, bought that book. I also got us a *huge* 110-year-old art nouveau photo album, all bound in leather and brass, with softly browning pages and gilt edges. We'd talked about starting a scrapbook of our life together, and I figured that now was a good time to start.

Lastly, I picked out an engagement ring for *him*. I'd told him, back when he slipped mine on my finger, that I wanted to.

"I don't get why the woman has all the fun and gets all the tokens of eternal love and affection. I want *you* to have one, too." He thought it was the sweetest thing ever, and told me that it was just another thing he loved about me. Never before had he been with a woman who would have even considered that.

He already had a signet ring that his mother had given him ages ago, upon his graduation. I'd asked him if he wanted to pick out his own engagement ring, but he asked me to surprise him. The only guidelines that he offered me were that it be unique, and preferably a Georgian antique.

It took ages for me to find. The Georgians weren't as big on rings as the later Victorians and Edwardians, especially not rings made of precious metals. In the Georgian era, I learned, those sorts of rings were liable to get you mugged and to get your throat cut. But finally, after an excruciating search, I found it. It suited Matt and his taste to a tee.

The ring dated to the 1820s. It was gold with a dark patina and an oval bloodstone, a deep green stone flecked with shimmering bits of red. Either side of the shank boasted two serpents, twisted into figure eights that called to mind the infinity symbol. Serpents, I learned in my research, were Georgian-era symbols of eternal love and commitment. In other cultures, they also represented fertility and wisdom. The bloodstone, on the other hand, was used in healing and protection by the ancient Egyptians, Aztecs and Greeks. It used to be the birthstone for both March and December (our birth months). It is also known as the "Stone of Courage" and supposedly revitalizes love, relationships and friendships. This was Matt's ring, all right. Symbology was important to the Georgians. He'd love it.

Right around this time, a neighbor also held a garage sale. Included among the boxes of random junk were hundreds of her granddaughter's baby clothes. I bought as many of the cute ones as I could afford. Some still had tags on them; some had clearly only been worn once or twice. I stocked up on outfits in sizes ranging from newborn to two years old. Matt would be putting a lot of his money into child support for Lori, who had never had a job in her life and would, he assured me, be living the rest of her life in a council flat and receiving benefits. I was sure that these clothes would come in very handy. Perhaps Lori would even see them as a peace offering. Over gtalk that night, I listed all the new clothes to him and told him I would try to get them shipped over in time for Christmas. He was excited about the clothes, sad that we wouldn't be together for Christmas, but at least he'd get to be with Kelsey. We'd waited this long to be married, though, and we could hold out a smidge or two longer. All the waiting and hassle would be worth it.

I'd noticed, a few months earlier, that I'd been putting on a lot of weight, and that my skin, already not in the greatest state, had erupted into the worst series of acne breakouts I'd ever had. I was also tired and listless a lot, and when I wasn't doing temp work, I stayed in bed sleeping for up to eighteen hours at a time—instead of sending out résumés for permanent jobs, as I should have been doing. I just didn't want to move. Half the time, I felt too exhausted to drive back to Riverside from my temp job in Irvine. At one point, I pulled off the road into a post office parking lot, crawled into the back of my car and slept for hours until I felt as if I could make it home without veering off the road.

I figured it was a residual effect of the crummy diet I'd been on for nearly a year. Living off affordable stuff like ramen noodles and fast food had taken its toll. I had been slowly gaining weight over my year of homelessness, but now my weight was skyrocketing up. I was bloating all over, and my breasts and thighs and stomach were beginning to boast the beginning of stretch marks. Even the bones in my nose felt as if they were spreading across my face—I felt paranoid and gross. I cut out coffee, sweets and burgers altogether, and forced myself to drag my ass to Costco, stocking up on every type of fruit and vegetable I could fit into my shopping cart, along with cartons and cartons of fruit juice and water. Surely, this would help.

But as the months floated by in a quasi-haze, I was still putting on weight, and I was still exhausted. None of it made sense.

My belly, in particular, was expanding, and it didn't feel squishy and wobbly like fat, but hard and distended. I laid flat on my back in bed one night, staring down at it. Could I have cancer of the belly? Was there even such a thing as cancer of the belly? I pressed my finger into it as hard as possible. It felt numb. Numb and hard. A terrifying thought flashed across my mind, but I pushed it out as fast as I could. Surely I couldn't be. I had my IUD. Those suckers were more reliable than the Pill. They were, like, 99.9999 percent reliable, right?

Just to put my mind at ease, I decided to take a pregnancy test the next day. It was stupid, really—a complete waste of money. There was absolutely no way. I'd made sure to cover my bases. But then, I'd take the test and I'd feel better, and you can't put a price on peace of mind.

I stared down at the pink line on the test.

There was absolutely no way this was possible.

I took a second test the following morning. It was supposed to be slightly more accurate in the morning.

That little fucking pink line was still there. I wanted to go haywire on it, smash it in a million pieces like I was Arnold Schwarzenegger or Chuck Norris.

Hysterically, I thought of what Matt had told me, that he and his first wife had tried to have children, but couldn't. Though the doctors did tests and told him it was she who was infertile, he secretly harbored a ton of guilt and uncertainty over it. He was always half-sure that they had been wrong, that he was the one to blame. When we found out about Lori's pregnancy, I had tried to lighten the mood by laughing nervously.

"Hey, at least we know now that you're not the infertile one!"

I wasn't laughing at the moment, though. This was absolutely surreal.

Clearly, Matt has the most fertile sperm in the entire world.

The first thing I thought to do was to call Planned Parenthood. I wanted *somebody* to give me an explanation, dammit!

It seemed to take forever to get a nurse on the line. She immediately asked me a bunch of questions about my cycle to determine just *how* far along I was.

Well, let's see. That was kind of hard for me to figure out. I'd still been having a period, but it had transitioned from a monthly, hard-core, bloody tidal wave lasting ten days at a time, into light, pink, irregular spotting. I'd been under the impression that this was normal; they'd told me this was a possibility when I'd had the IUD inserted. Most women started out with a few months of longer, crampier, heavier periods, and then it often tapered off into normal or even lighter periods, only lasting for a few days. This had sounded all right to me at the time; I figured I could deal with a little extra pain for a few months. I just took more aspirin until my uterus felt so dead you could probably kick me in the gut and I wouldn't have noticed.

I tried to think back to the last time I'd had one of the heavy periods. I thought it might have been twelve or fourteen weeks earlier...maybe sixteen? I'd never kept particularly close track of such things. I didn't need to. I had safe sex, right?

I vaguely thought I might have had some light spotting the week before Matt flew back to the States, the week I was on CNN with Nicole Lapin. My head hurt. I couldn't remember.

"OK, so you think you might be somewhere between twelve and sixteen weeks? Then you're just finishing up your first trimester."

"Screw that. More importantly, *why am I pregnant?!*" Clearly, this woman didn't grasp the gravity of the situation, or the real issue here. "I have an IUD in! That's supposed to be absolutely the most effective form of birth control to date! *It sits there in your uterus, there's nothing to forget, and you don't get pregnant! The end!*"

"Well, this happens occasionally. It's more common than you might think. Many nulliparous women find that their IUD can be dislodged or expelled within the first year."

It sounded like she'd said *leprous*. I was a leper now? I sure felt like one.

"Nulliparous. Women who've never had children before. About 10 percent of them, within the first year, lose their IUDs. Either their body expels it or it is placed incorrectly and can move up into your uterus. Once it's dislodged from your cervix, all bets are off. So while you may have been operating under the assumption that you were 99.9 percent covered, for your first year you're really only 90 percent likely to avoid pregnancy. And if it was somehow dislodged, then you're just as likely to get pregnant as if you were using nothing at all."

"So what do I *do?!*"

"You should probably see a doctor for an ultrasound."

And how was I supposed to do that? *I live in a trailer.* I have no health insurance. I just spent most of my money on Christmas presents. "The IUD may still be inside you, up in the uterus with the fetus. Unless it's been expelled. There's no danger of miscarriage if it's in your uterus, though. IUDs don't pose any harm to embryos or fetuses; that's a common myth. In fact, they probably won't try to remove it until you're much further along in your pregnancy, or even until after the baby is born, if you decide to carry it full term. Trying to remove a migrated IUD during pregnancy can actually *cause* a spontaneous miscarriage, so it's generally safer to just leave it there. But, yeah, you should get an ultrasound."

"Right," I muttered dully. "OK. I guess that's it."

"Have a nice day, good luck and congratulaaations!"

She sounded very singsong-y and perky. I wanted to

punch her. *Congratulations?* This couldn't possibly have come at a worse time.

Instead, I heard myself replying, "Thank you very much." Even stranger, I kind of realized I meant it. I should have been angrier, but through the complete shock, I was feeling a bit of elation? Excitement? Anticipation? Whatever it was, it came with a hefty side helping of terror. But still. Not entirely unhappy.

Chapter Twenty

I had to tell Matt, somehow. He'd had some problem the previous week: His internet connection had stopped working, and the company was telling him they'd have to deliver a new SIM card, or something. He'd taken my laptop back to Scotland with him, since his was ancient and on its last legs, and I'd managed to pick up a cheap, tiny Netbook. The 92 percent–sized keyboard took some getting used to, as did reading on a tinier screen, but I actually found it adorable and much lighter to carry around, so I didn't mind the downgrade.

Matt couldn't get online now from his home, though, and had to visit the town library if he wanted to contact me, or text me from the corner of his street, since he couldn't get cell reception in his flat. The library would be closing down very soon for Christmas, and he hated to bring Kelsey outside the flat if it was snowing, which it often was now. Huntly was having the worst winter in thirty years. Normally, it frosted over a bit, maybe snowed in February for a week or two, and then it was over. But here it was mid-December, and flurries of snow were burying the town, and more was predicted. Matt worried about Kelsey getting too cold. So, for a week, there had been very little contact, though he sent me loving texts and emails every couple of days. His birthday was in a few days, also, a week before Christmas, and I wouldn't even be able to reach him on that day, except via email.

It didn't seem right to tell him something so important online or in a text. I knew that he wouldn't want to hear it that way, though I also knew that he'd probably be thrilled to hear it at all. He was, after all, the one who had been pushing for me to have kids ASAP. His desire for children with me hadn't seemed to lessen with Kelsey's arrival. I'd sort of hoped that it would, that all the screaming and diaper-changing and spitting up would make him think twice about having another baby so soon, but I'd been wrong. He still brought it up far too often. I was still batting around all the pragmatic considerations, but I imagined in response to this news, he would only get as far as hearing "I'm pregnant," and probably hit the ceiling with joy, the way he went on about having babies with me. He was always waxing poetic about it.

"You'll be adorable! And we can have pregnancy sex! You with your little humpable pregnant belly. You'll be glowing and just as sexy as you are now, don't worry."

I didn't feel sexy, or glowy. I felt greasy and exhausted and queasy and as if I had giant cratering acne scars popping up all over my face. As excited as I was allowing myself to become, I hated the actual feeling of being pregnant.

In any event, I had to tell him in person, somehow. It's what he'd want, and it would be one of those moments you remember forever, right? Like that *I Love Lucy* episode where Lucy wants to settle heftily on Ricky's lap, wrap her arms around his neck, and whisper softly, "Ricky, darling, we're going to have a baby!"

That's how he'd want it to be, and how I wanted it to be. But I had no idea how to make it happen.

OK, that's a lie. I totally did know how to make it happen. I'd go to the person I always went to in dire straits. Brandon.

"You need to borrow how much this time?"

"Enough to get me on a plane to Scotland. Maybe for about three weeks. I've got a few hundred to last me for food and stuff while I'm there, but I don't have enough for plane fare."

Brandon always lent me money when I was in an extra tight spot, because I always paid him back. And I'd also take him out to dinner a few times to make up for it, and maybe to a couple of movies.

He didn't bat an eyelid.

"No problem."

"Thank you sooooo much. I really appreciate it. I'm sorry to ask right before Christmas, and I'll totally understand if you can't swing it, but this way I can surprise him, and he can still be with Kelsey for the holiday the way he wants!"

"It's totally no problem. Come over tomorrow and I'll give you the money."

"Thank you again. Thank you, thank you, thank you. You know I'll pay you back as soon as I can."

"Shut up."

"OK. I love ya."

I had ten days to prepare for my flight. I'd arrive on Christmas Eve, I decided. Matt would *love* the surprise.

When he proposed to his first wife, he'd secretly made arrangements with her boss to have her take time off, and then he'd "kidnapped" her and spirited her away to Prague, where he proposed at the top of some elaborate architectural tower. He loved grand, romantic, spontaneous gestures, and often lamented that he'd always wished a woman would do something like that for him. Well, this was my chance.

I spent a stressful eight hours in the Los Angeles passport office to pick up my first passport. I'd only ever been to Canada and Mexico in my life, before passports were required. This would be my first time off the continent. My first stamp in my passport. Despite all the stress and exhaustion, I allowed myself to get more and more excited. I would fly from LAX to Dallas to Paris to Manchester to Aberdeen. Only the longest flight and the furthest trip away from California I'd ever been on. Nothing to it.

Meanwhile, things were pretty silent on the Matt front. His birthday came and went, and it took him a couple of days to respond to my "Happy Birthday" email. He was thirty-seven. Later that day, he bundled Kelsey up in a coat and walked down to the corner for a surprise phone call.

He loved and missed me so much, and he was *so* sorry about all this technical trouble. Soon the internet company would replace his SIM card, and things could get back to normal. In the meantime, he was worried. What if they didn't fix it by Christmas?

I giggled to myself.

"It's OK, baby. You can send me a text or something. I've shipped your Christmas presents, so expect them any day now!"

"I can't wait! I'm so excited! I'm going to wait to give you yours in person, though. I know what I want to get you, but I haven't been able to buy it yet. Things have been tight, with Kelsey. Do you think you can wait until I come out to California?"

"Of course, I understand. Enjoy your Christmas. Talk soon. I love you."

"I love you more."

After I hung up, I emailed a couple of his Homeless Tales writers. *Shhh, don't tell Matt, but I'm surprising him for Christmas!*

They all thought it was a fabulous idea, as did Sage. *Have a safe flight; enjoy yourself!*

I'd already finished my internship with E. Jean, but we chatted occasionally on gtalk. I let her know where I'd be.

"Wonderful, have lots of fun in Europe, darling! Enjoy your man, and for heaven's sake, don't get pregnant," she added cheekily.

Oops. Well. Um.

My friends, Ben and Aubrey, picked me up and drove me to the airport. I had packed lightly as far as clothing went. It was mainly stretchy, warm flannel pajama bottoms, cotton robes and sweatshirts. I figured I wouldn't be wearing all that much clothing in Matt's flat anyway, and all I really needed were a few things for outside in the snow. All my clothes fit in a tiny rolling suitcase. My Netbook and cell phone I shoved into my purse, which I slung over my shoulder.

The only heavy item, which would need to be checked, was a large metal trunk I'd bought at a thrift store for $5.

Most of the Christmas presents went into it, and all the clothes that I'd bought for Kelsey

I wore an empire-waist top and tied the arms of a hoodie around my waist. Nobody would suspect anything. I just looked like I'd eaten a couple too many burritos lately.

Ben had been slightly miffed at me when the media storm broke, and he found out that I'd been homeless all this time. A couple of years before, when I was in between places to live for a couple of weeks, he and Aubrey had let me crash on a mattress on their dining room floor until I was ready to move into my new place.

"We could have done that again, you know! You're always welcome to stay with us!"

I supposed I believed it, too. Following the publication of my story, people I hadn't seen or heard from since junior high school had contacted me.

Remember me? From Mr. Dotson's seventh-grade science class? You were, like, my best friend in that class.

I vaguely remembered most of them, although many of them I couldn't recall ever actually speaking to. I was just amazed that anybody had noticed me or remembered my name, much less made the connection so many years later.

But things weren't like that with me and Ben. I had always considered him one of my best friends, and I adore Aubrey. It was just that things were somewhat strained in the recession; they, too, had both been laid off and were busy with their own lives, it had been a couple of months since we'd really spoken, and it never occurred to me to put even more strain on them now, with both of them out of work themselves. I'd simply, I explained to Ben, made use of what I had.

"I guess," he said quietly. "But if this ever happens again, you need to call us first. We would have taken care of you."

I'd nearly made it. I was on the flight from Manchester to Aberdeen, and two women in front of me were chatting.

"Yes, I'm going home to Huntly for Christmas!" exclaimed one in her thick Scottish brogue. What sheer luck! This lady could tell me how to get to Huntly. I tapped her on the shoulder.

"Excuse me, but I couldn't help overhearing. You're going to Huntly? So am I. I've never been there before. Is there a bus or train from the airport that I can take to get there?" I hadn't thought that far ahead. I figured I'd just ask the help desk once we landed.

"There's a bus, though there probably won't be a train this late at night. But you know what, my brothers are picking me up at the airport. You can just hitch a ride with us!"

"Oh, you mean it? Wow, that's so kind of you! Thanks!" My luck was running high.

We landed in Aberdeen and I made my way to the baggage claim. My trunk with the Christmas presents didn't come out on the conveyor belt. The kind lady and I went to the help desk. I'd been delayed in Manchester and put on a later flight, and apparently the trunk had been lost. They'd find it and deliver it to Matt's address, but probably not until Boxing Day. I had the Jules Verne book and the ring, but Kelsey's clothes and the photo album would miss Christmas. Oh, well! It wasn't that big a deal. I was in too optimistic a mood to worry much about it. I gave the clerk

Matt's address, I was bundled in the woman's car with her brothers, and we were on our way, making the one-hour drive to Huntly.

Chapter Twenty-One

Huntly was an adorable little town—I could tell that even in the dark. A tall clock tower, a charming square with cobblestone streets, an old library hundreds of years old, everything crafted of stone. It was exactly how you'd picture a sleepy little rural town in Scotland. It had a population of only four thousand people. I loved it on sight. Snow began to fall in great flurries. Snow on Christmas Eve. It was too perfect.

The car screeched to a halt outside Matt's flat, and the two men pulled my rolling suitcase from the "boot," as they called the car trunk. Then they each kissed me dramatically on each cheek, loudly proclaiming, "Good luck to ye, lass!"

My heart pounded as I climbed the stairs to Matt's flat. Seconds to go. Somehow I had pulled it off!

I knocked.

Footsteps.

Then he opened the door.

He looked so good I could have jumped his bones right there. He had grown a stubbly beard, which made him look a little rough and edgy. He was so sexy I immediately felt self-conscious of my tired, bloated appearance and blushed, staring at my toes. His eyes widened in shock. He just stood there. He didn't say anything.

Why was he just standing there? *Say something!*

Finally, I shuffled my toes and looked up at him, smiling shyly. I had no idea why, after all this time, I was suddenly bashful, but my heart overflowed with love.

"Merry Christmas."

He still just stood there, looking at me with the oddest expression on his face. It took me a moment to realize what it was. It was panic.

"You can't come in here."

The overwhelming initial sensation was that of finding oneself in a Coen brothers' movie—like everything had been going absolutely swell, not perfect perhaps, but damn close to it...then one day, one tiny, seemingly insignificant thing goes wrong, and you barely notice at first, but suddenly it all snowballs and does a plummeting death spiral until before you know it, someone's bludgeoning your head open with a hatchet or feeding your body into a wood chipper, and you're too stunned to react or defend yourself, because you're busy wondering just exactly where and when life so dramatically shifted course, to bring you to this point.

Yeah. I was *there.*

"What are you talking about? Why can't I come in? I've come all this way to surprise you..."

He interrupted me.

"Lori's here."

Nothing had happened, he started to explain. It wasn't what I thought. She'd just shown up, said it would be too hard for her to spend Christmas without her daughter. He didn't feel right sending her away, and the buses wouldn't be running again until Boxing Day. He'd agreed to let her stay on the couch.

"You promised you'd never do that! You *promised!*"

"Look, I would have told you. I'm sure I would have, in a couple of days. But I had to make the decision *now*. She's Kelsey's mother. I couldn't be cruel! I'm sorry, I didn't mean to lie to you. It just happened. But nothing inappropriate has happened or will happen. You *know* I would have been happy to see you, if it weren't for these circumstances. But now you've put me in an awkward position." He glanced over his shoulder furtively.

"Where am I supposed to go? What am I supposed to do tonight? I brought a little money for the trip, but I haven't exchanged it yet!" I heard Kelsey stirring in the living room behind him, and tried to keep my voice to a whisper, even though my impulse was to scream at the top of my lungs and brain him with my Netbook.

He reached into his pocket and pulled out £40 ($65).

"The post office won't be open until Monday, probably. You can exchange your money then. Here. That's all I've got on me right now. Go find a hotel for tonight. There are a few in the town square. I'll try to get rid of her in the morning."

I took the money.

"I'll come back in a few minutes and let you know where I'm staying and how long this'll buy me." Tears were streaming down my face. None of this was going as I'd planned it.

The first two hotels I tried shook their heads.

"We don't take people in on Christmas Eve." I figured it must be some local custom I didn't know about.

The largest (and most expensive) hotel in town, the Huntly Hotel, did give me a room. The girl at the desk looked like she was about seventeen years old, as if she was on her way home, and as if she thought I was the stupidest and weirdest person in the world for asking for a room on Christmas Eve. *Crazy Americans.* She took me upstairs and let me into a tiny, bare room. There was no telephone and no internet access, but that didn't matter. I'd only be here for a night. She handed me the room key.

I dropped my suitcase and ran back around the corner to Matt's flat.

"I'm at the Huntly Hotel. It's the only place that would take me on Christmas Eve. That's only enough money to pay for one night."

"I'll see what I can do."

"Does she know that it's me at the door?"

"Yes, I've explained it to her. She's not taking it well."

"What the hell do you mean she's not taking it well? You're *my* fiancé! You've spent months telling her that you're my fiancé! Hell, you've spent months telling *me* you already consider me your wife!"

"I do—it's just—you shouldn't have done this! You shouldn't have come here."

"*Why not?* Since when is it considered improper for a wife to surprise her husband, or even for two engaged people to surprise each other for Christmas? It's not! You're only upset now because you've been caught in a lie!"

"Look, I'm sorry. I don't know what to tell you...."

Lori stormed up to the door. I turned my head. I didn't want to see her; didn't want to know what she looked like. Somehow it would just make it that much more painful. Out of the corner of my eye, though, I saw her throw a giant garbage bag of trash at Matt violently.

"Take out the fookin' trash!" she screamed. It was a possessive scream. As though she considered him hers. Kelsey began to cry in the background, and Lori ran back into the living room.

Matt looked away from me helplessly, turning to pick up the garbage bag. He didn't even notice me flee. By the time he looked back up, I was already down the stairs and gone. I didn't want him to see me fall to pieces.

There was no sleeping that night. In the morning, ordered to check out by 10:00 a.m., I headed downstairs with my luggage.

There was nobody at the front desk. The lights were out; all was silent. I decided I'd just leave the key at the front desk and slip out.

The front door to the hotel was locked. I was locked in. All the doors I tried in the hotel were likewise locked—no access to any other area. I'd mistakenly hoped that perhaps I could gain access to the manager's room behind the front desk and use the phone to call for help. No luck.

Since there was no phone in my room, and no internet access, I couldn't call or email anybody. I kept checking downstairs all day to see if anybody had showed up to the hotel, but there was nobody. It's as if they'd all gone home, forgotten that they had a guest and taken Christmas Day off.

I went back to my room, sobbed some more, showered and drank all the coffee creamers in the little basket on the nightstand. There was no other food to be found. I hoped that Matt would come looking for me; perhaps call the police when I didn't show up. But everything was silent—for the rest of Christmas Day and all that night.

. . .

On the day after Christmas, the front door to the hotel was unlocked, though there was still nobody at the front desk. *Does anybody actually come to work in this town?* I left the room key on the counter and left with my luggage, figuring that at least I'd gotten an extra night's stay for free in exchange for the hassle. It was freezing outside, so I pulled on an oversized, shaggy blue coat that made me look like the unholy spawn of the Cookie Monster. It was the warmest thing I had found at the thrift store.

I walked back to Matt's flat and knocked. There was no answer. It was about 11:00 a.m., so I figured he shouldn't still be asleep. I waited a bit, and then knocked again. I could hear some shuffling around inside, so I knew *somebody* was there. I had no intention of leaving. I kept knocking, at five-minute intervals, until I heard a door slam inside, and Lori screaming in her thick Scottish accent for him to answer the door. She threw in a few curses for good measure. Matt came to the door.

"Wow. She's…charming," I spat, looking him dead in the eye. He pulled his jacket on.

"Let's take a walk."

We wandered until we found an empty church parking lot.

"I got locked in the hotel all day yesterday. They locked up for Christmas and forgot about me."

"Oh, my God. You poor thing. I'd wondered where you were!"

But you didn't come looking for me.

"Yeah, well, I guess at least I got a free night's stay. So… Lori sure made a point of coming to the door the other night." He smirked a bit. I couldn't see why. I didn't find any of this funny at all.

"Yeah, she sure did, didn't she? Your being here really winds her up, for some reason."

I can tell you exactly why it's winding her up.

"I looked up and you were gone," he continued.

"You wanted me to go."

If circumstances had been different, he insisted, he'd have been ecstatic to see me. He'd have happily taken me in and we'd have celebrated Christmas and I'd have met Kelsey. He still hoped I'd get to meet Kelsey soon. He was so sorry about all this. He hadn't meant to lie to me.

He started to shiver violently from the cold.

"Oh, my god, you're freezing…I want to hold you, but…I don't know if…" *if you still love me.*

He opened his jacket and pulled me into him.

"I love you so much. And now I've fucked everything up."

"It's OK. We'll figure it out. Will she be leaving soon?"

He looked uncomfortable.

"Last night, she called her entire family and told them to come down to Huntly. I only found out this morning. They're arriving later today. I don't know how long they'll be staying."

What? What?! But it was *his flat!* She'd had her Christmas with Kelsey; now it was Boxing Day and she was supposed to be going home. He hadn't even invited her to stay this long in the first place, had he? I was his *fiancé!* I'd spent the previous two days in panic, freaking out, because I had no idea what was going on. He'd just shoved me off his doorstep and treated me like a near stranger. We had made *every single possible concession* in order for Lori to feel comfortable, but this was the part where he was supposed to put his foot down and stand up for me, for us.

That's when he lowered the boom on me.

"It's not my flat anymore. That's the problem."

Oh, my god. Oh. My. God.

"You didn't. You didn't sign over the flat to her already."
Silence. "*When* did you sign over the flat to her? *Why?*"
Why, why, why would you be so fucking stupid?

A couple of months back—he couldn't really remember exactly when. She was getting paranoid and starting to push him. Asking when he was leaving for California already, when she could have the flat and be with her daughter. Her aunts were freaking her out, too, saying that Matt would go back on his promise. So he'd put the flat in her name to keep her from worrying. It was a gesture of good faith, he insisted. So that she *knew* beyond a shadow of a doubt that she could move in after we were married.

How could you not tell me this?! Every single major life decision I had made since we'd been together, I had talked out with him. We were partners. He had gone on and on about how he could never be with someone who didn't treat him as an equal, wasn't completely honest with him. And yet he'd hidden this from me for *months*. It was too much to take in all at once.

He started to cry.

"I'm sorry. It was supposed to be a surprise. The *good* kind of surprise, to show you how serious I was about making a life with you. I was going to tell you when I came out to marry you. Everything would have been all taken care of already."

Oh, for fuck's sake. It was like a perverse, not-at-all touching version of *Gift of the Magi.* We'd each planned a surprise for the other and now everything was all shot to hell. *Still, my surprise would have been relatively harmless if he hadn't broken his promise and let her stay,* I thought. *My sur-*

prise was sweet and romantic and thoughtful. His was dangerous. Reckless disregard for our future.

I didn't want to rub it in, though. I mean, the guy was weeping in front of me. I was really starting to resent having to be the sane, rational, pregnant one, though. Pregnant women got to throw tantrums and demand foot rubs and be smug and self-righteous and bitchy, and then blame it all on their fluctuating hormones, from what I'd seen. I thought of a former dance teacher, who'd brought his eight-months' pregnant girlfriend to the Big Bear Jazz Festival with my swing team when we'd performed there. She spent an entire weekend making nineteen people crammed into a six-person cabin absolutely miserable, tiptoeing around her like she was some dormant dragon not to be awakened. And everybody took it for granted. *She's pregnant. That's what pregnant women do.*

Not that I wanted to be a sanctimonious bitch. But I was really beginning to see the irony—and feel the strain—of holding it together, as Matt fell apart in front of me. What could I do, though? *By the way, I'm pregnant, you well-intentioned dimwit. Put that in your pipe and smoke it. Mull that one over, in addition to all the angst you're feeling right now.* No, it had to be a happy occasion, when I told him. It had to be right. Now was not the right time. We had to tackle this first.

"And now," he continued, "she's threatening to take me to court! She's saying she'll throw me out of the flat and take Kelsey away if I don't get rid of you! Every time I try to talk or reason with her, she either screams and throws things, or refuses to speak to me."

You idiot. You fucking, goddamn idiot. I love you, but right now I have no idea why. You've put our entire future at risk. You disregarded every last thing I ever said. You laughed off all my fears as completely irrational and did exactly what you were going to do, and now we're fucked.

He said it for me.

"You were right. You were 100 percent right about *everything*. Everything you said was going to happen has happened. I'm so, so sorry."

I held him and let him cry.

"What'll we *do*, Bri?" *We. We* was good. He was still thinking *we*.

We'd figure something out, I told him. But the first thing he needed to realize was that she had no right to tell him whom he was allowed to love and whom he was allowed to marry. There were no excuses for her behavior. He needed to stand up to her.

I couldn't process his sudden (or maybe not-so-sudden) spinelessness. A horrible thought struck me. "Matt, I don't mean to sound like I'm attacking you. I'm not. But your actions have put us in a very bad position, and it all seems completely out of character for you. So I have to ask. Are you still off your medication?"

He gave me a deer-in-the-headlights look.

"Yes. You were right. I should have gone back on it. I've made bad decision after bad decision. That's probably got a whole lot to do with what's happened so far."

Of course. It's just one other thing I said that you disregarded. Why on earth would you be on the meds that keep you healthy and rational? Brilliant.

I began to formulate a plan of action, outlining each step for him. First, he needed to get back on his meds. I knew they took about a month to kick in, but that was all the more reason to get started now. Then, he needed to go to the council and see if there was any way of getting the flat back in his name. He could sign it back over to her later on, once they had a binding custody agreement, but as long as she was threatening to take him to court, it was not a smart idea to give her that kind of leverage. He didn't want to be homeless again, right?

"I don't think it's possible to reverse. It's all completed."

"You've been off your medication for several months now. When you go to the doctor, get a note from him explaining this. I'll bet if you show that note to the council, you can get the transfer canceled on the grounds that you weren't in your right mind. You weren't taking the meds necessary for you to function and make rational decisions."

"I don't know if that will work!" He was getting agitated. "She's going to throw me out and take Kelsey! And her family's coming! Her mother's coming!"

I wanted to shake him like a bobblehead doll, until his teeth chattered. *Focus, Matt. You got us into this by underestimating my input in the first place. Now I'm trying to get us out of it.*

I promised him I'd see what I could find out about custody law in Scotland. He just needed to try to convince Lori and her family to leave and go back to Peterhead for the time being. He'd been Kelsey's sole caregiver since she was born. Most likely, Lori couldn't just take her away from him without a court order, I figured. I encouraged him to sit Lori down and talk to her, and not to take no for an answer.

"Don't cower when she throws things and screams, and don't give up and let her ignore you. You're a grown man. You can handle this."

"I'll try."

If he *did* end up having to go to court to resolve this, we could work around it. Instead of us going to New York, I could come to the UK instead, if that would make things easier. We could use the book advance money to rent a flat in town, so that he and Lori could be within a couple of blocks of each other and share custody of Kelsey until everything was mediated between them. There was no rush for New York. We could set up house in the UK instead. Or we could even make that permanent, so that he could be close to Kelsey year-round.

He insisted vehemently, though, that he still wanted to move to New York with me, even now. He'd talk to her.

"You're right. You've been right all this time and I was a stupid fool, and you've been the most loving, supportive girlfriend any man could ever have. I don't deserve you, but I'm going to try so much harder to." He was crying again in my arms.

"Stop it, honey. I love you. It's all going to be OK."

He took me up the street to a small bed-and-breakfast, the Dunedin Guest House. It was the most affordable place in town; half the price of the Huntly Hotel in the main square. I couldn't figure out why it should be cheaper to get a larger room, internet access *and* free breakfast, but I wasn't complaining.

The post office wouldn't be open for two more days, so Matt paid for the next two nights. He would meet me in the square on Monday morning, I could exchange my currency, and by then he was sure he'd have dealt with Lori and I could come back to the flat with him. He seemed renewed with optimism and relief that I had been so understanding and supportive. I was feeling pretty optimistic myself.

He walked me upstairs to the room, and pushed me up against the wall, kissing me deep and hard. It was the first time he'd kissed me since I'd arrived, and I immediately knew it would all be fine. Over and over again he kissed me, and I thought that maybe this would be a perfect time to tell him that I was pregnant. We were both happy again.

I sat down on the bed and patted the covers next to me.

"Can you stay for a little bit? There's some stuff I'd like to talk to you about. I have so much to tell you."

"I can't. I need to get back to the flat. I've been away so long already—she's probably fuming."

My face fell. For fuck's sake, we *just* had the conversation about standing up and being a man! He explained that every time he'd tried to leave the flat the day before, even if it was just for an errand, Lori had gone on a screaming rampage, accusing him of visiting me.

"*Accusing* you? What's there to accuse you of? So what if you were seeing me? I mean, I'd assume that'd be a given. She knows that we're together…right?"

Of course, but he couldn't really explain it. My presence was setting her off. There'd always been an undertone of her wanting him back, but for a few weeks, he said, she'd started talking about it openly, pushing him to leave me and reconcile with her.

"Why wouldn't you tell me something of that magnitude? You *promised* you'd tell me if she ever tried to make a move on you!" I was right back to feeling betrayed.

"Look, I haven't given her any hope whatsoever, OK? I've told her that it's never going to happen."

That wasn't enough, I insisted. She needed to be told, flat out, "I don't love you—I never have and I never can—and I'm marrying somebody else. Case closed. Now we need to focus on parenting our daughter in a healthy manner." I couldn't believe that I needed to spell this out for him, and then I felt guilty for being frustrated with my lover when he was off his medication and falling to pieces in front of my eyes.

He sighed.

"I suppose you're right. It probably does need to be said."

He would tell her. He'd wait until her family left that night: He didn't want to humiliate her in front of them. But he would tell her. I agreed that that was fair.

Just like that, back to happy again. My brain couldn't keep up with the emotional pendulum. I was getting a headache.

"But I need to go. It's going to be hard enough telling her if I get her upset at me today. I love you. I'll see you on Monday."

Deep kisses, and then he bolted down the hallway.

Chapter Twenty-Two

On Monday, I exchanged my currency at the post office, and Matt met me outside. He was lugging my heavy trunk full of Christmas gifts, which had been delivered over the weekend.

I stood on my tiptoes and kissed him. He looked distant.

"Homeless Tales is down, I noticed yesterday. It looks like Michael forgot to pay the bill again."

Michael Abehsera hosted Matt's website on his Media Temple server, in exchange for Matt promoting his social media work. Matt more than fulfilled his end of the bargain, but Michael often forgot to pay the $20 hosting fee, and we had several times known the frustration of a flurry of panicked emails from the HT crew: *Why is the site down?* More often than not, Michael would plead that money was tight that month, and I would end up buying a prepaid debit card from Walmart and logging in to the Media Temple account to pay the $20 myself.

"Oh, crap. Can you pay it?"

"No, I don't have a debit card with me. I didn't know this was going to happen."

"*Shit.* I don't have internet access yet. Can you try to get hold of Michael and get him to pay it, or ask around and maybe find a friend to front us the money? We need to get that site back up. Ask around, and when you find somebody, give them the Media Temple login info."

"I'll do my best."

I turned my attention to my trunk. "Why'd you bother bringing that? Those are gifts for you and Kelsey. You can just keep it at the house."

"I can't do that."

Oh, come on. Not another problem.

"You didn't talk to her." I said it flatly. I could have slugged him.

"I've tried! I've tried everything! She refuses to talk! The rest of her family went home, but her mother stayed. They've set up camp in the flat and are refusing to leave! I can't go anywhere without them screaming at me, and then when they start to scream, Kelsey gets terribly frightened and starts to cry! Bri, I love you and I want to marry you, but I…I hold my daughter and I just realize that it's not possible. I can't have you both. Lori won't let me."

What the fuck?!

I was watching the scene as if floating high above myself. It was the very first time that, gazing into his eyes, I saw nothing of the Matt I knew. There was no sign of the man who'd spooned with me tight all night long discussing quantum physics, and taken such giddy, boyish pleasure in sharing memories of his childhood with me—the man who'd laughed over my shoulder as we watched *Paddington Bear* and *Bagpuss* together, or who'd insisted on reciprocating my favorite classic black-and-white movies, *The Ghost and Mrs. Muir* and *Roman Holiday,* with his own, *Brief Encounter.* It was like trying to get through to a stranger.

His eyes were blank with panic, like a drowning man whose only thought is to save himself.

"You're going back to her."

"No! No, I'm not going back to her. I'd never go back to her. I'm not saying *anything* about going back to her. But maybe if I live in the same flat as her and coparent Kelsey, you know, living like roommates, she'll back off and things will calm down. She'll stop freaking out and Kelsey can have a quiet life, instead of all this constant conflict."

I stamped my foot hard in the snow. Perhaps a childish gesture, in retrospect, but I felt completely and thoroughly provoked, and I'd reached my breaking point.

Was he crazy? Was he listening to himself? Her behavior was so far over the line, *beyond* abusive and insane and irrational, and he was caving to it. He was pandering to her. *Appeasing* her. Did he honestly believe that allowing this kind of insanity to dominate their lives was creating a healthy environment for his daughter? If he loved me and wanted to marry me, then he should fucking well *do* it. She had no right to make such a demand. I begged him to stand up to her *now,* draw the line and set boundaries with her *now,* while Kelsey was still a baby. For the umpteenth time, I wished he'd done it before Kelsey's birth as he'd promised…but he had waited too long and put us all in jeopardy. Still, if he stood up for himself now, he could get the unpleasant part over with while his daughter was too young to remember all the fighting and conflict. I thought back to my own mother, and knew that if Matt allowed this craziness to continue, Kelsey would grow up thinking that her mom's warped, twisted power plays were normal. The realization was like a dagger in my heart.

"I'm sorry. I'm sorry I did this. I don't know what to do anymore."

"Yes, you do. You know what to do, you're just too scared of her to do it. But think about this, Matt: Single parents fall in love and get remarried every day. It happens. Normal, healthy people don't allow their exes to dictate their choice of partner. Lori is the *only person* in this entire scenario who's told you that you need to give up one of the people you love—your wife-to-be or your daughter. *I* haven't asked you to, and *Kelsey* hasn't asked you to."

"You're right."

He kept *saying* that he knew I was right, but I needed to see some action from him. *Be an adult, already. You're thirty-seven years old. Time to grow up.*

"You know what I spent the past two days doing, Matt? Calling all the Scottish child law center hotlines I could locate, asking them what to do. And you know what? *Every last one* has verified what I suspected before."

He could get his flat back in a heartbeat. He just needed a doctor's note. He was considered the parent of residence, not Lori. He was entitled to status-quo custody until a court ordered otherwise, and that was highly unlikely, especially with both their names on the birth certificate, and with Lori's unstable actions. He was even entitled to free legal representation if she took him to court.

And the most frustrating thing? She didn't need his flat. She had *never* needed his flat. All the wheedling and emotional blackmail, pushing him to sign the flat over to her—and all she had to do to get one from the local council… was *ask*. She could *still* ask, I stressed to Matt. *Any* single mother with no job gets a free flat within a matter of weeks, just by *asking*. She could have asked the moment she found out she was pregnant. There was never *any* need for all this drama and manipulation. But instead, she had done her best to fuck up *all* our lives, just so she could have another shot with a man who never loved her in the first place; a man she had to lie to and trick into pregnancy, all in hopes that he'd come back to her. And now that it had exploded in her face, he was just going to *let* her do this to us?

I hated him at that moment. It was simultaneous with loving him, but I think I can safely say that in that instant, there was no room in my body or mind for anything else but rage. What had we worked so hard for? Why had we bothered going to all the trouble of building a life and happiness together, if he was just going to go off his meds, roll over, wave a white flag and die?

He repeated the *You're right, I know you're right* mantra over and over.

"I swear I love you and want to marry you. I know that I'm making all these stupid, bungling decisions because I'm off my meds. You're absolutely right. I shouldn't make any more rash decisions until I'm back on them."

"So don't. Go home and do the right thing. The smart thing. And take this." I drew my engagement ring off my finger, clenching it in my palm sadly before handing it to him. "Put it back on my finger once you've proven that you can keep a promise."

"You should hold onto this."

"No, I trust you with it. Earn my trust, please."

He pocketed the ring.

"I will."

I had enough money to last me through New Year's Eve. After that, I had nothing, not even enough for bus fare to take me back to the airport in a couple of weeks. I'd brought only enough to pay for three weeks of meals while on vacation, not hotel fare, because I had planned to stay with Matt the entire time.

"You know, kind of like I put you up for free for months on end in California?" I reminded him. Now the entirety of my food money had been repurposed to put me up at the Dunedin Guest House. "Was it really all that unreasonable to assume I'd be staying with you for a couple of weeks here in Scotland?" I figured at this point, a smidge of extra guilt-mongering couldn't possibly do any more damage than had already been done.

"No, of course not. I'll have her out by then, I should think." He would come back to the Dunedin and get me once she was out. He should get his benefits check in the mail the next day. He would come get me and take care of me, he promised. He loved me.

"I love you, too. Please, *please* be strong for us. I know this might be a lot to ask of you right now, in your frame of mind. I know you love your daughter and you're out of your mind with worry. But please be strong. And hurry back. We have a lot of important things to talk over. I keep trying to get you to sit down with me, but it seems like I only see you for fifteen or twenty minutes at a time, and then you're running back to the flat. Be strong, do it quickly, like ripping off a Band-Aid, and hurry back."

"I will. Do me a favor, though. It's going to be hard enough to force her to listen. I don't want to rub it in her face. I'll come get you at the Dunedin once I get her and her mother to leave. Please don't come knocking at the door. It'll only make her angrier and more irrational, and she'll get more stubborn. I'll be back at the Dunedin within the next couple of days."

"OK."

"If something goes wrong, and for whatever reason I'm not able to get rid of her that quickly, there's a train station half a mile up the street, on the outskirts of town. If you have to check out of the Dunedin on New Year's, and I haven't gotten here yet, go wait for me there. I'll come and get you. There's no heater or anything, but there's a raised roof that can provide you with some shelter from the snow."

"Do you seriously not see the irony, as a homeless activist, in telling your fiancée that she may have to go wait out in the freezing cold for you?"

"Yes, I do, and I'm sorry. Don't worry, though. I don't think it'll be necessary, but if it is, I'll find a way to come and get you as quickly as possible. You won't have to wait there for long."

My mind flashed back to Dennis, to every man who had ever hurt, lied to and abandoned me. The darkest suspicion I ever could have imagined clouded my thoughts.

"Matt...you'd never...you'd never just disappear and leave me here, would you? You *will* come and get me, right? You couldn't chicken out and abandon me, could you?"

He looked wounded and horrified.

"No! I could never do that. That's not possible. I don't have it in me to do something so cruel." *You've done a lot of things lately that you said you could never do,* I thought. But I chose to believe him, because, after all, what option did I have? I was at every possible disadvantage here. And I also loved him and wanted to believe that, as fucked up as he was in the head right now, he wasn't *evil* or anything. Screwing up—making a few mistakes—was a world apart from intentionally putting someone's life at risk.

"Of course. I'm sorry. It was a ridiculous question, I guess. I'm just scared, is all. I didn't mean to insinuate that you'd ever purposely be cruel. How should I contact you? My cell phone isn't working here. I've already tried it."

"Email me. Keep me updated. Maybe in the next day or so my SIM card will arrive, or I can go to the library. They're reopening before New Year's, I think."

He hurried up the snow-covered street, and I went back to the Dunedin Guest House, and forked over the last of my funds, until the book advance came through, whenever that was. It would be enough for a few more days, but he had promised to take care of me.

I trusted him.

Christine and Keith Best owned the Dunedin Guest House. They were two kindly souls from Leeds, England. He had worked for the government for many years and when they retired, they decided to pursue their dream of owning an inn. They soon realized that I had no money left, and was living off the Bourbon cookies they placed in my room every morning, so they began inviting me to dinner with them nightly. They were also hearty drinkers, and encouraged me to have another glass of wine, and another. I knew enough about pregnancy to know that a glass of wine or so was supposed to be OK, but much more than that could be dangerous. After three or four times saying, "No, thank you," followed by their continued insistence, I would allow them to refill the glass and then offer to take my own plate into the kitchen as they spoke, taking the glass with me and quietly pouring the wine down the sink. I felt bad wasting their wine, but I felt worse turning them down for the fifth time. I didn't want them to take it personally, as though I were refusing their hospitality.

Keith was a Yorkshireman, so I privately associated him with the James Herriot books I'd loved as a kid, always imagining him in a tweed cap or something. He was very funny, social and loud. I am the complete opposite, but for some reason we really connected as friends. I filled the Bests in on some of my story, and they were fascinated, especially that I used to be one of "those crazy Jehovah's Witnesses."

Keith had already introduced me to haggis (which was surprisingly tasty!), and now he had it in his head that he needed to make me blood pudding. Next morning at breakfast, in addition to the usual gut-busting, heaping platter of sausage, eggs, bacon, ham, stewed tomatoes, toast and cereal, lay five thick, black slices of…well, fried blood. Those Scots really know how to eat.

I would eat the blood first, I decided. Get it over with quickly, and then all the remaining "normal" food would wash the taste from my mouth. Keith hovered over me, awaiting my reaction. I speared a blood slice with my fork and tentatively placed it on my tongue. It was heavy, crumbly, metallic-tasting…and, surprisingly, it didn't taste too bad. I suppressed a shudder or two as I ate it, but only because I was working on disassociating myself from the concept, rather than the taste…like overcoming the mental block of eating brains or octopus or escargot or something. In junior high school, my Bangladeshi friend Sonia's mother had served me lamb heart, a Bengali delicacy, without telling me beforehand, and although it was delicious, once I found out what I'd consumed, from then on I was always a tad suspicious and careful to ask what I was being served up front. Culinary surprises aren't my thing.

I was so proud when I'd finished my blood pudding. Though I far preferred the taste of haggis, what was more important was that I'd done it. It felt like breaking the last

Witness taboo. I couldn't wait to tell Matt. I was sure that when we saw each other again, *he'd* be superproud, too. If I could eat clearly labeled blood of my own free will, then I could overcome anything.

Chapter Twenty-Three

New Year's Eve came, and no Matt. By about 7:00 p.m., I'd given up waiting. It was the train station for me. It was cold and snowing out, but I figured it wouldn't be too bad to handle if I layered up on clothing. I couldn't bring the trunk along with me to the station, so I began to lug it up the street toward his flat. I knew I couldn't knock on Matt's door, but I could leave it outside. They were his presents, after all. Before leaving, I emailed him to let him know why I had to leave it for him. I wasn't sure if, in his frame of mind, he'd make the connection. I also reminded him that I'd be at the train station, as per his instructions.

It took me a half hour just to reach the end of the street. The trunk was incredibly heavy and awkward. Some young boys, maybe thirteen or fourteen years old, stopped and asked me if I needed a hand. I gratefully accepted, and they each grabbed an end and walked it the next half mile to Matt's flat, where I dragged it up the stairs and dropped it outside his door, slinking away quietly and quickly. The lights were out and there was no sound from the inside. I assumed that since he hadn't shown up, he was still trying to shake Lori and her mother, so I didn't want to disturb them. I didn't want to put extra pressure on him and make it harder for him to do what he had to do. I was warm and even sweating a bit from all the walking and lugging of the trunk, which reassured me that with a few extra layers of jackets, I wouldn't be too cold at the train station.

I returned to the Dunedin and gathered up my things. The Bests were going to a New Year's Eve party at Huntly Castle up the street and asked, with some concern, if I'd be OK.

"Oh, yes. Matt said he'd meet me at the train station, so I'm off to wait for him," I said cheerily. "Thank you again, so much, for your hospitality!"

I shook their hands and trudged up the road, over the bridge across Huntly River, and into the isolated train station. The ground was all freezing stone. I pulled out my ragged copy of *Gone with the Wind* and began to read. Despite my thick socks and hiking boots, within an hour my toes were completely numb, and the numbness was starting to creep up my legs. As it got colder, I unpacked the contents of my suitcase, adding another layer, and then another. Before long, I was wearing three pairs of jeans and six pairs of pajama pants, one on top of the other, and every shirt, sweatshirt and jacket in my suitcase, topped off with the shaggy blue coat. I looked like a swollen, roly-poly Violet Beauregarde from *Charlie and the Chocolate Factory*. The layering distorted my size to the point where anybody looking at me would have thought I weighed 350 pounds. But there was nobody around to see.

The hours dragged by and I tried to sleep, stretching myself out on the stone and using my suitcase and purse as pillows. But despite the layering, I was soon shivering again. It started snowing lightly, but soon turned into a full-fledged snowstorm. The whirls of white outside were beautiful, but menacing. Eventually, of course, I had to pee. It was early in the morning, and there would be no local restaurants or bars open. Full of shame, I peeled off all my bottom layers except for the last pair of jeans, and climbed down onto the railroad tracks, squatting to piss, a dark yellow stream against the whiteness. My face burned, and I hoped there was no CCTV recording me. Crouching to pee with your jeans half on was incredibly awkward, and I couldn't avoid getting some on my pants. *Fuck.*

I hoisted myself back up the side of the railroad tracks, my hands freezing from the snow. Gloves were the only thing I hadn't thought to pack. I hadn't counted on spending the night in a snowstorm. *How silly of me.* I wadded the jeans up and threw them into a nearby trash can, then ran bare-bottomed back into the station, pulling all the remaining pants back on as fast as I could. One less layer of clothing, but at least the running and the embarrassment forced a little blood through my body, and I felt warmer for just under an hour. I tried to sleep again, drifting in and out of consciousness, and occasionally standing to walk briskly in circles, pulling my sleeves over my hands and crossing my arms, hiding my fingers in my armpits.

Day came and went. Occasionally, I heard people nearby, walking their dogs or taking a lovers' stroll on New Year's Day. I pulled myself into as small a ball as I could in the corner of the station. Once or twice, I heard footsteps stop, and quiet murmurs, as though a passerby were staring at me, but then the footsteps would fade as they moved on. Matt never came, although I was still convinced he would. Darkness fell again, and the snow continued unabated. I had stopped shivering, and was beginning to feel only numbness and a kind of hazy peace. I didn't realize at the time that I was entering the intermediate stages of hypothermia. I was just glad not to be shaking violently anymore. Hallucinations set in, and I spent hours alternately sleeping and speaking to voices that weren't really there, or huddling in the corner terrified, certain that an angry mob was stalking me with torches and pitchforks, then falling back to sleep.

At some point, I came around in a daze. The wind was cutting through my clothes to the bone, whipping snow into the station's shelter. It occurred to me, through my brain fog, that perhaps it was a bad strategy to remain down here, close to the river. Everything was colder by bodies of water, right? Thickly, I staggered to my feet and gathered up my suitcase and purse. The suitcase was nearly empty now—I was still wearing all the clothing I had— but my arms felt heavy and dead, and it was a struggle to lift *anything*.

I would head up to the town square, I decided. There was a bus stop there. That would provide shelter, and perhaps it would be warmer at higher ground.

It took nearly an hour to reach the town square. Every footstep felt like the most tremendous effort. I just wanted to sleep....

Finally, I reached the bus shelter and collapsed onto the bench, passing out within minutes. It *did* feel warmer here, although that may also have been from the exertion of my long trudge upwards from the train station. I don't know how long I was unconscious before I awoke to a man, maybe in his late thirties, patting my shoulder.

"Miss? MISS? Are you all right?"

I opened my eyes very slowly. My eyelids hurt. *Leave me alone. Can't you tell I want to sleep?*

"I'm...fine. Really."

"Are you sure? Should I call someone? I don't feel right just leaving you here. Do you have anywhere to sleep? It's freezing out. You shouldn't be trying to sleep out here. You could get yourself killed."

"Someone will come to get me...I'll be OK."

He protested a little more, but finally left. I went back to sleep. *Sleep? Die? I almost don't care anymore. Sleep is warm, or at least not cold.*

I was jolted awake again by a female police officer shining a flashlight at me. Again, I tried to tell her that I would be OK, but she wasn't having any of it. *Damn, that man called the police,* I surmised. I didn't know what time it was, but it was still dark and I would later learn that the police had found me around 2:00 or 3:00 a.m., early in the morning on January 2.

Before I knew it, the woman bundled me into a police car with her partner. He drove us back to the town police station, where I was offered hot chocolate and a blanket. They wanted to know why I was sleeping outside in the snow. They couldn't leave me there. I needed to tell them who did this to me, and they would find a place for me to stay for the night.

I started to cry. I tried to explain the situation to them, but I could tell that they didn't understand, or at least I thought they didn't. They exchanged glances.

They think I'm an abused woman. They think this is a domestic abuse case. They're going to treat him like an abusive boyfriend. They think I'm spouting off all the typical abuse victim BS.

"You stay here with my partner," the female officer said. "I'm going over there to his flat. Don't worry, we're not going to arrest him or anything. I'm just going to talk to both of them. What they've done to you is *not* all right, not under any circumstances."

The woman left, and I cried harder. It was all my fault. He'd never love me again. What if they took away Kelsey because they thought he wasn't a fit parent? I began to shiver uncontrollably as I warmed, and the hypothermia slowly wore off.

Her partner leaned over and put his hands on my shoulders.

"I want you to know something. I've never met this Matt Barnes of yours. But I can tell you right now, he is *scum*. He is the biggest asshole I've ever heard of, and you deserve much better. I've never heard of anyone doing something so disgusting to his fiancée." I tried to smile at him through my tears, but I was paralyzed with fear. Once they were done speaking with Matt, he'd hate me. He'd never speak to me again. He'd think that I'd gone to the police myself. I was stuck here with no money, no phone, no way to get back home for weeks, and Matt would never trust me again, certainly not enough to ask Lori to leave and put me up in the flat.

The female officer returned quickly. In Huntly, everything was a two-minute drive away or less.

"There's nobody at that flat. From what we can tell, nobody's been there for days. There's a suitcase outside, a big, blue metal trunk. Is that yours?"

"Yes. It's got our Christmas presents in it. It was too heavy and awkward to take to the train station."

"It's outside still, covered in snow. There are no footprints on the stairs, nothing. When was the last time you saw him, again?"

"Monday. A few days ago."

"I'd say nobody's been there for several days. That flat's vacant. He must have left right after you saw him."

My mind exploded. I couldn't accept this. There was no way that Matt had told me he loved me and wanted to marry me, and then turned around and fled the city immediately afterwards. There must be some mistake.

"We've called the Dunedin, and they've said to bring you back. They're going to keep you there on the honor system until you can pay them. They trust you. Get your suitcase."

I couldn't believe the kindness of the Bests. Christine answered the door and fussed over me, loading me up with extra blankets and instructing me to put my clothes, wet from the snow, over the radiator to dry. I was tucked into bed with extra cookies in my basket.

"Don't worry about a thing. We don't have a moment's doubt that you'll pay us as soon as you can. Nobody's going to kick you out on the street. You can stay here as long as you need to, and you'll be well fed while you're at it."

If I hadn't been so tired and cried out, I would have wept at their kindness. As it was, I thanked them profusely as much as I could before passing out and sleeping the sleep of the dead.

I awoke to emails from several members of the Homeless Tales crew. The website was still down, Matt wasn't returning any of their concerned emails—was everything all right? I was the first person they all thought to turn to, since I was Matt's girlfriend.

Most of them I told very little. I didn't want to embarrass Matt in front of his crew. I just explained that the host had forgotten to pay the bill, I was working on fixing it, and that Matt had had to go deal with some personal issues. I was fine, but was having a hard time getting hold of him, since he had internet trouble. I didn't have all the crew members' email addresses, so I asked them to spread the word.

To a handful of the crew members who contributed the most, and to whom Matt felt the closest, I told more of the story. I explained that he had gone missing and I was very worried about him. I filled them in on the sequence of events after I'd shown up. I didn't know where he'd gone, if he was hurt or in the hospital, or what had happened to make him leave.

There was wide variation among their reactions, and it mostly seemed to be split along gender lines. The women were shocked, and though they didn't believe any of it sounded like Matt, they were quick to brand his actions abusive and urge me to give him up as a lost cause. The men, on the other hand, suggested that perhaps he had tried to stand up to Lori, and she and her mother had absconded with the baby. Perhaps, they continued, he was forced to go after them with no notice, to ensure his child's safety.

"Men can do some stupid, crazy things if they feel that their child is in danger," said Michael Ian, one of our good friends, who ran an excellent website called SLO Homeless. "But I know Matt, and I have no doubt that he loves you, even if what he's doing is wrong and has put you in danger. I have a feeling he'll eventually get back on his medication and realize the magnitude of how he's hurt you. Give it time. Keep emailing him, letting him know what's going on. He loves you, I know it."

wo nights after my snowbound adventure, I lounged recumbent on the floor of the living room, chatting and watching *Hell's Kitchen* with a couple of other guests, Christine and Keith. We had all had a glass or two of wine; the tone of the room was cheerful, lighthearted, the teasing lilts of Yorkshire and Highland accents twining about me and buoying me up. My cheeks blushed warmly like two impish coals, and I wondered if this was what having a family, or at least a group of close friends, was like. I was optimistic, happy even. Everything would turn out fine. Matt had been delayed for some reason, but everything would be fine; he would show up soon, we would talk and work everything out. If the men in his crew thought so, that was good enough for me. They understood the male mind better than I did.

Without warning, the room was suddenly pinwheeling and my brain felt as though it had flipped lazily to one side. Moments before, it had felt as though I were pleasantly toasting marshmallows across an open campfire on a metal skewer; now it was as though the skewer had been heated to a lusty, insidious orange in the flames, and I was poked through the back with it, flesh cauterizing as it slid through my spine and womb like butter, emerging through my pelvis.

In shock, I staggered to my feet and excused myself. Every movement was agony and sent shocks radiating up my body into my skull, but I had to conquer the stairs. Making it safely to my room, I collapsed to my knees before the all-knowing porcelain goddess and, as proof of my veneration, spewed a suitably regal amount of burning vomit into it. I hauled myself to my feet, but the nausea struck again and I retched into the white pedestal sink this time. My pajama bottoms began to seep vile liquid, and I pulled them off, crawling clumsily into the shower and huddling in the corner. I grasped at my hip bones as the blazing poker of agony stabbed me over and over. I recognized the feeling of a dilated cervix from having my IUD put in, but now it was coming in stabbing, shuddering waves. I knew instinctively that these must be contractions, and that they shouldn't be happening, and that I was miscarrying.

I held my dead fetus, mere inches long, in my bloody palm. It was a tiny, weightless boy, at the end of my twisted, detached cord like some oddly deflated balloon. He looked like a baby but, at the same time, not a baby. He was the color of deep burgundy jelly; wizened like a tiny, defeated old man from a fairy tale, but with perfect translucent eyelids and fingers and veins in floppy, sylph-like limbs. I stroked the bottom of his little foot, soft and cushiony like an animal's pad.

In a dreamlike state of shock, I gently laid my baby in the shower and set about tidying up. I rinsed my leaking body as best I could, pulled on a new pair of black sweatpants and stuffed them with great pillowing wads of toilet paper, stripped off my stained green fleece sweatshirt and used it to mop up the horrific mess. I set about bailing my vomit from the sink with a plastic cup, wrapped my desecrated sweatshirt into a ball and stuffed it into the trash can. I had no idea what to do next, so I climbed into bed.

He needed a name. This thought came to me as clearly and inexplicably as anything. I was ragged and feeble, but I couldn't just leave him without a name. I wanted to think hard, to give the question proper weight, but I couldn't. My mind was clouding over and I was sinking fast. Only then did the tears begin to flow; I wrapped my arms around myself, heaving and quavering violently as though I were breathing chandelier shards of glass. *Hurry, hurry*...Matt had wanted his son named after his grandfather, hadn't he? *Or was it his great-grandfather? Uncle?* I knew there was a family name that was incredibly important to him, but in my stupor it was elusive, beyond my grasp. It started with a *J* though, I knew that much. It was John, wasn't it? James? John or James...just before sleep roared up and engulfed me whole, I decided, just to be safe, on John Tristan James Barnes.

The following morning, when Christine knocked on the door of my room, I said I didn't feel well and passed on breakfast. I remained in bed all day, occasionally refreshing my makeshift sanitary pads, staring numbly like a zombie. I finally emerged for dinner, where I smiled as best I could, but believed myself broken and transparent, sure the shameful scent of death clung to me, as obvious and clear as a foghorn.

I left the hotel on the pretense of going for a walk the next afternoon, my child in my sweatshirt pocket, wrapped in a frivolous, sheer blue scarf from my suitcase. I felt I should give him a proper burial of some sort, but the entire town was thigh deep in ice and snow. I waded onwards, coming to a rest on the outskirts of town a half mile away, under an arching, skeletal tree at the banks of the River Deveron. I had no idea what a water burial entailed. Should I say something? There was nobody to hear, and I no longer believed in God or an afterlife, so I wasn't sure who to appeal to in any event, or why. The crisp air bit into my face like an apple. I settled for a few nonsensical sobs of love and regret, clutched the blue scarf to me and then gently placed it on the river. It bobbed once before the current ripped it from my grasp, sweeping him swiftly away, tumbling, then lost from sight forever.

I'm a social drinker. I only like fruity, nonalcoholic-tasting drinks, and I usually only have one at a time. I can count on one hand the number of times in my life that I've been even tipsy, much less drunk (two, by the way). But that night, the Bests broke out the whiskey, and I downed over half the bottle. They exchanged playful "She's going to be *hella* sick tomorrow" glances, and cheered me on, offering me shot after shot, finally bestowing me with the empty bottle as a souvenir. It tasted disgusting and it burned, but I kept drinking until I felt like I was moving through a bubble of water. Then I crawled upstairs and puked my guts out, and spent all of the following day with my first hangover. Perhaps not so strangely, it was preferable to having any room in my pounding head to think about anything else.

. . .

I contacted Vicki Day in London. If anybody would know what I should do next, she would.

After I explained my situation to her, she insisted that I come stay with her in London until Matt turned up. She would keep me busy. She asked to speak to Christine, and I put her on the phone. They spoke for a while and she assured Christine that she personally would make sure that I sent them all the money for my stay, as soon as I could. The two of them seemed to hit it off, and both of them trusted me. After Matt had demonstrated his heretofore hidden mistrust of me, his own fiancée, it was sweet to know that even people who were nearly complete strangers could trust me.

I chose to remain in Huntly until January 13, the date I had originally been scheduled to return to the United States. I still held out hope that Matt would turn up, or at least contact me somehow and let me know what was wrong. I continued emailing him every few nights, as he'd asked me to, letting him know everything that was going on, so that if he suddenly gained internet access, he wouldn't be at a loss.

I'm sorry about the police. I didn't call them, I swear. They just found me out there, waiting for you. Why, why, WHY would you ask me to go there and sleep in the snow, and then never come for me? I understand if something bad happened and you had to leave suddenly. I understand. Just please let me know you're OK. Let me know you're not hurt. Unless you're hurt or in the hospital, there must be some way for you to contact me, or use a pay phone to call the Dunedin.

But there was only silence.

Meanwhile, Michael Malloy, a hard-core follower of Homeless Tales (though not a writer), offered to pay the

$20 monthly fee to restore the site. Michael had stumbled across the site several months earlier. He'd been having a bad day and had left an angry comment on an article by a writer with a somewhat controversial opinion. Quick to defend Matt and his writers, I lashed out at him. It was OK to disagree, but geez, at least be polite about it! We didn't always agree with one another on this site, but we were courteous to one another, and we didn't sling insults as he'd done. Personal attacks weren't welcome on this site. Jerk. Jerky jerk jerk troll. So there.

We'd expected him never to come back, but he did. And he'd even apologized. It was the strangest thing. He kept coming back daily from then on; commenting and offering proactive and constructive solutions on articles. He was never again nasty to any of us. He became one of Matt's and my fast friends, and though he didn't submit articles of his own, he became just as much a part of the Homeless Tales crew as the rest of the writers.

Michael was one of the few crew members I'd given the whole story of Matt's disappearance to. And now, for the sake of the rest of the writers, he was willing to lend the $20 to get the site back up.

"Poor Cynthia's going crazy," Michael wrote. Cynthia was Matt's first writer, a deeply spiritual woman, a non-denominational reverend in San Luis Obispo who had recently been housed after two bouts of homelessness and years on California housing lists. Cynthia was the eternal peacemaker of the group, and had one of the kindest hearts I'd ever seen. She worried incessantly for others, and never for herself. I'd also let her know about the situation, and I could almost *see* her wringing her hands, panicking at the thought of me freezing in the Scottish winter.

Homeless Tales was the center of most of these people's lives. It was their support network, their social club, their outlet. I could conjure up all sorts of imaginary reasons for Matt abandoning *me,* if I tried hard enough, but I couldn't understand him forsaking his innocent crew. These people, many of them with no family or close friends, deeply loved and respected him. Why would he just vanish and ignore all their emails, too? None of it made sense.

I gave Michael the login info, but he was unable to access the Media Temple site. The password had changed. I contacted the *other* Michael, Michael Abehsera, who hosted the site, to find out what the problem was. It took him nearly a week to respond.

Why hadn't I contacted him sooner, he demanded. He berated me as though it were somehow all *my* fault that he hadn't paid the bill, as though it were my site and my responsibility, instead of Matt's. Hey, I was just the messenger. And I'd been dealing with my own crap. Like hypothermia and bleeding out my insides.

After he'd chewed me out enough, he confessed that a former business associate, with whom he'd just parted ways abruptly, had hacked into his Media Temple account and changed all the login info. He'd have to call Media Temple directly and deal with it.

It was several days before he bothered. Meanwhile, the crew was getting more and more angst-ridden. All I could tell them was what I knew…and that was basically nothing. Finally, Michael Abehsera got back to me. He'd taken too long, although he was careful to tell me that *I'd* taken too long to notify him. It was *my* fault. Media Temple had deleted the website. It was gone forever. Michael Malloy could call and pay the $20, but then we'd have to pay an extra $120 on top of that for Media Temple to retrieve the files.

"Wait…retrieve the files that are gone forever?" I asked skeptically.

"That's what they said. They're gone forever, but they can get them back."

Trouble was, I didn't *have* $120. Jon, in Ireland, was in touch with me and knew about the Matt crisis—after all, Matt considered him his best friend—and he told me that he could scrape up the money somehow, so that the writers wouldn't lose all their hard work. By this time, though, Michael Abehsera was having second thoughts.

"My loyalty is to Matt. If he's gone somewhere without telling you where he is, then I can't give you those files. It's his website."

"I don't *want* the files. You don't have to send them to me. Just send them back to their writers. It's *their* intellectual property." But he wouldn't budge. Matt would have to give him the OK, and Matt was nowhere to be found.

On January 13, I took the train from Huntly to London. Vicki Day met me at Kensington Station, thick blonde hair blowing in the chilly air, and spirited me away to her flat.

Vicki is like a Fellini muse crossed with the no-nonsense business sense of Anna Wintour. Minus the meanness. She became something of a surrogate mother to me. Her daughter, Alice, was magnanimous enough to give up her room to me for a month and a half, and even their Chihuahua, Biggie, deeply suspicious and snarly at first, took a liking to me after a couple of days.

I went through random bouts of depression—my moods swung high and low. Half the time, I needed to be near somebody, to feel human contact, and I padded around from room to room, following Vicki like a stray dog. She never once complained or showed any irritation with me, and neither did Alice, though I imagine there must have been moments when I got on their nerves. In turn, they gamely dragged me all over London during my clingy phases, showing me parks and museums and Buckingham Palace—anything to keep my spirits up.

Then I would feel the deep, dark urge to be alone for days, and I would retreat to Alice's room, shut the door and sleep for vast periods, locking myself away from the world. I watched endless viral YouTube videos until a classic *Sesame Street* video of a curly-haired toddler mischievously singing the alphabet with Kermit triggered gales of tears for hours on end. I couldn't tell what would set me off anymore, what would make me think of babies or of cherished memories I'd shared with Matt, so I tried to stick to things that would make me laugh, like old episodes of *The Chaser's War on Everything* and *Futurama*.

I probably should have been writing the book, but I couldn't bring myself to touch it. How could I? I had no idea where my own life was, or where it was going anymore. Matt had been gone for over a month, and still none of the crew had heard from him. I managed to track down his first wife via Facebook, hoping that perhaps she'd either heard from him, or could put me in touch with his mother somehow. Surely, his parents would be the first ones contacted if he had somehow gotten hurt, right? Victoria was kind to me, much kinder than any first wife could ever be expected to be, but she was sorry, she didn't know anything. She hadn't seen or heard from him in years.

I was also still bleeding heavily. Miscarriages were pretty common in my family, I knew. My mother had had at least two that I am aware of, and was herself the twin of a stillborn sister. My great-grandmother had also miscarried a boy, the twin of a girl who had lived, my great-aunt Anne. Still, for all that miscarrying, I didn't know anything about the actual process. It had never occurred to me that I would bleed for three weeks. I ruined three of my pairs of pajama bottoms at Vicki's house, and soaked Alice's sheets until they looked as though someone had been murdered on them. Ashamed, I continued to sleep on them for a week and a half, until the bleeding finally stopped. I approached Vicki and told her that I'd accidentally had my period on the sheets. She must have wondered at the vast amount of blood, but never once did she even raise an eyebrow, or act with anything other than kindness and compassion. She assured me that she wouldn't say anything to Alice, bundled the sheets up in a wad, and threw them away. Then she asked me if I needed to toss my pajamas in the wash.

Sage was in touch, and was also shocked about Matt's actions, though she, too, continued assuring me that this *wasn't* him, she had *seen* the way he looked at me, she just *knew* he loved me and would turn up eventually. She would continue to talk me down from my skyscraper, so to speak, for several weeks. She still occasionally does. I'm lucky to have her.

Sage also asked if I was willing to allow another homeless man to stay in my trailer while I was gone. He was a friend of Emese's, another homeless woman at the ranch who lived out of a trailer with her daughter and a neighborhood girl from a dysfunctional family she'd "adopted." Emese was the epitome of a giving person. Sage assured me that she and Emese would go through my trailer and put my belongings into one of the storage sheds. My mind flashed to the second pregnancy test, still sitting on the sink.

"Er...the trailer is a bit messy...of course I want to help out another homeless person...but, you know, it's kind of embarrassingly messy...."

"Really, it's OK! We'll take care of it. We don't mind at all!"

I felt like the worst kind of hypocrite. I was going to deny another homeless person temporary shelter because I was afraid that someone would find out I'd been pregnant? I sighed and told Sage that she and Emese could go ahead. I hoped that Emese would just sweep the test into the garbage with a bunch of other random stuff without noticing, so that I wouldn't need to talk about it.

A couple of days later, Sage emailed and tactfully brought the conversation around to asking if I might perhaps be pregnant. "I was. I miscarried in Scotland."

Instinctively, she seemed to know what to do. She told me how sorry she was, and then changed the subject. She didn't leave room for self-pity, just buoyed the conversation onward and upward. That was Sage. Ever true to her name.

Just before Valentine's Day, I checked my email inbox and my heart stopped. There was a message from Matt.

I clicked it open, and there was only one sentence.

"Please accept that it is over, and perhaps we can both move on."

Emails began to roll in from the Homeless Tales crew. He'd sent them all two-line emails, before he even emailed me, saying simply that he and Brianna were no longer together, he was sorry about the website and he'd be in touch. There was no further explanation of any kind. I had no idea how to answer their questions. I didn't know myself. For my part, I didn't know what exactly I was supposed to be accepting—or why—or where he'd been or why our lives had just imploded.

Matt responded to my pleas for an explanation, after a couple of days. He was staying with Lori's family for the time being. They were together as a couple and were moving on. He was sorry: If it was any consolation, he hated himself right now, and knew that there was absolutely no excuse for his behavior, but his decisions were final and irreversible. He hoped that we could remain in contact and stay friends. He had very fond memories of our time together, and hoped that we didn't have to hate each other. But, he added, he had to request that I not try to come find him. He didn't want to involve the police in this matter, but if I came looking for him, he'd do whatever was necessary to protect his family.

At no point did he acknowledge the specifics or the magnitude of the events that he'd set in motion. He spoke in vagaries, as though it had all been a mere unpleasantness instead of having nearly killed a woman. A woman whose hand he'd held, whose eyes he'd gazed deeply into and promised to marry.

What?! What was he talking about? What had happened? "Protect his family?" I had never threatened him or Kelsey or even Lori in any way, and now he was acting paranoid when *he* was the one who had lied, who had abandoned me, who could have gotten me killed. He'd disappeared and sacrificed all of us on the altar of his selfishness—his crew, his friends, and me...the woman he said he'd loved more than anything. For all his supposed *love,* it was easy enough for him to trade my life as a mildly regrettable casualty, just to make his choices easier. I was shocked to realize that he'd rather stay with a woman he claimed to pity and loathe, just so that he wouldn't have to

stand up for himself. And he "knew there was no excuse?"
Fuck you, try anyway! For all the havoc he'd wreaked, the
least he could have done, I felt, was *try* to come up with an
excuse, no matter how pathetic! He wanted us to remain
friends? Fuck him. He could take his fond memories and
shove them.

There would be no friendship, I told him. Indeed, why
would he wish for us to remain friends? So that once Lori
and he imploded, I'd still be around for him to weasel back
into my life, so that I could support him again? Did Lori
have any idea that he was sending this email? It was nearly
3:00 a.m. when he sent it. Wow, nice going, waiting until
Lori's asleep to send a conniving, pitiful email, hoping to
keep me in his life. I guess it was good for them to know
they could trust each other. Oh, wait. They couldn't.
Return my belongings to Vicki Day's address, immediately. My laptop, the engagement ring I'd bought and the
Christmas photo album. The baby clothes he could keep.
I no longer had any use for them. Go back to your whore.
Douche bag.

He responded defensively that, by all means, I could go
ahead and hate him. I was certainly entitled. He back-
pedaled rapidly, angered at being called out. He didn't see
any reason to keep in contact—it was just a *gesture*. A gesture? I had a gesture or two for him myself.

He would send my items at some point, but not until he
was good and ready, he continued. He wasn't in Huntly at
the moment and didn't know when he'd find the time to
get back there and send my things.

I knew he was lying. He definitely wouldn't have left
without at least my laptop, at any rate. I responded that I
didn't care for his pitiful excuses. He would get himself
on the first train to Huntly if he had to beg, borrow or

steal from Lori's family—I didn't give a flying fuck. But my items would be in the post immediately, unless he wanted me to call the police and charge him with theft. The ring, especially, could land him in a lot of trouble, I knew. I still had the receipt for it. There was no room for negotiation. He should have thought of that before he knowingly told me to wait for him in a snowstorm, and then left me to die.

As for hating him? Ha.

"I don't hate you *or* love you. I nothing you. You're worthy of neither hate nor love." It was a lie, of course. I both loved and hated him. But he was no longer entitled to the truth from me, I thought wildly. He'd fed me nothing but lies. I hoped he choked on them.

"Vicki Day and Jon Glackin will facilitate the return of my belongings. Don't ever contact me again."

Jon Glackin was in London, coincidentally, meeting with some English street folk in preparation for World Homeless Day, a global event we were coordinating, to take place on 10-10-10, catchily enough. He had amassed supporters from all over the globe, even including several high-profile celebrities. We were hoping to make it into an annual event, geared toward raising homeless awareness and combating negative, judgmental stereotypes.

Yet, he proved himself a true friend by putting much of it on the back burner to walk me through the next several days. We met up in person in Camden, and hugged like old friends. He was furious with Matt, and disavowed their friendship to high heaven. He was sickened by what he'd done. He'd make sure that Matt returned my things, and right quick.

Vicki wrote to Matt, instructing that he send my things back immediately, and that no excuse would be accepted. He didn't even do her the courtesy of responding. It was awfully chauvinistic of him, I found myself thinking, a quality I'd never before seen in Matt.

Instead, Matt tried his luck with Jon, calling him "bro," and speaking intimately as though they were still the best of friends and allies. Jon was displeased by the feigned chumminess, and Matt's underhanded statement that "Obviously, Brianna and I are having trouble communicating effectively at the moment"—the intimation being that I was the silly, overreacting woman who just couldn't accept a breakup and move on. *Women, eh? Wink, wink, nudge, nudge.*

What Matt didn't know was that Jon had asked to read all the correspondence that had gone on between us thus far. He wanted to know the full situation before taking a stand against his former best friend and I certainly understood. For all he knew, I really *could* be a woman just having a hard time dealing with a breakup. Once he read all our emails back and forth, though, there was no doubt. Jon took it *very* personally that his "friend" would not only treat his wife-to-be that way, but then try to play it as though he'd done nothing wrong, as though it were all perfectly sane and rational and understandable.

Jon ripped into Matt, and after reiterating that my belongings must be returned, ended his email with the following statement:

"You left our friend Bri out in the cold, at the mercy of nature, and relying upon the kindness of strangers to get by. For a 'homeless activist,' that is shameful for sure. 'Bro.'"

The following day, I began to receive emails about some story on me in a Scottish tabloid called *News of the World*. I

was confused. The *News of the World* writer, Siobhan Mc-
Fadyen, had contacted me several weeks earlier and offered me £500 ($810) to interview me and Matt for a
Valentine's Day story. He was still missing, and I still had
no idea what was going on at the time, so I told her, "No,
thank you. He's busy with personal matters at the moment
and I'm doing business in London. But, again, thanks for
the interest." Besides, Matt had already told me, back when
we were first navigating the media storm, that *News of the
World* was a cheap rag of a tabloid, the British version of
the *National Enquirer*. We didn't need to lower ourselves to
that standard, he'd said. We wanted to keep our reputa-
tions clean. The paltry amount of money it might bring
in would never be worth it in the long run. It would only
tarnish the opportunities for advancement that legitimate,
reputable news outlets would hold out. I agreed with him.

The writer had apparently gone ahead and contacted
Matt. And he had accepted her offer. I located the article.
Matt and Lori posed with Kelsey in a baby carriage. Most
of the article was complete fiction. The writer quoted
anonymous "sources close to Brianna"—none of whom
existed. These "sources" were clearly bogus because as
far as nearly everybody in my life knew, I was OK. Mc-
Fadyen and her colleague Nicola Stow created a completely
botched time line of events that included me coming to
Scotland to be with Matt for Valentine's Day, and him
dumping me. To be honest, simply by reading my blog
they would have gotten closer to the truth. For *months,*
my readers had been aware that I'd come to Scotland to
surprise Matt for Christmas, even though I'd played everything cool as though it were all going swimmingly. The
writers even got our ages wrong.

"There was no infidelity," Matt lied to the tabloid. "We just broke up—that's life…I'm back with Lori for now."

The *for now* caught the attention of a lot of people, though I suspect it flew right over Lori's head. In her photo, she looked thrilled and somewhat bewildered at being photographed for a tabloid. It was probably the most interesting thing ever to happen to her. Looking at her dull face, I almost pitied her. But not quite. They deserved each other.

The writer concluded by quoting an anonymous source: "[Bri] is devastated. She feels really foolish." I didn't feel foolish, though. How could I? I had believed I could trust my fiancé, the one person I loved more than anyone in the world—a completely normal assumption, right? It had never occurred to me that there was any other option.

The tabloid photos were posed in Huntly. Matt had been lying all along when he swore that he was in Peterhead, fifty miles away, and had no access to my belongings. Jon emailed and called him out on it, and for selling his morals and ethics to a tabloid—and for such a paltry sum, too. He called it the "thirty pieces of silver *News of the World* article," intimating that Matt was nothing but a Judas. Matt never replied. He seemed to realize he'd burned all his bridges.

So I went back to California, kept picking up work wherever I could find it from temp agencies I'd signed up with, and used the advance money from this book to pay back Brandon, Vicki, the Bests…everybody I owed money to, who had taken me in as though I were their daughter, their sister or their friend. Me, a virtual stranger. Whenever I'm tempted to think back on the heartache that Matt caused me and become cynical, I remember all the good people who came through for me in a heartbeat, without a second thought, when my own family had disowned me, as though I'd never existed. And I realize something perhaps not very profound or original, but comforting: People in general are not so bad after all.

It had been a year since I wrote my first blog post. On February 26, 2010, I opened my Netbook and typed:

One year ago today, a very scared girl with a lot of bravado opened a plain little no-frills blog and tapped out the following:

"In three days, I will be homeless."

As they say, what a long, strange ride it's been....

Epilogue

I set out to write this book in a very different frame of mind than the one in which I finish it. I was excited, naïve perhaps. The world was my oyster and I felt like I was headed for, if not a fairy tale ending, at least a fulfilling one. All I wanted was a house to live in with a man who loved me, and, finally, to leave my past behind and create a life of my own.

As you know, it didn't quite turn out that way.

Matt did send my belongings back, with the exception of the Christmas photo album. I can't imagine what he could possibly want to keep it for, so I simply don't. I wrote it off as a loss, and was simply happy to retrieve my laptop and ring. When I turned on the computer I discovered that he'd deleted every single one of my personal files—three years' worth of photos, documents, bookmarks, records, contracts, tax paperwork, music, piano sheets, the templates for a vintage clothing site that I'd slaved for hours over—all gone. My memories, my life for three years, long before I'd met him, wiped away. Ben, my brilliant technogeek friend, spent days running a recovery program on my laptop. Over twenty thousand files were recovered, many of them junk and many of them corrupted beyond retrieval. I'm still sorting through them, seeing what I can save.

I haven't had any contact with my family in nearly two years at this point, and I don't expect that I will anytime soon. I still love them very much, as I suspect I always will. But I realize and accept that they are not going to change, and I can't force my will or perspective on them. As a result, we are destined to live separate lives.

The members of the Homeless Tales crew have been largely supportive, and are working through their own grief. Most of them have been clear that they don't blame me for the loss of the site and of their work, which I'm still partially compiling as I stumble across it, so that I can send it back to its rightful owners.

I do still believe in love, as odd as that may seem, even if I'm liable to be a lot more gun-shy moving forward. Maybe eventually I will find someone to share my life with. It may not be the next relationship I enter, or the next several, but I do hope that I deserve the happiness that comes with love, and that I will find it.

For now, though, I'm doing my best to make lemons into lemonade and I'm focusing my energies into pursuing my passions. As of this writing, I'm building my own company and network of websites; some of them creative, some of them recessionista-centric, some of them humanitarian. There's a beautifully exhausting amount of work involved in starting my own business, and I'm loving every minute of it. Believe it or not, there's very little time to allow myself to feel lonely or sad. How can I? I am constantly on the go these days, and I've befriended multiple people, communities and subcultures (especially online) who constantly check in to reassure me that they've got my back—and the sentiment is assuredly mutual.

The recession has dragged on longer than nearly anybody anticipated, and after being unemployed for more than a year, I have just started an amazing job at a prestigious Orange County theatre—a stroke of luck that has left me thrilled and hopeful. But there's an overwhelming sense of it all being the end of an era. The world and economy have evolved and moved on in many ways, and we're struggling to regain our breath and catch up. I suspect that even if or when the ship rights itself, things will never be quite the same. Not that I believe the economic collapse is a harbinger of Armageddon and impending doom-and-gloom and the zombie apocalypse, or any of that sensationalist, panicky nonsense that those more disposed to fear-mongering seem to drum up...just that the atmosphere will be (and this is not necessarily a bad thing) *different*. Americans have now collectively watched the fabled American Dream crumble around our ears, taken a major hit and been reminded in a big way, just in case we forgot, that our country and our government have feet of clay. We are not immune.

I have high hopes for Americans as a whole working together to rebuild what we've lost. And I have a hunch that my faith in our resiliency will be justified in the end. One of my takeaways from a year spent navigating the seamier underbelly of the American Dream is this: If I've only got this one life, it's important to me to spend it advocating for causes I believe in, and making some kind of difference in the world, no matter how small.

. . .

Brandon once joked that becoming homeless was the best thing that ever happened to me. In a way, he was right. Because I have experienced such an odd and often fulfilling journey while homeless, new doors have been opened and new opportunities created. If I hadn't lost my job and my house, I never would have found my passion and a calling to help give others a voice. My hope is that this book inspires discussion about homelessness, and what we, as individuals and as a society, can do to end it.

It's been just over a year since I've lived in a house, but I realize, with not a small amount of melancholy, that I can't remember the last time I ever felt that I had a home. All my life I've longed for someplace to call my own—and not just a physical building, but a niche, somewhere that I fit in and feel a sense of harmony and *belonging*. While I would love the opportunity to see the world, and travel to exotic lands, I wish to do it knowing that there's a solid, permanent base awaiting my return, that nest where a warm, fuzzy robe is always hanging on a hook for me and my dog is sitting at the front door waiting for me.

Perhaps it's not all tied up in a neat little bow with sparkles and ribbons on top. But that's OK; life rarely is. It's a start. I know who I am and where I want to go. I deeply want a home, quite possibly more than anything in the world. And that's the next, most important step for this homeless girl.

Acknowledgments

Extra special thanks to Chris Schelling, who walked me through this entire daunting process—and taught me how to write a book. I wish I could come up with a more fitting synonym than "thanks" to express my gratitude for your awesomeness. You, sir, are a rock star. Additional special thanks to Deb Brody, Shara Alexander, Alex Colon and everybody at Harlequin for all the work you've put into helping me improve and polish the manuscript. Phenomenal amounts of thanks to E. Jean Carroll for doing a complete stranger such a kindness, mentoring her and always telling it like it is…blunt and straight, but with gobs of compassion.

They say it takes a village to raise a child; I suppose for particularly difficult children like me it occasionally takes a little extra push from additional continents. Vicki Day, you are the best adopted British mother a girl could ever hope for. I am eternally in your debt. Alice Smith and Biggie Fudgecakes, thank you for your complete grace and class during the time I was occupying your bedroom. Jon Glackin, if Vicki is my adopted mom, you're at least my adopted uncle (I'd say dad, but you might get upset because you're too young at heart). Maryse-Noelle Sage, you are like my crazy fantabulous hippie aunt and I adore you. Thank you so much for all you've done, and for being "the family I chose."

All the love in the world to Brandon Quan, Sonia Jahan and Ben Choy for being my best friends and having my back for so many years. Shoutout to David Roth, Josh Bogy and the rest of our high school circle for picking me up and taking me in more than once when I was a kid, and for tolerating my utterly age-inappropriate crushes and general social ineptitude with your typical sardonic humor. I've learned more from you than I care to admit!

Much appreciation for the constant and unwavering support of Cynthia Eastman and the former Homeless Tales/ Street Voices crew, Jul Gorman, Michael Ian, Michael Malloy, Keith and Christine Best, the Huntly Police Station and its kind officers, Adam Warner, Rande Levine and Barbara DeSantis of Karma Rescue, Lindsay Johnston, Amy Norris, Kyria Abrahams, Aubrey Gonzaga, Robbie Myers at *ELLE* magazine, every SoCal Starbucks barista who ever let me leech internet on a daily basis, my Facebook friends, Twitter followers, blog readers and especially all my fellow homeless/street people/vehicle dwellers/ activists for your letters of solidarity. I shudder to think of how much poorer my coping skills would be without you.

To my half sisters and their mom, my most heartfelt thanks for your warmth and generosity from the day we met, despite the unfortunate circumstances that brought us in touch. You are such brilliant, talented and resilient women and you are going places! I admire you deeply.

I would like to extend my appreciation to my family and former religion, for providing me with an eventful and interesting childhood, and for imbuing me (albeit perhaps unwittingly) with such handy qualities as determination and adaptability in the face of less than desirable circumstances.

And lastly, hugs and pets to Fezzik, for being such a kickass monster goober of a dog, loving me no matter what and always being happy to see me. As long as I'm carrying a bowl of large breed kibble.

The
Girl's Guide
to
Homelessness

1. What ideas did you have about homelessness/homeless people before you read *The Girl's Guide to Homelessness?* Have your ideas changed after reading about Brianna's experiences? How so?

2. Brianna had an enormous number of odds stacked against her throughout her life. To say that her childhood was difficult would be an understatement. How do you think she was able to overcome her past and survive? What qualities in Brianna have allowed her to be particularly resilient?

3. How did religion play a role in shaping Brianna's relationship with her family? She says that Jehovah's Witnesses is a cult. Do you think her life would be different if she had stayed on and tried to be a member of the community as her sister did? Would it be better or worse?

4. Regarding her religious education, Brianna writes: "Even as a child, I recognized hypocrisy and prejudice at play, but I was at my most impressionable and, inevitably, whether I liked it or not, I retained bits of it." How has Brianna attempted to deprogram herself from religious indoctrination? If she was raised to embrace certain prejudices, do you think she can ever be truly free of them?

5. Brianna says that she has tried to forgive her family, including her mother, for the wrongs they have done her. If you were in her position, would you be able to forgive? Why or why not?

6. Brianna has a vehicle, a trailer, a mobile phone, a laptop and a dog. Does she still "count" as being homeless? Are there different levels of homelessness? Do you think she's made good use of the "comforts" available to her?

7. Throughout her experience being homeless, Brianna is adamant that she will not accept charity—that there are people worse off who need help more than she does. If you were in her shoes, would you feel the same? Is Brianna wrong to forego such assistance?

8. Having fun is still a priority for Brianna, even though she's homeless. Should homeless people be singly focused on altering their circumstances? Is there anything else she could or should do? Is having fun a luxury, or a basic need?

9. When daily survival was Brianna's number one goal, she met and got involved with Matt. What do you

think initially attracted her to Matt? Do you think her relationship with him shifted her priorities in a negative way?

10. At first, Brianna presents Matt as a kind of savior, a true kindred spirit who gives her support and guidance. Did you detect any warning signs that Matt might not be the upstanding, selfless person that Brianna wanted him to be?

11. *The Girl's Guide to Homelessness* was written while Brianna was going through the events she describes in the book. How might her memoir have been different if it had been written at a later date, looking back on past experiences?

12. The title *The Girl's Guide to Homelessness* brings a sense of humor and a bit of irony to a serious subject. How does its tongue-in-cheek title affect your impression of Brianna and of the book?

13. On one of the final pages of the book, Brianna says, "People in general are not so bad after all." Were you surprised that she would say this, after all the hardships and betrayals she faced? Do you agree with her?

14. Now that you've read about Brianna's struggles, what do you think we can do about the homelessness epidemic? How can the average reader help?

Resources

If you need help, or would like to help others in need, or if you'd simply like to hear more stories from people like Brianna, please visit the websites below.

Brianna's Blog
http://girlsguidetohomelessness.com

Change.org
http://uspoverty.change.org/blog/category/homelessness

Homeless.us—United States Department of Social Services; Emergency Shelter http://homeless.us

211 National Human Services Information & Referral Hotline http://211.org; http://211us.org or dial 2-1-1 toll-free from any U.S. phone to be connected with an operator

National Coalition for the Homeless
http://nationalhomeless.org

Homeless Blogs Project
http://homelessblogs.org

The International Homeless Forum
http://homelessforums.org

World Homeless Day
http://worldhomelessday.org

I Hate My Life
http://www.ihatemylife.us/index2.html

SLO Homeless
http://slohomeless.wordpress.com

The Homeless Guy
http://thehomelessguy.blogspot.com